NINO KEBADZE

ROMANCE AND EXEMPLARITY IN POST-WAR SPANISH WOMEN'S NARRATIVES

TAMESIS

First published 2009 by Tamesis, Woodbridge

ISBN 978 1 85566 192 9

Tamesis is an imprint of Boydell & Brewer Ltd
PO Box 9, Woodbridge, Suffolk IP12 3DF, UK
and of Boydell & Brewer Inc.
668 Mt Hope Avenue, Rochester, NY 14620, USA
website: www.boydellandbrewer.com

A CIP catalogue record for this book is available
from the British Library

This publication is printed on acid-free paper

Printed in Great Britain by
CPI Antony Rowe, Chippenham and Eastbourne

Colección Támesis

SERIE A: MONOGRAFÍAS, 279

ROMANCE AND EXEMPLARITY IN POST-WAR SPANISH WOMEN'S NARRATIVES

The effects of General Francisco Franco's authoritarian rule (1939–75) on the production and reception of cultural texts can be gauged by the silence that now surrounds them. This is especially true of works that enjoyed considerable popularity when first published. Most of the novels in question belong to the sentimental genre known as *novela rosa*, whose authors—mostly women—and heroines Academe has consistently treated as literary pariahs. This volume represents the first serious effort to question the categories used to assess the value and meaning of texts previously presumed to be devoid of both. It does so by bringing to the fore the operative premise of Francoist cultural politics, wherein fictional works have the power to mould individual character and conduct. Narratives by Luisa-María Linares, Concha Linares-Becerra, Carmen de Icaza, and María Mercedes Ortoll are thus examined in terms of the effects that they were expected to have on their readers, and the constraints that such expectations placed on the works' production and reception. The result is a paradox: while the study of women's bestselling novels is by definition a study of the constraints that shape them, careful reading reveals the limitations of those selfsame constraints.

NINO KEBADZE is an Assistant Professor in the Hispanic Studies Department of the University of Massachusetts Boston.

CONTENTS

The author and publishers are grateful to the University of Massachusetts Boston for assistance with the production costs of this volume

The author is grateful for permission to develop material previously published as "The Right to be Selfless and Other Prerogatives of the Weak in the Rhetoric of Sección Femenina' in Romance Quarterly, Volume 55, Number 2, Spring 2008, pp. 109–127. This is reprinted with permission of the Helen Dwight Reid Educational Foundation. It was published by Heldref Publications, 1319 Eighteenth St., NW, Washington, DC 20036-1802. Copyright © 2008.

INTRODUCTION

Drawing on the Francoist use of literature as a means of social control and edification,[1] this book examines post-war romance fictions by Spanish women novelists as narratives of female exemplarity.[2] Under the label of exemplarity—which here denotes both a narrative modality and an interpretative strategy—are examined models of conduct that receive positive or negative sanction within the chosen texts. I contend that the practice of conferring meaning and value to given female representations is conditioned by prescribed gender and cultural norms found in a vast body of prescriptive texts (conduct manuals, treatises, and sermons)[3] intended for the female audience of the time.

Because censorship controls not only the production but also the reception of literary works, any reading of the selected texts must take into account

[1] On the Francoist definition and uses of literary texts, see Fernando Valls, *La enseñanza de la literatura en el franquismo (1936–1951)* (Barcelona: Antoni Bosch, 1983). On post-war edifying literature, see Jordi Roca i Girona, "Del clero para el pueblo. La Literatura Edificante de Postguerra: un instrumento de divulgación y socialización religiosa," *Revista de dialectología y tradiciones populares* 48.2 (1993): 5–29.

[2] My use of the term "exemplarity" is informed by Susan Suleiman's study of the *roman à thèse* in her *Authoritarian Fictions: The Ideological Novel as a Literary Genre* (1983; Princeton: Princeton UP, 1992). As Suleiman convincingly argues, narratives with an embedded exemplary structure are made up of so-called "closed" texts, and entail a lesson to be derived. However, one can read them choosing to ignore the "message." When this happens, the texts lose part of their "value" contingent upon the fulfillment of their pedagogic purpose. Conversely, didactic readings are not limited to didactic texts and can produce didactic interpretations by willfully glossing over any ambiguities that could jeopardize the validity of such readings. Similar reading practices often proliferate under the closed systems of representation that characterize authoritarian regimes. The texts that promote alternative interpretations of national life and value systems from the ones that are being prescribed may be subject to censorship. Under such conditions, exemplarity becomes an accepted form of encoding and decoding cultural artifacts.

[3] Foucault defines "'prescriptive' texts" as "texts written for the purpose of offering rules, opinions, and advice on how to behave as one should: 'practical' texts, which are themselves objects of a 'practice' in that they were designed to be read, learned, reflected upon, and tested out, and they were intended to constitute the eventual framework of everyday conduct. These texts thus served as functional devices that would enable individuals to question their own conduct, to watch over and give shape to it, and to shape themselves as ethical subject." See *The Uses of Pleasure: The History of Sexuality*, vol. 2 (1985; New York: Vintage Books, 1990) 12–13.

the constraints that regulate their meaning and interpretation. Among these constraints are the normative and normalizing tenets of womanhood, which constitute a shared body of knowledge between the novelists and their readers. Hence, the first part of this study examines the dominant, national-Catholic system of values pertaining to the conventions of representing women, while Part II demonstrates its relevance to women's literary production of the time through the analysis of selected novels. Its aim is ultimately to explore the relationship between dominant gender representations and their conditions of emergence, between authorized forms of female socialization and modes of expression, between national prerogatives and cultural expectations, between lived experiences and literary constructs.

By and large, both the novels and the authors studied here form a blind spot of literary scholarship. This neglect is sustained on one or both of two grounds: first, the alleged lack of literary merit of the selected corpus; and second, its ideological affiliation with Franco's authoritarian regime. The exceptions are made up of those authors and texts that lend themselves to counter-hegemonic readings, combining the resistance to imposed cultural and gender norms with the type of writing privileged by literary institutions. In view of the existing valorizations, the present study assumes the task of expanding the active corpus of women's writing to texts that defy the operative conventions of interpretation. With few exceptions, the choice of women-authored texts for scholarly investigation has helped to naturalize a correspondence between cultural marginality and liberal ideologies, gender and politics, women's writing and the literature of resistance and/or exile.[4] Victoria L. Enders identifies a parallel trend in historical research whereby "[d]edicated to the recovery of women's voices that were silenced through political, economic, and social oppression, historians have overwhelmingly chosen women linked to political parties of the left as their sympathetic subjects" ("Problematic Portraits," 377). While these correspondences are not without foundation, their institution has the obvious drawback of converting them into ready-made assumptions. As givens, they become criteria for the selection and analysis of texts that serve to validate and reproduce the starting premise.

Despite the prevailing attempts to shift the focus of literary criticism to non-canonical texts, women's fictional works from the 1940s to the early-to-mid 1950s—prior to the regime's relative aperture—remain outside the scope of existing scholarship. More systematic and fertile in this respect have been cultural and gender studies conducted from other disciplines, namely history and sociology. These include essays edited by Victoria L. Enders and Pamela

---

[4] Erin Carlston makes a similar point in reference to women and fascism, arguing that the prevailing trend is to "assume that women writers were necessarily antagonistic to fascist ideologies." See *Thinking Fascism: Sapphic Modernism and Fascist Modernity* (Stanford, CA: Stanford UP, 1998) 4.

Beth Radcliff in *Constructing Spanish Womanhood*, and Aurora G. Morcillo's monograph *True Catholic Womanhood*. The bulk of the work on the period comes from investigations of female socialization and educational policies, women and fascism in comparative perspective, and the role and activities of the *Sección Femenina*.[5] What persists, however, is the neat separation between the aforementioned inquiries into the production and representation of post-war cultural and gender norms and the literary output of the time. Here, too, one can speak of exceptions. Giuliana Di Febo's unpublished paper, "El tiempo de las mujeres durante el franquismo: De los manuales 'de formación' a la narrativa femenina," offers a useful juxtaposition of two ostensibly incompatible discourses from the period: the prescriptive (in the form of male-authored conduct manuals) and the novelistic (in the form of canonical narratives by women authors). However, Di Febo's discussion of the works in question presupposes the existence of "true" and "false" representations of womanhood corresponding to male vs female constructs, which lead her to a "truth distorted → distortion subverted → truth restored" model. The resulting dichotomy of compulsory/false vs. subversive/authentic feminine models is, to say the least, problematic. Moreover, it seems to corroborate the ascendancy of literature over other forms of cultural production, suggesting that literary texts are somehow autonomous and, as such, impervious to political and ideological currents. An alternative would be to view "Spanish womanhood" (and its myriad representations) as a cultural construct comprised of enunciations across the board (whether "political," "religious," "literary," or otherwise). Such an approach allows the study of texts that in the past have formed part of a separate field of inquiry from that of literary studies, without implicitly endorsing the hierarchy alluded to above.

At the interstices of various disciplines lies Carmen Martín Gaite's insightful essay, *Usos amorosos de la postguerra* (1986), whose contributions include having legitimized the study of the popular romance novel, or *novela rosa*, as a form of cultural expression engaged in the shaping of female subjectivity. What is singular about Martín Gaite's typology of post-war feminine representations is that it is carried out from the perspective of the reader: the narrator is at once a contemporary and a consumer of the cultural artifacts that constitute the object of her study. As such, *Usos amorosos* presents an audi-

---

[5] Among others, see Alicia Alted Vigil, "La mujer en las coordenadas educativas del régimen franquista" in *Ordenamiento jurídico y realidad social de las mujeres*; Pilar Ballarín Domingo, *La educación de las mujeres en la España contemporánea*; Victoria De Grazia, *How Fascism Ruled Women*; Giuliana Di Febo, "La condición de la mujer y el papel de la iglesia en la Italia fascista y en la España franquista: Ideologías, leyes y asociaciones femeninas" in *Ordenamiento jurídico y realidad social de las mujeres*; María Teresa Gallego Méndez, *Mujer, falange y franquismo*; Kathleen Richmond, *Women and Spanish Fascism*; Rosario Sánchez López, *Mujer española, una sombra de destino en lo universal*; Geraldine Scanlon, *La polémica feminista en la España contemporánea. 1868–1974*.

ence-based model of analysis in which the operating models of female comportment are gauged by the impact and expectations (themselves mediated
and culturally constructed) that they bore on their narrator-reader. What
Martín Gaite's examination of post-war courtship practices signals, beyond
the stated objective, is the presence of exemplarity as a prevailing template
for decoding given cultural representations. Accordingly, the female protagonists are perceived by the readers as models worthy of emulation or rejection.
In this way, her analysis invites the study of popular cultural artifacts as sites
for negotiating women's conventional societal and gender roles.[6]

One of the fundamental characteristics of exemplary narratives is their
teleological design endemic to the post-war representations of womanhood.
Women's "sexuality, work and education" were interpreted in terms of their
ultimate function, which was to become model wives and mothers (Nash,
"Moral Order" 298). That women were ostensibly defined by their relationship to men is manifest through countless references to courtship, marriage,
and motherhood, which assume an almost obligatory character in most discourses of the period, literary or otherwise.

Life before marriage was conceived of as a period of formation during
which women underwent a mandatory socialization. A successful formation
was the key to happiness, which for women meant marriage and maternity.
These normative expectations find expression in women's literary representations through the structure of romance and *bildung*. In fact, as I shall argue, it
is the normative subtext (here constituted by the aforementioned body of prescriptive texts) that vests the protagonists' conduct with positive or negative
meaning, thereby turning them into exemplary figures by promotion or nega-
tion. Following this contention, they become subject to what French sociolo-
gist Pierre Bourdieu calls symbolic violence. Such violence entails the
imposition of a dominant cultural arbitrary as legitimate, disguising the power
relations that are at the base of its force (*Reproduction* 5). The instances of
symbolic violence in given texts are most readily observable in the construction of the heroines' subjectivity and in the narratives' resolutions, tacitly
"misrecognized" as logical, causal successions and exigencies of the plot.
Furthermore, if we bear in mind, as does Alda Blanco, that "la escritura es una
práctica social que crea significados y no meramente los comunica" ("writing
is a social practice which creates meanings rather than merely communicate
them") (*Escritoras virtuosas* 30), then perhaps the texts, which have previously been dismissed for their transparent adhesion to the established norms,

---

[6] As Mary Nash contends: "Gender identities are, to a large extent consolidated and disseminated
through images of women. These models of femininity become decisive in manifestations of
informal social control and help channel women into historically constructed gender relationships."
See "Un/Contested Identities," *Constructing Spanish Womanhood* (New York: State U of New
York P, 1999) 26.

will warrant a second, or as may be the case with most of the novels in question, careful first reading.

In light of these observations I shall begin my study by examining the pre-scribed gender roles and "arts of existence"[7] that inform the selected post-war narratives by women.

---

[7] Foucault, *Uses of Pleasure* 10–11.

PART I
TOWARDS FEMALE EXEMPLARITY:
SETTING THE NORM

1

From Nationalist Victory to New Signifying Practices

The Nationalist victory in the Civil War (1936–39) inaugurated a new order founded on the union of authoritarian politics and reactionary Catholic values. The years preceding the war were marked by significant political and socio-economic changes for Spain, which at the turn of the century was still undergoing the parallel processes of industrialization and urbanization. The rise of anarchist, socialist, and communist currents made evident the increasing fissures in the existing order, laying bare the insufficiencies surrounding the growing sectors of wage laborers and the landless population. The Church's failure to take an active initiative in response to these demands, advocating piety and conformity instead of reforming policies, betrayed its own interests in the swelling class conflict. However, the sources of local tensions were not confined to the national borders, as the effects of the First World War, the Bolshevik Revolution, and the rising Fascist regimes reverberated throughout Europe. Spain's response to the mounting pressures from within and without were two brief and ideologically disparate tenures, represented by the military dictatorship of Primo de Rivera and a liberal rule of the Second Republic.

After the two-party Restoration system[1] had been replaced by a series of coalition governments, the nation received its first "iron surgeon" as a result of the military coup staged by General Miguel Primo de Rivera. The ensuing dictatorship (1923–30) was an authoritarian response to the preceding period of political instability and the increasing fear of those whose stakes lay in the preservation of the existing order. While intent on protecting the conservative status quo, the regime sought credibility in the Regenerationist discourse of middle-class liberal intellectuals who, in the aftermath of the Disaster of 1898, attempted national revival through a series of modernizing agrarian and educational reforms. One of the most prominent figures of the group, Joaquín

---

[1] Otherwise known as *turno pacífico*, it gave the two dynastic parties, Conservatives and Liberals, the right to alternate in power. The First Republic (1873–74) was succeeded by the Bourbon heir to the throne, Alfonso XII, inaugurating a Restoration regime that would last nearly fifty years.

Costa, disillusioned by the movement's failure to implement the desired changes, hàd claimed the need for an "iron surgeon" who could single-handedly change the course of the nation through a revolution from above.[2] In consonance with Regenerationist thought, "[t]he new dictator affirmed that his aims were . . . . to purify the political world through the establishment of a temporary authoritarian regime and . . . relieve the nation's ills" (Tusell and Queipo de Llano 208). The subsequent economic and social reforms founded on the state interventionist policies and the system, which had initially enjoyed some support, failed to achieve the necessary consolidation. Although "the link between Costa's ideas and twentieth-century authoritarianism is problematic," it is important to recognize, as does Balfour, that the Regenerationist views regarding "Spain's spiritual mission, the distrust of parliamentary politics, and the belief in an essential, as opposed to plural, Spain whose roots lay in Castile and Catholicism" were recast as sources of cultural and political legitimacy under the dictatorships of Miguel Primo de Rivera and Francisco Franco.[3] Both dictatorships relied on the hermeneutics of Spain's history and national identity for political and cultural legitimation. Popular interpretation and representation of the imperial past drew heavily on the ideas of Menéndez y Pelayo, whereby the nation's present "was seen as the tragic culmination of misguided policies and philosophical currents fundamentally alien to Spain's historical identity" (Balfour, *The End* 231). Its true self was defined in teleological and providential terms epitomized by two singular historic events: the Reconquest and the Colonization. Such a genealogy served at once as an explanation and a determinant for the role that Spain was to assume as a spiritual crusader in the ongoing battle against the reviled spread of materialism and moral degeneration of reputed capitalist and communist heresies.[4]

According to Stanley Payne, if a case were to be made for Spain's unique course in history during this time, it would be for the ascendancy, however brief, of a liberal rather than reactionary order. While authoritarianism was on the rise in Europe, the discredited military leadership in Spain had been succeeded by the parliamentary government of the Second Republic (1931–36). The result was a "sweeping reversal of traditions and values" manifest in the separation of Church and state, the institution of civil marriage and divorce, the laicization of education, the implementation of labor and agrarian reforms, and a general secularization of national life (Lannon 181).

---

[2] For the appropriation of Costa's ostensibly harmless and idealized portrayal of a longed-for national leader and a savior by different political groups, and especially by the authoritarian right, see Sebastian Balfour, *The End of the Spanish Empire: 1898–1923* (Oxford: Clarendon P, 1997).

[3] Sebastian Balfour, "The Loss of Empire, Regenerationism, and the Forging of a Myth of National Identity," *Spanish Cultural Studies* (Oxford: Oxford UP, 1995) 29.

[4] See Balfour, *The End.*

Regardless of whether the revolutionary principles underlying the new constitution ever fully materialized, an understanding of the kind of unprecedented political and cultural shift it advocated is necessary in order to appraise the ensuing nationalist counter-revolution. Among some of the most innovative reforms were the Republic's policies addressing women's social, political, juridical, and cultural status:

> In an astonishingly short time, in one of Europe's most backward societies and polities women became the *legal* equals of men. Under the December 1931 Constitution, they could vote and stand for parliament (the legal majority being set at 23 years for both men and women). In addition, a package of progressive social reforms, including one of the most liberal divorce laws in existence (February 1932), significantly enhanced their civil and employment rights. For the first time women could legally act as witnesses and guardians, sign contracts, and administer estates. Employers were no longer formally able to dismiss women merely because they had married. (Graham 101)

Following Payne, the nationalist insurgents began to employ the term "true Catholic Spain" at the start of the war as a way of eliciting and displaying support from conservative and religious groups. For the Church, the military uprising against the lay government provided a singular opportunity to reassert its authority through the resacralization of national life. For the insurgents, the espousal of the Church's cause proved to be a critical move for the forging and consolidation of the nationalist culture.[5] As early as 1936 the bishop of Salamanca, Pla y Daniel, issued a pastoral letter, *The Two Cities*, in which he justified the uprising by calling it a crusade. In its 1939 sequel, *The Triumph of the City of God*, he claimed "that the war was neither a class war nor a conflict over politics, but a confrontation between two civilizations, Catholic Spain on the one hand and foreign, Marxist, anti-Spain on the other" (qtd in Lannon 203). The invocations of "order" against "anarchy," of "hierarchical government" against "dissolvent communism," of "Christian civilization and its bases, religion, fatherland and family, against those without God and against God, and without fatherland" became the litany of the counter-revolutionary right.[6] The representation of the nationalist cause as a struggle of good against evil, and the subsequent division of Spanish society into "the victors" and "the vanquished,"[7] propitiated new

---

[5] See Stanley Payne, "National Catholicism" in *Spanish Catholicism: An Historical Overview* (Madison: U of Wisconsin P, 1987) 171–91.

[6] See Stanley Payne, *The Franco Regime: 1936–1975* (Madison: U of Wisconsin P, 1987) 198–9.

[7] See Raymond Carr, and Juan Pablo Fusi Aizpurua, *Spain: Dictatorship to Democracy* (London: George Allen & Unwin, 1981) 18.

historiographic accounts and the rise of "authoritarian fictions" as part of the state pedagogic machinery.[8]

According to Carolyn Boyd, the Nationalist victory in the Civil War was the culmination of a century-long contest between liberalism and Catholic traditionalism over who should have the right to educate. Already in 1936, the insurgents called for the revision of textbooks (in light of Catholic doctrine) and for the suspension of co-education (licensed by the Republic) in favor of traditional gender-segregated learning. As the authors of the ensuing scholastic reform averred:

> Contra la tendencia niveladora de los sexos, nosotros postulamos una educación específicamente distinta para cada uno. Pilar esencial de la reforma es la creación de una *Escuela de niñas* que permita llevar a cimas de plenitud el invaluable tesoro de afectividad e intuición que guarda el alma de la mujer española.
>
> (Contrary to the trend toward equalizing the sexes, we propose a specifically differentiated education for each. An essential pillar of our reform is the creation of a *Girl's School* which would allow the invaluable treasure of emotion and intuition that is preserved within the Spanish woman's soul to come to full fruition.) (qtd in Alted 429)

By the end of the war, religious instruction became mandatory in public schools and the new curriculum founded on the prevailing national-Catholic principles of authority, obedience, and discipline—the founding principles of "national spirit" (*el espíritu nacional*)—was well under way (Payne, *Franco* 172, 192).

The country's "spiritual and material reconstruction" was undertaken by Francisco Franco, a man who came to embody the nationalist ethos as a "crusader" for and a "savior" of authentically Spanish values (Payne, *Franco* 171). The supreme commander of the Armed Forces and head of the single political party *el Movimiento* (or, the Movement),[9] his unlimited authority was subject only to God and history.[10] Buttressed by a series of cultural sym-

---

[8] Susan Suleiman posits that the ideologically polarized climate is particularly propitious for the proliferation of narratives with an "unambiguous, dualistic system of values" in the tradition of *exemplum*. See *Authoritarian Fictions* 56, 69.

[9] The Movement, or *FET y de las JONS (Falange Española Tradicionalista y de las Juntas Ofensivas Nacional Sindicalista)*, represented a mandatory coalition of different right-wing forces among which were the Carlists who sought the restoration of monarchy and the Falangists who modeled themselves after Italian fascism. Its creation obeyed the Francoist objective of neutralization through unification.

[10] See *Doctrina e historia de la revolución nacional española* (Barcelona: Editora Nacional, 1939). Statutes of *FET y de las JONS*, articles 47 and 48 (August 4, 1937). On the role of Falange, see Sheelagh M. Ellwood, *Spanish Fascism in the Franco Era: Falange Española de las Jons, 1936–76* (New York: St Martin's P, 1987) and Stanley Payne, *Fascism in Spain: 1923–1977* (Madison: U of Wisconsin P, 1999).

bols, among them the famous arm of national saint and mystic Teresa of Avila, which stood for the providential force behind the general's military campaigns,[11] Franco came to enjoy the quasi-mythical status of a divinely ordained leader whose goal was to restore Spain's grandeur through the fulfillment of its imperial purpose as "unidad del destino en lo universal" ("unity of destiny in universal affairs").[12] His ascendance to power was to mark the dawn of a new era, which signified "the end of transformation through the final epiphany of truth," the condensation of past and future into post-apocalyptic present, and hence the suspension of time as a catalyst of change (Herzberger 34, 71).[13]

The consolidation of the new order was thus contingent upon the successful instrumentation of language as a closed system of signification. Prompted by the need for self-preservation and perpetuation, the state called for normalization, or a return to the (conservative) status quo, which aimed at "the elimination of all social and psychological irregularities and the production of useful and docile subjects through a refashioning of minds and bodies" (Best and Kellner 47). At the heart of nationalist counter-revolution was the state monopolization of all signifying practices. The subsequent control over the production of meaning and interpretation of everyday life played a central role in the process of national reconfiguration. These new signifying practices presupposed restoration of the traditional and conservative values upheld by the state and the Church. Their alliance, which came to be known as "national Catholicism," produced, in Payne's words, "the most remarkable traditionalist restoration in religion and culture witnessed in any twentieth-century European country" (*Spanish Catholicism* 171).

The official interpretations of Spain's past, present and future substantiated the view that history was a succession of authentic and inauthentic manifestations of national essence.[14] Perceived as spiritual, chivalrous, and imperial, this essence was at once a by-product of such interpretations, and a starting point for further conjectures. Historical events were judged in accordance with this allegedly ahistorical and atemporal notion that in turn allowed for claims of historical objectivity. National or authentic history mirrored the

[11] See Giuliana Di Febo, *Ritos de Guerra y de Victoria en la España franquista* (Bilbao: Desclée de Brouwer, 2002).

[12] "A unity of destiny in universal affairs," a term derived from Ortega y Gasset and popularized by José Antonio Primo de Rivera—the son of the former dictator and the founder of the Spanish Falange—echoed the sixteenth-century conception of Spaniards as "the new chosen people of God, charged with a broader world-historical mission." *Franco* 8, 58.

[13] See also Carmen Martín Gaite, *El cuarto de atrás* (1978; Barcelona: Destinolibro, 1994) 133.

[14] On the role of national history, or rather histories, in the founding of different "imagined identities," see the excellent study by Carolyn Boyd, *Historia Patria: Politics, History, and National Identity in Spain, 1875–1975* (Princeton: Princeton UP, 1997).

true, unitary, and unchanging character of Spain. The rest discredited itself as an aberration, a perfidious trajectory bound to culminate in national disasters like that of 1898. The most recent example of such historical deviation from authentic selfhood was the Second Republic. Its sole and inevitable legacy, according to Francoist ideologues, was the country's moral degeneration perceived as particularly dangerous to the feminine psyche. The wartime relaxation of the status quo regarding normative gender roles was conventionally deemed pernicious and at best unorthodox.[15] Subsumed under the category of "moral degeneracy" were the "changes in traditional cultural values, irreligiosity and most especially . . . the changing status of women and the degradation of family" (Nash, *Pronatalism* 161). The term "moral degeneracy" further echoed the turn-of-the-century Regenerationist movement that had once validated Primo de Rivera's authoritarian claims and served to legitimize subsequent calls for "regeneration."[16]

Central to the project of national reconfiguration was the production, diffusion, and naturalization of new national and gender identities, which informed and shaped the social relations of the time (and permeate the corpus of the present study). The result was a conflation of Catholicity with a set of mostly traditional and essentializing notions about what it meant to be Spanish. To such long-standing national classifiers as chivalry, valor, piety, honor, and loyalty, were added bourgeois tenets of decorum, respectability, decency and industriousness on one hand, and on the other, order, discipline, asceticism, and respect for authority preached with renewed zeal by Falangist doctrine. Finally, while "national-Catholic" identity was consistent with the principles of unity and continuity advocated by the state, and while neither religious nor national allegiance was limited to any one group, ultimately, the variables of class and gender (when not region) determined how exactly one was called to live one's life as an "authentic" Spaniard.

[15] The mobilization of a female force in the Nationalist zone was portrayed as an exception to the rule, and the subsequent calls for the return to "normality" demanded that it be further recognized as an heroic, and therefore a singular event, rather than a precedent for change.

[16] The notion of "regeneration" within fascist ideology designates a process "whereby present systems and values are replaced by a 'new order,' which itself finds its inspiration in defining moments or eras in the nation's history": Kathleen Richmond, *Women and Spanish Fascism* (London: Routledge, 2003) 3. Such a process rests on the principle of putative causality—a commonly employed narrative and self-legitimating strategy—wherein the coherence and organization of past events are subordinated to the historical present of the discourse responsible for their production. See Hayden White, "The Value of Narrativity in the Representation of Reality," *On Narrative*, ed. W.J.T. Mitchell (Chicago: U of Chicago P, 1981).

2

Engendering Exemplary Women

As we have seen, the new state warranted new subjects. Implicit in the struggle for power was "the struggle to impose certain meanings at the expense of others" (Graham and Labanyi 6). Fittingly, Sebastian Balfour stresses the significance of "value-systems" as "a battleground for the regime" ("The *Desarrollo*" 283), and Mary Nash locates the ideological underpinnings of post-war cultural and gender policies in the regime's national-Catholic orientation, "defined as a Spanish essentialism based on Catholicity" ("Moral Order" 289). Unity, sought on national and individual levels (as a milestone of the new state), presupposed exclusion, conformity, and ideological homogeneity. In spite of Franco's reputation as a monolith, the regime's makeup was heterogeneous, owing to the concomitant presence of contesting and often conflicting ideologies. The advocated models of womanhood were not uniform, either. Instead, the normative and therefore normalizing representations varied according to their loci of enunciation and according to the self-legitimating objectives of given discourses (as we shall see from the example of *Sección Femenina*). By and large, for a model to qualify as "official" it either had to stem from an authoritative source (such as the state or the Church) or bear the Church's seal of approval through the presence of a vast paratextual material (dedications, prefaces, introductions, etc.).

The ensuing attempts to at once fix and institutionalize Francoist definitions of national and gender identities produced a large body of prescriptive texts. While their study further invalidates the argument for the existence of a coherent and monolithic model of Francoist womanhood, it is nonetheless both feasible and useful to trace the premises about the role and alleged nature of the Spanish woman that they share, albeit in varying degrees. In the following pages, I shall briefly outline the constituent elements of a model that, without being attributed to a single discursive practice, was common to all of them.

The new state called its subjects, both male and female, to order (through observance of authorized practices), discipline (through compliance with instituted hierarchies), and service (through surrender of individual will for the benefit of the state). However, being "Spanish" entailed a mode of life that differed substantially for men and women. Each had an assigned role, or a "mission," to use the official rhetoric of the time, defined by state interests, which enjoyed religious and scientific validation. Hence, the allegation made by Morcillo Gómez that at the crux of national-Catholic identity— conjugating principles of unity and continuity with biological essentialism—lay a gender distinction:

> Franco's state viewed women as its indispensable partner in nation building. It put in place institutions and promulgated laws to officiate women's duties as mothers and daughters of the fatherland. . . . As the regime (and the Catholic Church) saw it, gender difference constituted the very essence of selfhood; it rendered stability and social order to the nation, and clarity of purpose to the individual. (*Construction* 51)

The prescribed gender roles functioned as normative and coercive categories that helped consolidate the new order by restoring the conservative status quo. Implicit in their production and circulation was "the refusal or repression of alternative possibilities": the normative models were passed off as ideal and therefore "desired," and the only legitimate, and therefore "natural" realizations of feminine essence (Scott 1068).[1] The spontaneity ascribed to the practice of given tenets rendered them immanent, while the deployment of "nature" as an alleged source of endorsed norms made their observance seem inevitable and their rejection a sign of anomalous development. The wide circulation of these "ideals" rested on the tradition of exemplarity, which served to induce, if not a desire to emulate, at least a pressure to conform. The making of female formation a stipulation for successful womanhood, however, betrayed the latter's socially and historically constructed makeup.

For all practical purposes, the state *was* Spain, hailed as *una, grande y libre*—one, great, and free. But not unlike woman, Spain was also a repository of sacred ideals, contaminated by the hands of the enemies, and in want of sanitization best achieved through isolation (as manifest in the politics of autarchy). And while the regime passed off its colonizing tendencies as Spain's moral imperative, the country's own spiritual regeneration was imparted to women. In a time of political upheaval, economic instability, and shifting cultural codes, Spanish woman became a symbol of permanence and a custodian of virtue.[2] In the tradition of the nineteenth-century exponents of bourgeois morality, she was extolled as an "archivo viviente de nuestras mejores tradiciones" ("a living archive of our best traditions"), "depositaria y guardadora de lo más intenso y notable de la tradición cristiana" ("repository

---

[1] For the definition and reformulation of the category of gender, see also Judith Butler, who defines gender as "the repeated stylization of the body, a set of repeated acts within a highly rigid regulatory frame that congeal over time to produce the appearance of substance, of a natural sort of being": *Gender Trouble* (New York: Routledge, 1999) 44–5.

[2] On the valence of stable, unitary constructs at the time of flux, see, among others, Susan Kirkpatrick, *Las Románticas* (Berkeley: U of California P, 1989) 366.

and guardian of the most vital and noteworthy aspects of the Christian tradition"), "garantía de la pureza de la institución familiar y depositaria del honor de la familia" ("guarantee of the purity of the family institution and repository of family honor") (qtd in Pastor i Homs 33).

As Mary Nash notes, "[m]any of the propagandists of the 'National Revolution' saw themselves as moral regenerators engaged in the purification of public morality" ("Moral Order" 299). Their project targeted women at once as passive recipients and partisans of the peremptory moral code. It was incumbent upon women to preserve their virtue above all, for the sake of men, whom it was their duty made destiny to nurture and serve. This, as the bellicose rhetoric of the time never tired of pointing out, meant waging a war against their own perceived shortcomings, desires, and ambitions, not to mention the pressures from without, capable of tarnishing women physically or morally:

> La casa es el más seguro santuario de la inocencia y la pureza . . . la joven que ama la casa y la ama como su más caro y natural reino, evita peligros que pudieran serle fatales.
>
> (The home is the safest sanctuary of innocence and purity . . . the young woman who loves her home as her dearest and most natural kingdom avoids dangers that could be fatal for her.)
>
> Que ningún cuadro o imagen pueda turbar vuestra mirada pura. Que ningún periódico con la procacidad de su lenguaje, de sus grabados ofenda la más bella virtud. Que ningún libro sea motivo de corrupción, de inmoralidad.
>
> (Let no painting or image cloud your pure vision. Let no newspaper with the indecency of its language [or] drawings, offend your most precious virtue. Let no book be a cause of corruption [or] immorality.) (qtd in Pastor i Homs 33–4)

"Docile bodies," women were "subjected, used, transformed, and improved" so as to become purveyors of national-Catholic values (Rabinow, *Foucault Reader* 180). As the periodicals of the time assured, "[s]ólo así, hecha estatua, podrás estar tranquila, porque el bronce es sólido y el diablo no tienta el mármol" ("[o]nly in this way, turned into a statue, will you be able to be at peace, because bronze is solid and the devil does not tempt marble") (qtd in Pastor i Homs 30). By dint of such discursive practices, compulsory attitudes gained the semblance of a compulsion and arbitrary qualities were transformed into indelible marks of femininity.

The new identity politics were buttressed by the state legislation that between 1938 and 1939 annulled the Republican laws on civil matrimony and divorce and reinstated Title IV, Book I of the 1889 Civil Code. Under the restored regulation, all marriages had to be authorized by the Church, contraception was illegal and abortion a crime, the dissolution of marriage was feasible only upon the death of one of the spouses, and the civil union was reserved for couples who either did not profess or abdicated from Catholic faith. A 1950 exegesis of women's legal rights offers no explanation on the regulations for civil marriage. According to its author, the lawyer Francisco Malo Segura:

> Si bien en España la ley reconoce dos formas de matrimonio: el canónico, que deben contraer todos los que profesen la religión católica, y el civil, que se celebrará del modo que determina el Código Civil, se ha considerado innecesario mencionar las disposiciones relativas a este último, por reservarse solamente para aquellos que prueban su acatolicidad por no haber sido bautizados.

> (Even though Spanish legislation recognizes two types of marriage—the canonical, by which all those who profess the Catholic religion must be married, and the civil, which is carried out as stipulated in the Civil Code—there is no need here to refer to the regulations concerning the latter, as it is reserved only for those who demonstrate their non-Catholicism by not having been baptized.)[3]

Implicitly, these words reinforce the endorsed homology between non-Catholics and non-Spaniards. In stark contrast to the Republican legislation, which had granted men and women equal rights within marriage, the civil code in question "enshrined women's juridical inferiority, married women becoming minors before the law" (Graham 184). The wife was obliged to obey (Article 57) and follow her husband wherever he chose to reside (Article 58). In turn, the husband was the administrator of all matrimonial property (Article 59) unless the wife had belongings that did not form part of the dowry, in which case the profits were automatically converted into joint property (Article 1.382). Like minors and delinquents, women could not be legal guardians (Article 237), and if married, they needed the consent of their husbands—as their representatives—to appear in court (Article 60). Women's conjugal rights, or lack thereof, were founded on the principle of separate spheres, which misrecognized women's socially and historically constructed role as their natural inclination and their subordinate position as a by-product of biological difference:

> [S]ería indigno halagar hipócritamente el orgullo femenino clamando por que se le conceda la autoridad marital o iguales prerrogativas que al marido, pues es un hecho innegable que su menor experiencia, su debilidad natural,

---

[3] See *Los derechos de la mujer en la legislación española: Contiene las disposiciones canónicas, civiles, penales y mercantiles relacionadas con los derechos de la mujer, expuestas en forma práctica y de fácil comprensión* (Santander [Sp.]: Fasan, 1950) 9.

su carácter antojadizo y su misma naturaleza, hecha más bien para el cuidado del hogar y amor de la familia que para la lucha de la vida y dificultades de la existencia, obligan a reconocer la supremacía del marido en la dirección y administración de la sociedad conyugal.

([I]t would be unseemly to falsely flatter feminine pride by demanding that she be granted marital authority, or prerogatives equal to those of the husband, when the undeniable fact is that her lesser experience, her natural weakness, her capricious character and her very nature—better suited to care of the home and love of the family than for the struggles of life and the difficulties of survival—oblige one to recognize the supremacy of the husband in the management and administration of marital property.) (Malo Segura 8)[4]

In a seemingly paradoxical contrast to the state legislation, women's return to the hearth was couched in redemptive and liberatory rhetoric. Both the state and the Church claimed to have rescued women from their condition of slavery (imposed by other religious and pagan practices), exploitation (encouraged by capitalism), and corruption (fomented by communists and anarchists). Motherhood, within the sacrament of marriage, was a task that ennobled women and made them men's equal in their shared Christian and national endeavor. While the mobilization of female forces, before and during the war, was seen as a direct response to circumstances, the "restoration" of the bourgeois model of domesticity was interpreted as a recovery of true feminine "essence," displacing the link between the advocated ideals and the exigencies of the established order:

¿Ves aquel tipo exótico, de boina, dejando ver un fleco de cabellos recortado, sobretodo, medias gruesas, calzado holgado, tacón bajo, bastón en mano y guía de turista?
Tiene envidia al hombre; pretende corregir al artífice del sexo y superarse.
Vano y ridículo conato. No caigas en la tentación de imitarlo.
El Catolicismo te libró de la esclavitud y abyección que tenías en el paganismo, te devolvió tu dignidad, te hizo compañera del hombre, reina del hogar. No quieras ir más allá y usurpar la masculinidad.

(Do you see that exotic character, wearing a beret, revealing a tuft of cropped hair, with an overcoat, thick stockings, loose-fitting shoes, low heels, cane in hand, and a tourist guidebook?
She is envious of men; she purports to correct the Maker of sexes and rise above herself.

---

[4] On women's legal status under the 1889 Civil Code, see also Mary Nash, *Mujer, familia y trabajo en España (1875–1936)* (Barcelona: Anthropos, 1983) and Rosario Ruiz Franco, "La situación legal: Discriminación y reforma," *Mujeres y hombres en la España franquista*, ed. Gloria Nielfa Cristóbal (Madrid: Complutense, 2003) 117–44.

What a vain and ridiculous attempt. Do not yield to the temptation of imitating her.
Catholicism freed you from the slavery and abjection to which you were subject in paganism, it restored your dignity, it made you man's companion, queen of the hearth. Do not wish to go further and usurp masculinity.)[5]

The routine infantilization of female audiences on the alleged grounds of their low educational level had the added benefit of bolstering the state mandate to eradicate all traces of liberal formation and generate "una masa limpia de resabios y totalmente dócil y dispuesta a recibir [sus] enseñanzas" ("an untainted mass, completely docile and disposed to receive [its] teachings") (Primo de Rivera 251).

The main purpose of female education was the formation of exemplary wives and mothers. "According to Francoist ideologues, the model woman, the 'Perfecta Casada', the dedicated and submissive spouse and mother, had been transformed when women were granted political rights" even when these were expressed on paper more often than in practice (Nash, "Pronatalism" 162). Likewise, "[w]omen's aspirations to social advancement, female emancipation and economic independence," observes Nash, were repudiated as vestiges of the Second Republic; that is to say, inauthentic manifestations of true Spanish womanhood ("Moral Order" 296). For these officiators of national-Catholic gender ideology, female socialization was key to enabling women to fulfill their mission as propitiators and perpetuators of the established order, to improve their performance as wives and mothers, and to impose on them the relation of "utility–docility."

Thus, in Francoist rhetoric, femininity and maternity were coterminous. The single, most widely upheld contribution of the national-Catholic woman was to produce "hijos católicos con la mentalidad del 'nuevo estado'" ("Catholic children with the mentality of the 'new state'"), possible only within the legal institution of marriage (Pastor i Homs 38). In view of this function, women were encouraged to take courses and obtain certificates at national schools of childrearing (escuelas nacionales de puericultura). One objective of these courses was demographic growth. According to Kathleen Richmond, the "demographic problem" served as justification for restoring the ideal of domesticity once the "[i]mproved social legislation and changes to the Civil Code had given women more rights in the workplace and within the family structure, challenging the traditional authority of the male" (14). Motherhood, or the realization of womanly destiny, became a duty rather than a choice. Consequently, marriage was defined in terms of procreation:

---

[5] See Francisco Esteve Blanes, Hacia tu ideal: Unas palabras a una joven (Barcelona: Subirana, 1939) 9.

Etimológicamente, la palabra matrimonio se deriva de los voces latinas 'matris et munium', que significan oficio de madre. Por tanto, con estas palabras se quiso señalar que, dentro del matrimonio, son insustituíbles las funciones que desempeña la madre y la que soporta el mayor trabajo.

(Etymologically, the word 'matrimony' derives from the Latin words 'matris et munium' denoting 'a mother's duty.' Hence, these words were meant to establish that, within marriage, the functions that the mother carries out are indispensable and she is the one who bears the greater amount of work.) (Malo Segura 20)

The cult of motherhood was thus supported by the state and religious authorities whose prescribed code of actions implied control over desires and expectations. Their doctrines insisted on a way of life, a *modus operandi*, which would perpetuate itself. It was not enough to follow the set precepts; these had to be internalized so that their realization appeared to be a subjective necessity rather than a compulsion from without. By extension, the sacred mission of motherhood was to enable Spanish women to achieve not the prescribed condition, but their own ambition of serving God and Fatherland. In consonance with these objectives, women were encouraged to become proficient in the only science that the state deemed indispensable for the realization of their feminine purpose: the science of motherhood (*la ciencia maternal*). "El mundo podía progresar sin mujeres científicas, doctoras, abogadas, etc." ("The world was able to progress without women scientists, doctors, lawyers, etc."), but, according to the regime's contemporary, Carmen Buj, it could not go on without "'madres que sean reinas del hogar, sacerdotisas . . . que alumbren el espíritu familiar con la luz de las celestiales enseñanzas, dirigiendo a sus hijos hacia el bien, la verdad y la belleza'" ("mothers, who are queens of the hearth, priestesses, . . . who illuminate the family spirit with the light of celestial teachings, guiding their children towards goodness, truth, and beauty") (qtd in Palacio Lis 175). Ironically, the exaltation of feminine essence and the cult of motherhood, which imbued women with a considerable degree of symbolic capital, allowed for broader interpretations of the type of training that women required and hence were entitled to receive. While classes on domestic economy and hygiene, needlework, and childcare could not be foregone, there were those who claimed that higher education in fields that enhanced innate feminine qualities could make women better companions and more valuable partners in the common enterprise of "hacer patria" ("building the fatherland") (Palacio Lis 176).[6]

---

[6] While the members of the *Sección Femenina* played a central role in promoting traditional gender roles (as representatives of the primary state organization responsible for women's social and political formation), they also advocated female participation in national life and to an extent managed to legitimate their own initiative in the public sphere, provided that no woman claimed to compete for ascendancy with the opposite and dominant sex. For further discussion in this study, see Chapter 5, "Female formation and *la nueva mujer* of the Falange."

As an ideological state apparatus, education was the primary social institution responsible for the forging of new subjects in consonance with their national, gender, and class-specific roles. Accordingly, female instruction was conceived in traditional terms as primarily moral, religious, and domestic. The view propagated by the nineteenth-century conduct manuals that "la mujer 'mal educada' es aquella que ha rechazado el papel tradicional asignado a la mujer basado en la obediencia, la resignación y la castidad" ("the 'poorly educated' woman is the one who has rejected the traditional role assigned to women based on obedience, resignation, and chastity") (Andreu, *Galdós* 66) gained new currency in post-war debates on female socialization. In addition, women received mandatory political education under the directive of the *Sección Femenina,* the women's branch of the Falange.

Latent in all pedagogic work, according to Bourdieu, is "a process of inculcation which must last long enough to produce a durable training, i.e. a habitus, the product of internalization of the principles of a cultural arbitrary capable of perpetuating itself after pedagogic action has ceased and thereby of perpetuating in practices the principles of the internalized arbitrary" (*Reproduction* 31). A system of social reproduction, institutionalized education reinforced patriarchal authority and women's subordinate positions within the family and society at large. Furthermore, it sought "'formar en las niñas lo que debería ser la ambición básica de toda mujer: el hacer de la casa la extensión de su persona'" ("to instill within girls that which should be the basic ambition of every woman: making the home into an extension of her person").[7] Implicit in this phrasing, not atypical of Francoist edifying discourse, is an attempt at interiorizing the external. The prescription "el hacer de la casa la extensión de su persona" ("making the home into an extension of her person") must stem from the woman herself: "debería ser la ambición básica de toda mujer" ("should be the basic ambition of every woman").[8]

Although women were not entirely precluded from access to work and/or higher education, according to the institutionalized hierarchy both were considered ancillary (if not superfluous) to the exercise of their primary duty to the fatherland: "formar familias con la base exacta de la austeridad y alegría donde se fomente todo lo tradicional" ("to form families with the precise foundation of austerity and happiness upon which all that is traditional can be

---

[7] Enrique Herrera Oria, "Educar en la niña a la mujer" in *Atenas* (Burgos), 86 (Dec. 1939), p. 366. Qtd in Alted 428.

[8] Bourdieu's concept of "self-perpetuating and transposable dispositions" is instrumental for understanding why certain attitudes outlast the immediate circumstances responsible for their emergence, and may persist even after these material conditions have been discredited or cease to exist, as has been the case with the values instilled by the *Sección Femenina.* See *Reproduction in Education, Society and Culture* (1977; London: Sage, 2000).

built").[9] As Morcillo Gómez observes, the identity of university subjects according to the *Ley de Ordenación Universitaria* (University Regulatory Law) "was irreconcilable with the official discourse on Spanish femininity," being, as it was, intended for the formation of the state elites, which by definition were male ("Shaping Womanhood" 56). Those who sought university degrees or professional training were channeled into fields that were deemed more in tune with their feminine essence even as they were unlikely to pursue these fields once they got married:

> Ni que decir tiene que hay actividades que deben reservarse a las mujeres, como por ejemplo, las que guardan relación con labores de aguja, y todo trabajo que pueda llevarse a cabo en el hogar o en sus cercanías y alrededores, sin descuidar los deberes con aquel relacionado . . . es evidente que cierta clase de labores, por su feminidad, algunas especies de trabajos, por la relación que ha de estarse con el público, por la agilidad y destreza de las mujeres, y en suma por la delicadeza y afán de orden de que están poseídas, constituyen profesiones aptas para ellas.

> (It goes without saying that there are activities that should be reserved for women, for example, those related to needlework, and any work that can be carried out in the home or nearby, without neglecting the duties related to it . . . it is obvious that a certain kind of labor, due to its femininity, and certain types of employment, due to their requisite relationship with the public or to the nimbleness and skill of women—and, in sum, because of the delicacy and penchant for order which women possess—make apt professions for them.)[10]

Within the family—the bedrock of normative and normalizing power relations founded on patriarchal authority and conservative Christian mores— women had the ambiguous role of a subordinate party imbued with unsurpassed responsibilities. The state familial policies formed part of the political campaign toward demographic growth and national consolidation.[11] Women's work was regulated accordingly, so as not to interfere with their primordial function as breeders and their ensuing responsibilities as socializers of future subjects. In consonance with this exigency, and in exchange for their cooperation, Spanish women were relieved from all the allegedly fastidious tasks that drew them out of the house and away from their obligations. Under the 1938

---

[9] Pilar Primo de Rivera, qtd in Luis Suárez Fernández, *Crónica de la Sección Femenina y su tiempo* 76 and Irene Palacio Lis, *Madres culpables* 175.

[10] J. Pérez Serrano, *El retorno al hogar de la mujer trabajadora* (Barcelona: Ministerio de Trabajo-Patronato Escuela Social de Barcelona, 1945), qtd in Ruiz Franco 129.

[11] Although the fertility index had been dropping steadily since the early 1920s, its two accepted causes were the licentious policies of the Second Republic and the Civil War victims, who by definition were Nationalist.

Labor Charter (*Fuero del trabajo*) they were "delivered" from nightshifts, workshops, and factories:

> Es consigna rigurosa de nuestra Revolución elevar y fortalecer la familia en su tradición cristiana, sociedad natural, perfecta, y cimiento de la nación.
>
> En cumplimiento de la anterior misión ha de otorgarse al trabajador—sin perjuicio del salario justo y remunerador de su esfuerzo—la cantidad de bienes, para que aunque su prole sea numerosa—y así lo exige la patria—, no se rompa el equilibrio de su hogar y llegue a la miseria, obligando a la madre a buscar en la fábrica o taller un salario con que cubrir la insuficiencia del conseguido por el padre, apartándola de su función suprema e insustituible que es la de preparar a sus hijos, arma y base de la Nación en su doble aspecto espiritual y material.
>
> (It is a strict tenet of our Revolution to raise and strengthen the family in its Christian tradition, [as it is] a natural and perfect society, the foundation of the nation.
>
> To fulfill the aforementioned mission, the worker must be granted—without detriment to a salary that is just and remunerative of his labor—a sufficient quantity of goods, so that even though his offspring be numerous—as the fatherland demands it to be—the equilibrium of the home is not broken and the family driven into poverty, obliging the mother to seek a wage in factories or workshops with which to make up the insufficiency in the father's earnings, separating her from her supreme and irreplaceable function, which is raising her children, arm and foundation of the nation in its dual spiritual and material aspects.) (qtd in Scanlon, *La pólemica,* 320–1)

In addition, the state endorsed birth prizes (*premios de natalidad*, 1948) for women under the age of 30 and men under 35, family allowances (*subsidios familiares*, 1938) and bonuses (*plus de cargas familiares*, 1945) paid to the male breadwinner, and further concessions for families with numerous children, "from transport and school grants to tax exemptions, credit facilities, access to housing, [and] sanitary assistance" (Nash, "Moral Order" 299). The stipulation for these rewards was that women did not work outside the home. To this effect, state enterprises began to require that their female employees give up their positions after entering matrimony. In exchange, they were offered one-time monetary compensation in the form of a dowry or *dote*. A married woman needed her husband's consent to work, and this entitled him to her earnings. Interestingly, the average marriage age among employed women increased, suggesting that many were reluctant (or could not afford) to give up their jobs (Ruiz Franco 128).

Aside from promoting an increase in birth rate (which did not take place until much later when economic conditions improved) and a return to traditional values, familial policies facilitated the state surveillance of "private" practices. In this respect, what is noteworthy about Francoism is not so much the stipulated socialization of new political subjects, as the scale of control (manifestly authoritarian) that this process entailed. The adherents of national-Catholic doctrine were expected to "volcar su personalidad, si es que la tienen, dentro de las normas que se les dan, ajustándose a ellas exactamente, pero poniendo todas sus condiciones humanas en el servicio que realizan . . ." ("to pour their personality, if they have one, into the mold of given norms, fitting precisely into these while putting all of their human abilities into the service that they discharge . . .") (Primo de Rivera 257). Any suggestion of discrepancy between individual and national interests was tantamount to ideological heresy. A hierarchical relationship between the two required that private ambitions be defined by state interests, thereby coercing will and desire to signify will of obedience and desire of the legitimate. According to Helen Graham,

> In order to contain the growing material crisis and to avert any wider political repercussions, the Franco regime was obliged to adopt a level of intervention in the private sphere.
>
> This intervention, moreover, was also paradoxically generated by the very restorationist-patriarchal ideology underpinning the regime. On the one hand, it had sought to make a rigid division between public and private, closing down society . . ., promoting its 'privatization' or 'atomization' based on the 'haven' of the private household at whose center was the 'mother' . . .
>
> But, to ensure this outcome, the state could not really afford to let the private sphere remain entirely 'private'. Control, especially of women, had to be enforced. (186–7)

Consequently, for the purposes of state surveillance, the two gendered realms of operation, the private and the public, were indistinguishable.[12]

While it is not my intention here to discuss the effectiveness of the aforementioned policies—in fact, it could be argued that what they articulate is the want rather than the incidence of advocated practices—I would nonetheless like to acknowledge that most representations analyzed here (whether political, legal, religious, or literary) target middle-class women and not the urban poor (nor the agrarian sector) who, as Graham notes, were too hard pressed for survival not to work. But even as I concur with Mary Nash in that "neither normative ideology nor coercive legislation [is] a mirror of social reality"

---

[12] According to Althusser: "The distinction between the public and the private is a distinction internal to bourgeois law, and valid in the (subordinate) domains in which bourgeois law exercises its 'authority'. The domain of the State escapes it because the latter is 'above the law': the State, which is the State *of* the ruling class, is neither public nor private; on the contrary, it is the precondition for any distinction between public and private." See *Lenin and Philosophy and Other Essays* (1971; New York: Monthly Review P, 2001) 97.

("Pronatalism" 173), it would be wrong to underestimate the power that naturalized cultural representations exercise in the shaping of subjectivity and
structuring of self-representations (Sunder Rajan 129).

As we have seen, the normative correspondence between femininity and
motherhood presupposed observance of spatial constraints that drew women
back to home and hearth. This process was further buttressed by the state,
which viewed family as "the primary social unit of Spanish society," and the
mirror of its own vertical ordering ("Pronatalism" 160). The restoration of the
1889 Civil Code reinforced patriarchal authority and women's subordinate
legal status with the end result that "el sometimiento de la esposa a la autoridad marital invalidaba cualquier conato de independencia económica y
capacidad jurídica por parte de las mujeres" ("the wife's submission to marital authority invalidated any attempt at woman's economic independence or
juridical empowerment") (Ruiz Franco 123).

For its counter-revolutionary program, which defined women in terms of
their roles as wives and mothers, the regime drew on a vast archive of existing
traditional models, two of which, *la perfecta casada* and *el ángel del hogar*,
demand closer examination. To these we must add a third—perhaps the most
innovative—type promoted by the members of *Sección Femenina*, a woman's
branch of the Spanish Falange, and here studied under the label of *la nueva
mujer*. Although the stated objective of this organization was the enforcement
of traditional gender roles, the implementation of these roles entailed the
transgression of the prescribed norms. The values and practices exemplified
by each of the aforementioned models were guided by a shared nationalist
ethos, itself subject to dynamic socio-political and economic forces. The brief
introductions that follow identify the tenets that informed and shaped the
social relations of the time, and as such are embedded in the texts studied
below.

3

La perfecta casada: The Catholic Model of an Ideal Wife

Although post-war Spain produced an abundance of ecclesiastical writings, especially on the properties of the ideal woman and her societal role, Fray Luis de León's sixteenth-century moral treatise *La perfecta casada* (1583) was fundamental in legitimating the official Francoist model of womanhood, and enjoyed wide circulation as a staple wedding gift. An epistolary dedicated to María Varela Osorio (kin of Fray Luis), *La perfecta casada* presents a tropological exegesis of Proverbs 31: 10–31.[1] Each of the work's twenty

---

[1] The following verses, corresponding to Proverbs 31: 10–31, are taken from Félix García and Felicity Hubbard's respective editions of Fray Luis' treatise: "Mujer de valor, ¿quién la hallará? Raro y extremado es su precio./Confía en ella el corazón de su marido, no le harán mengua los despojos./Págole con bien y no con mal todos los días de su vida./Buscó lana y lino, y obró con el saber de sus manos./Fue como navío de mercader, que de lueñe trae su pan./ Madrugó y repartió a sus gañanes las raciones; la tarea de sus mozas./Vínole al gusto una heredad, y compróla, y del fruto de sus palmas plantó viña./Ciñóse de fortaleza, y fortificó su brazo. Tomó gusto en el granjear; su candela no se apagó de noche. Puso sus manos en la tortera, y sus dedos tomaron el huso./Sus palmas abrió para el afligido, y sus manos extendió para el menesteroso./No temerá de la nieve a su familia, porque toda su gente vestida con vestiduras dobladas./Hizo para sí aderezos de cama; holanda y púrpura es su vestido./Señalado en las puertas su marido cuando se asentare con los gobernadores del pueblo./Lienzo tejió y vendiólo; franjas dio al cananeo./Fortaleza y buena gracia su vestido reirá hasta el día postrero./Su boca abrió en sabiduría y ley de piedad en su lengua./Rodeó todos los rincones de su casa, y no comió el pan de balde./Levantáronse sus hijos y loáronla, y alabóla también su marido./Muchas hijas allegaron riquezas; mas tú subsiste sobre todas. /Engaño es el buen donaire, y burlería la hermosura: la mujer que teme a Dios ésa es digna de loor./Dalde del fruto de sus manos, y loenla en las puertas sus obras." ("Who can find a virtuous woman, for her price is far above rubies? / The heart of her husband doth safely trust in her, so that he shall have no need of spoil. /She will do him good and not evil all the days of her life. / She seeketh wool, and flax, and worketh willingly with her hands. / She is like the merchants' ships; she bringeth her food from afar. / She riseth also while it is yet night, and giveth meat to her household, and a portion to her maidens. / She considereth a field; and buyeth it: with the fruit of her hands she planteth a vineyard. / She girdeth her loins with strength, and strengtheneth her arms. She perceiveth that her merchandise is good: her candle goeth not out by night. She layeth her hands to the spindle, and her hands hold the distaff. / She stretcheth out her hand to the poor; yea, she reacheth forth her hands to the needy. / She is not afraid of the snow for her household: for all her household are clothed with scarlet. / She maketh herself coverings of tapestry; her clothing is silk and purple. / Her husband is known in the gates, when he sitteth among the elders of the land. / She maketh fine linen and

chapters opens with, and offers a gloss of, a particular verse (save chapter 8, which introduces verses 17–19). As such, the most obvious source for Fray Luis' model of a perfect wife is the Bible. In that sense, Fray Luis undoubtedly saw his work, *La perfecta casada,* as presenting a timeless model, and its persistence throughout centuries would seem to support this. In spite of this consideration, and notwithstanding the fact that Fray Luis considered his depiction of an ideal wife divinely inspired—if for no other reason than to stave off the criticism of those who claimed his knowledge of feminine mores all too accurate for a man of the cloth[2]—most studies point out the work's historicity, situating Fray Luis' rendition of Scripture within its relevant religious, cultural, and socio-economic contexts (or, perhaps, laying bare the historicity of religious thought as it is enmeshed in specific cultural, economic, political, and social contexts).

The assertion that "Fray Luis de León se inspiró en la Escritura para escribir *La perfecta casada.* Pero le pesó también ser hijo de su tiempo" ("Scripture was the inspiration for Fray Luis de León to write *La perfecta casada.* But he was also a child of his time") may, at first glance, seem too obvious to warrant repetition on its own merit (Castilla y Cortázar 193). It does, however, rather succinctly point us to two approaches discernible in the genealogy of Fray Luis' representation of women. While the Scriptural influence on his work is indisputable, the critics' sources of choice, when it comes to analyzing his model of perfection, range from St Paul to Erasmus. The problem, if we may so call it, stems from the perceived mismatch between Fray Luis' reputation as a "progressive" and contentious (because unconventional) thinker and his "retrograde" or, according to some, misogynistic view of women.[3] Since

selleth it; and delivereth girdles unto the merchant. / Strength and honour are her clothing, and she shall rejoice in time to come. / She openeth her mouth with wisdom; and in her tongue is the law of kindness. / She looketh well to the ways of her household, and eateth not the bread of idleness. / Her children arise up, and call her blessed; her husband also, and he praiseth her. / Many daughters have done virtuously, but thou excellest them all. / Favour is deceitful, and beauty is vain: but a woman that feareth the Lord, she shall be praised. / Give her of the fruit of her hands; and let her own works praise her in the gates."): See *Obras completas castellanas de Fray Luis de León*, ed. P. Félix García (Madrid: B.A.C., 1967) and *The Perfect Wife*, trans. Alice Philena Hubbard (Denton, TX: College P [T.S.C.W. Texas State College for Women], 1943).

[2] See Félix García's introduction to *La perfecta casada* in *Obras* 233.

[3] This tension forms Carroll Johnson's point of departure in "Ideology, Economy and Feminism," *San Juan de la Cruz and Fray Luis de León: A Commemorative International Symposium* (Newark, DE: Juan de la Cuesta, 1996) 129–44. For a reading that aligns Fray Luis' position with reactionary views of his time, see Josemi Lorenzo Arribas, "Fray Luis de León: un misógino progresista en la 'querella de las mujeres'. Relectura de *La perfecta casada,*" *Feminismo y misoginia en la literatura española: Fuentes literarias para la Historia de las Mujeres* (Madrid: Narcea, S.A., 2001) 76, 77, 78. For a critical perspective on the extent to which Fray Luis' model wife is faithful to its Biblical source, see Blanca Castillo y Cortázar's "Antropología bíblica de la feminidad en *La perfecta casada,*" *Fray Luis de León: IV centenario (1591–1991)* (Madrid: Ediciones escurialenses, 1992) 193–208. For an overview of the state of

entering this debate would lead us away from the present discussion, which itself is an interpretation of an interpretation or, as Barthes would have it, the second-degree meaning of the sign that is *la perfecta casada*, I shall limit my observations to what in Fray Luis' rendition of a Biblical text gave his work the status and legitimacy of a foundational discourse to the proponents of the post-war national and gender ideology.

For the propagators of Francoism, the appeal of Fray Luis' model wife, at least in part, lay in its endorsement of two principles of hierarchy: one having to do with marriage and the other with economy. The first drew on the then widely accepted premise of men's physical, moral and intellectual superiority, according to which women were expected to obey their husbands. The second may be attributed to the text's apparent privileging of agricultural and domestic (or self-sustained) modes of production over others.[4] Finally, one cannot ignore the transposability of those orthodox (Catholic) underpinnings that inform the work and that made religious discourse so appealing to Franco's rule.

From the state's perspective, there was no reason why teachings of self-sacrifice and denial, fear of and obedience to authority, conformity and submission of one's will had to be limited to the Church, when their widespread practice bore obvious advantages in the project of national reconfiguration. The seductive appeal of order in the aftermath of war made the conflation of political and religious doctrines all the more attractive. The following pages examine Fray Luis' spiritual injunctions against the backdrop of nationalist discourse that saw the utility of promoting them for its own benefit.

At a time when large sectors of the population were enduring hardship and penury, the Church's moral hegemony ensured that summons of resignation and perseverance received ample diffusion. Harmony (embedded in Fray Luis' notions of perfection) and order (promoted by the regime) were contingent upon the fulfillment by individual members of family and society at large of their unique purpose. The state and the Church spared no effort in elucidating this potentially ambivalent point, with the result that painstaking instructions abound as to the exact nature of the responsibilities that Spaniards were to assume in the name of God and Fatherland.

---

married women during the period in question, see Mariló Vigil's excellent study *La vida de las mujeres en los siglos XVI y XVII* (Madrid: Siglo XXI, 1986). A cogent discussion of the sixteenth-century cultural landscape with regard to Fray Luis' treatise can be found in Olga Rivera's *La mujer y el cuerpo femenino en* La perfecta casada *de Fray Luis de León* (Newark, DE: Juan de la Cuesta, 2006).

[4] In addition to the above-cited article by Carroll Johnson, see María Angeles Durán, "Lectura económica de Fray Luis de León," *Nuevas perspectivas sobre la mujer. Actas de las primeras jornadas de investigación interdisciplinaria organizadas por el Seminario de Estudios de la Mujer*, vol. 2 (Madrid: Universidad Autónoma, 1982) 257–73.

Consistent with Catholic ideology and post-war reality, the sixteenth-century guide to perfection by way of Christian virtues downplayed the significance of material conditions (even though markedly stratified social relations permeate the text) in favor of spiritual welfare. Those who read it found that contentment, as a mark of perfection, was not contingent upon one's circumstances, which were often volatile and seldom predictable, but upon the acceptance of one's cross. In Fray Luis' text,[5] "the cross" embodies a set of tenets, or principles determined by one's station in life: "Y la cruz que cada uno ha de llevar y por donde ha de llegar a juntarse con Cristo, propiamente es la obligación y la carga que cada uno tiene por razón del estado en que vive"; (13) ("And the cross which each one of us is bound to bear, and by means of which we are to attain union with our Lord, is the very duty and burden imposed on each one of us by virtue of that state of life in which we find ourselves") (Hubbard 6). The woman's "cross," like its secular equivalent, "mission," designated the functions that simultaneously bore out and reinforced the status quo. Since the prescribed roles were advocated as natural, God-given, or essential in some form, failure to embody them was regarded as a deviation from the norm. In the following passage, Fray Luis denounces the lack of chastity in women as an aberration, having previously extolled chastity itself as the basis of all feminine virtue:

> Que, como a las aves les es naturaleza el volar, así las casadas han de tener por dote natural, en que no puede haber quiebra, el ser buenas y honestas, y han de estar persuadidas que lo contrario es suceso aborrescible y desventurado, y hecho monstruoso, o, por mejor decir, no han de imaginar que puede suceder lo contrario, más que ser el fuego frío o la nieve caliente. (30)

> (Consider the birds, how it is their nature to fly; so married women must regard honour and goodness as their natural endowment, from which there must be not the least deviation. They must be convinced that the slightest lapse is an unfortunate and hateful occurrence, a most horrible deed. To put it more tellingly, no infringement must be considered possible, any more than it is in the nature of fire to be chilly, or snow to be hot.) (Hubbard 17)

---

[5] The quotations in Spanish correspond to a 1940 text of *La perfecta casada* (Buenos Aires: Espasa Calpe). For the English version, I have consulted the two available translations: the first by Alice Philena Hubbard (Sister Felicia of the Order of St Anne), see note 1 above, and the other by John A. Jones and Javier San José Lera (Lewiston, NY: Edwin Mellen, 1999). The pages at the end of each citation correspond to their respective sources. The brackets in the English text indicate instances of any minor discrepancy in judgment or choice of words on my part.

In contrast to the normative formulations, in which one's role was an extension of one's intrinsic condition, the discernible need for instruction and/or persuasion suggests that some dispositions were not as "natural" as others. The type of fulfillment that one was expected to achieve depended on variables of class, gender, and occasionally place, which in turn dictated the kind of formation one was to receive. Such a formation facilitated the internalization of conferred values and encouraged their respective essentialization in discourse. Consequently, the very circumstances responsible for the production of this so-called "second nature" were passed off as immaterial to its existence.

As a rule, normative representations of women were conceived in teleological terms and parted from claims about woman's ultimate purpose in life. If we were to condense this reasoning into a formula it would appear as follows: function → formation → essence (where the function determined the type of formation that a woman was to receive, misrecognizing the end-product for a manifestation of her essence). This, as we shall see, ran counter to the purported order of things, in which function was represented as a consequence of essence: essence → formation → function. According to Fray Luis:

> [A]sí como a la mujer buena y honesta la naturaleza no la hizo para el estudio de las ciencias ni para los negocios de dificultades, sino para un oficio simple y doméstico, así les limitó el entender, y por consiguiente, les tasó las palabras y las razones. Y así como es esto lo que su natural de la mujer y su oficio le pide, así por la misma causa es una de las cosas que más bien le está y que mejor le parece. (124)

> (Wherefore, as a good and honest woman was not endowed by nature for the study of the various branches of knowledge, nor for the difficulties of business affairs, but was created for one single duty, simple and domestic, so was her understanding circumscribed, and, in consequence, her words and arguments limited. And as this pertains to the nature of woman, and is what her calling demands, so likewise is it what is most to her credit and what becomes her best.) (Hubbard 70)

Such reasoning neither originated with Fray Luis, nor fell out of use after his time. Instead, what have varied are the definitions of womanhood based on women's historically and culturally constructed roles and identities, and with them the advocated models of formation. Thus, eighteenth- and nineteenth-century liberal thinkers used the changing function of women from child bearers to socializers of future subjects as grounds for the advancement of women's educational programs.

A given function or vocation presupposed an optimal conduct for its fulfillment. Perfection entailed complete identification with one's calling and was unattainable to those who failed to carry out the set precepts. This being the case, Fray Luis' *la perfecta casada* described the office of married women, and as such, set forth an ideal to be emulated. Following the model, women had to administer their homes, attend to their spouses, and rear their children. Of the three, Fray Luis gives precedence to the first, it being the function that encompasses the vast majority of virtues exalted in women: economy and assiduity, diligence and self-restraint, parsimony and vigilance, order and cleanliness, silence and temperance. With post-war necessities conveniently converted into virtues—poverty/abnegation, scarcity/austerity, misery/sacrifice, despair/perseverance—Fray Luis' perfect wife emerges as a model of the thrifty, industrious woman of modern times:

> Pues no sea la perfecta casada costosa, ni ponga la honra en gastar más que su vecina, sino tenga su casa más bien abastada que ella, y más reparada, y haga con su aliño y aseo que el vestido antiguo le esté como nuevo, y que, con la limpieza cualquiera cosa que se pusiere le parezca muy bien, y el traje usado y común cobre de su aseo de ella no usado ni común parecer. (39)

> (Wherefore, let not the perfect wife be extravagant; let her not stake her reputation on spending more than her neighbour; but let her house be better supplied, and more perfectly kept up than her neighbour's. Let her by her deftness and neatness make an old frock look like new; and see to it that by its spotlessness, any dress she puts on may look well on her. The worn, commonplace dress, because of her carefulness, may come to look fresh and unusual.) (Hubbard 22)

A perfect wife could never be idle. As a source of vice and temptation, idleness presented a threat to domestic economy through the squandering and neglect of housewifely duties, and what was worse, through awakening in women their potentially insatiable appetites:

> [A]unque el desorden y demasía, y el dar larga rienda al vano y no necesario deseo, es vituperable en todo linaje de gentes, en el de las mujeres, que nascieron para sujeción y humildad, es mucho más vicioso y vituperable . . . porque, si comienzan a destemplarse, se destemplan sin término, y son como un pozo sin suelo, que nada les basta, y como una carcoma, que de continuo roe, y como una llama encubierta, que se enciende sin sentir por la casa y por la hacienda, hasta que la consume. (37)

> ([A]lthough unrestraint and prodigality, and to give loose rein to vain and unnecessary desires is blameworthy in all sorts of people, in women, born as they are for submission and humility, all this is much more vicious and reprehensible . . . [for] once [they] begin to be immoderate . . . there is an end to moderation. They are like a bottomless well, never full, no matter how much is poured into it; or like a wood-borer perpetually boring; or like a hidden blaze which spreads silently throughout the house and property, until everything is in ashes.) (Hubbard 21)

A remedy against the pitfalls of idleness, as well as a source of countless other virtues, was industry. By being industrious, women were meant to overcome self-indulgence in favor of self-restraint, uphold order, shun slovenliness, and most importantly, avoid waste. In addition, by employing themselves in such quintessentially feminine occupations as weaving and embroidery, married women were expected to preserve and contribute to their household. Here we must bear in mind that in a pre-capitalist agrarian economy, wealth was non-renewable (Aldaraca, *El Ángel* 34). The repudiation of extravagance and lavish spending in favor of practices aimed at producing assets without external assistance, (through conservation, economy, thrift, needlework, and careful administration of the household) gain new significance under the post-Civil War cultural climate marked by the shared consciousness of the country's depleted resources, an increased stock in agrarian practices, and an emphasis on self-sufficiency.

Fray Luis' text extols industriousness in men and women of all segments of society. Here, labor is conceived of as an expression of virtue rather than a consequence of necessity. The members of the upper classes who were not constrained to the exercise of physical or manual labor by penury were impelled to it by their very standing, following the principle of *noblesse oblige*. Hence, "Fray Luis, cognizant of the disdain which upper-class women shared with upper-class men for manual labor, exhorts them to industry by arguing their obligation to serve as exemplar for the lower classes" (Aldaraca, *El Ángel* 37). The text's vindication of labor on the grounds of moral superiority[6] is of added consequence if we take into account the circumstances that, during and in the aftermath of the war, forced into wage labor those for whom previously it would not have been an option. This of course includes women. Even the official discourse, which discouraged female employment, recognized it as a temporary solution for those left with no other recourse. Curiously, the popular romance novels of the time are filled with heroines—impoverished members of high and upper-middle classes—who resolutely face up to their obligations, not in spite of their birth, but because of it. Their decision to take up wage labor (often as a last resort and never for too long) is represented as a sign of distinction, nobility of character and chivalry of spirit, in contrast to those who appear to be drawn to it by want of extraneous expectations, possibilities of material gain, or self-promotion.

While home is the designated place for the exercise of housewifely duties, in Fray Luis' times it was not yet separated from the field of production, as was the case after the Industrial Revolution. Women's circumscription to home was justified on the grounds of their natural proclivity and physical weakness. "¿Por qué les dio a las mujeres Dios las fuerzas flacas y los miem-

---

[6] José Antonio Maravall, *Estado moderno y mentalidad social*, vol. 2 (Madrid: Revista de Occidente, 1972) 392.

bros muelles, sino porque las crió no para ser postas, sino para estar en su rincón asentadas?" (129) ("Why, do you suppose, did God limit the strength of women, and give them fragile members? Certainly not that they might go posting about in every direction, but that they might remain quiet in their own corners") (Hubbard 73). The very place that ostensibly entitled women to governance also functioned as a guarantor of feminine virtue. Its breach supposed a perversion of nature—"su natural propio pervierte la mujer callejera" (129) ("A woman who roams the streets distorts her very nature") (Hubbard 73)—and an occasion for transgression:

> Y así es que, las que en sus casas cerradas y ocupadas las mejoraran, andando fuera de ellas las destruyen. Y las que con andar por sus rincones ganaran las voluntades y edificaran las conciencias de sus maridos, visitando las calles corrompen los corazones ajenos y enmollecen las almas de los que las ven. (131)

> (So it follows that women who, sheltered within their houses, and busy about their household duties, can and do accomplish wonders in improving their homes, once they take to gadding about, will inevitably wreck them. Likewise, those who by watchfulness and care gain the goodwill, and edify the conscience of their husbands, by betaking themselves to the streets will poison the hearts of others.) (Hubbard 74)

With post-war shortages and mandatory prophylaxis in sight, no discourse on feminine perfection could forgo at least a passing reference to cleanliness. In *La perfecta casada,* cleanliness is not a virtue *per se*, but a sign of one's inner disposition, supposing that "de la compostura secreta del ánimo, ha de nascer el buen traje exterior" (83) ("from the hidden orderliness of the soul, is to be born the beauty of the outer dress") (Hubbard 52). Hence, while slovenliness and disorder signaled the soul's impurity, tidiness and order were manifestations of virtue—and in this too Fray Luis' exemplary wife has much in common with other normative representations of the post-war period—perceptible not only in one's appearance, but above all in one's surroundings. In contrast to make-up and other devices by which women sought to embellish themselves physically, the text encouraged married women to practice hygiene both as a permissible means of personal upkeep and as a practice auspicious for conjugal accord:

> Así que, si no es virtud del ánimo la limpieza y aseo del cuerpo, es señal del ánimo concertado, y limpio y aseado; a lo menos es cuidado necesario en la mujer, para que se conserve y se acreciente el amor de su marido con ella, si ya no es él por ventura tal que se deleite y envicie en el cieno. Porque ¿cuál vida será la del que ha de traer a su lado siempre, en la mesa, donde se asienta para tomar gusto, y en la cama, que se ordena para descanso y reposo, un desaliño y un asco que ni se puede mirar sin torcer los ojos ni tocar sin atapar

las narices? O ¿cómo será posible que se allegue el corazón a lo que naturalmente aborrece y de que rehuye el sentido? Seréle sin duda un perpetuo
y duro freno al marido el desaseo de su mujer, que todas las veces que inclin-
are, o quisiere inclinar a ella su ánimo, le irá deteniendo, y le apartará y como
torcerá a otra parte. Y no será esto solamente cuando le viere, sino todas las
veces que entrare en su casa, aunque no la vea. Porque la casa, forzosamente,
y la limpieza de ella, olerá a la mujer, a cuyo cargo está su aliño y limpieza;
y cuando ella fuere aseada o desaseada, tanto así la casa, como la mesa y el
lecho, tendrán de sucio o de limpio. (145–6)

(Wherefore, if cleanliness and neatness of body are not virtues belonging to
the soul, they do indicate its harmony, and stainlessness, and perfect accord.
If a wife is to keep her husband's affection, and if his love for her is to
increase (unless, perchance, he is such a one as delights to wallow in mire)
she must give good heed to this matter of cleanliness. For, I ask you, what
sort of life is it for a man constantly to share bed and board, ordered in the
former case for restfulness and repose, and in the other to appease hunger
and be at one's ease, with a wife, unkempt and slovenly, so that he cannot
look without averting his eyes, or approach her except with nose pinched
between forefinger and thumb? How is it possible for him to draw close to
his heart what he instinctively loathes, and that from which his every sense
recoils? There is no doubt that a slatternly wife will prove a perpetual and
severe check upon her husband, for every time he is moved toward her, or
would willingly incline towards her, he will be repelled, and separated from
her, and, as it were, turned aside. And this, not only when he has her before
his eyes, but also when he enters his house and she is nowhere to be seen.
Because it is of necessity that the very house, the very neatness of it, will
give forth a sweet savour of the wife in whose keeping is its perfect order
and loveliness. The more slovenly she is, or the more meticulous, to that
same degree will house and bed and table be unkempt or immaculate.)
(Hubbard 83–4)

In short, not only did cleanliness in women denote spiritual purity, it was
also a pre-condition for marital harmony.

Here we may deviate from Fray Luis' text in favor of more general observations regarding the Church's stance on women's virginity and conjugal
duties. As Frances Lannon observes, by the 1940s, sex in Spain "was still
seen less as a normal part of human experience and development than as a
necessary function—if no longer a necessary evil—of married couples within
Church and society" (53). The sanctification of the matrimonial state did not
routinely replace virginity as a privileged category, which may explain why
spinsters, who did not fit the regime's ideal of womanhood, are portrayed in a
kinder light by more orthodox religious discourses. However, as is generally
known, reticence about female sexuality was no obstacle to promoting male
conjugal rights. As the study on women's prescriptive literature from Counter-
Reformation to Enlightenment shows,

> [p]articular emphasis is placed on the physical submission of wives to the sexual demands of their husbands. Even though the wife is continually exhorted to model her behaviour on that of the Virgin Mary, the Virgin's purity must not be a pretext for avoiding the payment of the wife's debt to her husband. (Aldaraca, *El Ángel* 42)

It should come as no surprise that the institution of national-Catholic gender ideology would enable the preservation of women's submissive roles in marital relations long after the end of the war.

Finally, vigilant against vainglory and wary lest they succumb to a false sense of entitlement, Fray Luis' treatise urges married women to be humble and silent at all times. A perfect wife had to demonstrate strength in the face of adversity and wisdom in knowing her station: that is to say, she had to be mindful not to employ her strength for self-promotion nor let herself be imbued with a sense of accomplishment on account of her virtues. Therefore, in her zeal to be perfect, she could not forget that even by doing all that was asked of her, she was merely complying with the duties of her office:

> Por donde, lo justo y lo natural es que cada uno sea aquello mismo para que es; y que la guarda sea guarda, y el descanso, paz, y el puerto, seguridad, y la mujer, dulce y perpetuo refrigerio y alegría de corazón. . . . [Y] no es gracia y libertad este negocio, sino justicia y deuda que la mujer al marido debe, y que su naturaleza cargó sobre ella, criándola para este oficio, que es agradar y servir, y alegrar, y ayudar en los trabajos de la vida y en la conservación de la hacienda a aquel con quien se desposa. (41)

> (But what is just and natural is that each of us should be whatever we were meant to be: the protector should be the protector; where restfulness was intended, there should be peace; security in port; the wife a sweet and constant refreshment, joy of heart. . . . [And] it is no mere condescension and liberality on the part of a woman, but a matter of justice, and a debt which she owes her husband, and which her very nature has imposed upon her by creating her for this very end: to please, to serve, to gladden, to assist in all the labours of life, and to conserve the resources of him to whom she is wedded.) (Hubbard 23–4)

In conclusion, we must mention the "strategies of persuasion" that Fray Luis finds admissible in women, and the reward entailed in the emulation of *la perfecta casada*. The good of their husband and children had to be a priority for all married women. In addition to the demands of exemplary housekeeping, a perfect wife had to apply herself to the material and spiritual needs of her spouse. The interest that a virtuous woman was expected to take in her husband's welfare entitled her, in turn, to a moderate exercise of influence, if she found him faltering in matters of faith. But even when reason and virtue vindicated her actions, gentleness and sweetness were her only valid tools.

For whatever his shortcomings, the husband's authority was never in dispute. Therefore, any pressure applied by the wife towards the progress of her spouse had to be accompanied by great meekness and discretion on her part, since in principle such an exercise represented a deviation from the norm, a deviation nonetheless legitimated by a wife's devotion and her Christian duty.

The initial and final chapters of Fray Luis' treatise eulogize the model wife, and in their praise they make known her reward. First and foremost, a woman who complies with her office is said to enjoy peace and contentment, which are the fruits of the Holy Spirit. She is showered with virtues, and granted a life in heaven:

> Los frutos de la virtud, quiénes y cuáles sean, San Pablo los pone en la *Epístola* que escribió a los gálatas, diciendo: 'Los frutos del Espíritu Santo son: amor, y gozo, y paz, y sufrimiento, y largueza, y bondad, y larga espera, y mansedumbre, y fe, y modestia, y templanza y limpieza' (Galat., 5). Y a esta rica compañía de bienes, que ella por sí sola parecía bastante, se añade o sigue otro fruto mejor, que es gozar en vida eterna de Dios. (151)
>
> (The Fruits of virtue, how many and whatsoever these may be, St. Paul has set down for us in the Epistle which he wrote to the Galatians. Here he says: the fruits of the Spirit are love, joy, peace, longsuffering, generosity, goodness, patient waiting, gentleness, faith, modesty, temperance, and purity. And to this boundless store of blessings, so rich that it would appear sufficient of itself, is added, or there follows, another even better recompense: the bliss of eternal life in God.) (Hubbard 87–8)

But even such blessings do not account for all the good fortune that befalls the perfect wife. In addition to what is here referred to as "provecho" (profit, or benefit), which, despite the material connotations that the word holds today, refers to celestial gifts, women also have "honra" (honor), or worldly praise, bestowed upon them. Thus, the virtues of a perfect wife are sung on earth as they are in heaven, and her memory is made eternal. And yet, instead of concluding our analysis with the prizes which, even with the added bonus of worldly praise, remain rather orthodox and ethereal, we must now turn to the beginning of Fray Luis' epistle, populated with terrestrial rewards that find their way well into twentieth-century treatises on womanhood and domesticity:

> Porque, a la verdad, cuando no hubiera otra cosa que inclinara a la casada a hacer el deber, si no es la paz y sosiego y gran bien que en esta vida sacan e interesan las buenas de serlo, esto sólo bastaba; porque sabida cosa es que, cuando la mujer asiste a su oficio, el marido la ama, y la familia anda en concierto, y aprenden virtud los hijos, y la paz reina, y la hacienda crece.[7] Y

---

[7] A dedication featuring the above-cited passage could still be found in the eleventh edition of a 1947 history textbook intended for the perusal of schoolgirls beyond the age of 10: *Guirnaldas*

... la buena en su casa reina y resplandece, y convierte así juntamente los
ojos y los corazones de todos; el descanso y la seguridad la acompañan a
dondequiera que endereza sus pasos, y, a cualquiera parte que mira, encuentra con el alegría y con el gozo; porque, si pone en el marido los ojos,
descansa en su amor; si los vuelve a sus hijos, alégrase con su virtud; . . .
Como, al contrario, a la que es mala casera todo se le convierte en amargura,
como se puede ver por infinitos ejemplos . . .
    ¿De cuántas mujeres sabe que, por no tener cuenta con su estado y tenerla
con sus antojos, están con sus maridos en perpetua lid y desgracia? ¿Cuántas
ha visto lastimadas y afeadas con los desconciertos de sus hijos e hijas, con
quien no quisieron tener cuenta?
    ¿Cuántas laceran en extrema pobreza porque no atendieron a la guarda de
sus haciendas, o, por mejor decir, porque fueron la perdición y la polilla de
ellas? Ello es así, que no hay cosa más rica ni más feliz que la buena mujer,
ni peor ni más desastrada que la casada que no lo es. (16–18)

(For in truth, were there no other reason to incite a woman to perform her
duties than the peace and the quietude and deep happiness which good
women enjoy in this life, and which make it worth their while to be virtuous,
these alone would furnish a sufficient reason for goodness. How well we all
know that when a wife is faithful to all her obligations, her husband is
devoted to her, her family lives in harmony, her children grow in grace,
peace reigns, and money affairs prosper. And . . . so does the virtuous wife
rule in her household, and shine out, and incline towards herself the eyes
and hearts of everyone. Restfulness and security wait upon her whithderso-
ever she may direct her steps, and turn her eyes where she may, she finds
only joy and gladness. For if her eyes look toward her husband, she will rest
in his love; if she regards her children, it is to rejoice in their goodness; . . .
But the bad housekeeper! How many instances there are that show that for
her everything turns to gall and wormwood! . . . How many women you
know who, because they have been unmindful of their calling, and very
mindful indeed of their own caprices, are perpetually quarrelling with their
husbands, and out of favour with them? How many have you seen rendered
ugly and cut to the heart by the disagreements of sons and daughters with
whom they refused to be bothered? How many are suffering dire poverty
because they had no care to the frugal management of their finances, but
rather wasted and squandered them? The plain fact is that there is nothing

de la Historia. Historia de la cultura española contada a las niñas. As we may surmise from the
words of its author, Agustín Serrano de Haro, being likened to the sixteenth-century feminine
ideal was high praise well into the mid-twentieth century "A mi mujer, en la que se han cumplido
al pie de letra aquellas hermosas palabras de fray Luis de León: 'Cuando la mujer asiste a su
oficio, el marido la ama, y la familia anda en concierto, y aprenden virtud los hijos, y la paz
reina.'" ("To my wife, in whom Fray Luis' beautiful words find a perfect reflection: 'when a
married woman attends to her duties, the husband loves her, and the family works in harmony,
and the children learn virtues, and peace reigns.'") Qtd in Lorenzo Arribas 62. The above
translation of Fray Luis' words belongs to John A. Jones and Javier San José Lera, 19.

more precious, no one happier than a good wife, nor is there anyone worse or more wretched than a [married woman who is not good].) (Hubbard 8–9)

Unlike religious discourse, which saw marriage and motherhood as the primary but not the sole realization of femininity, the bourgeois ideal known as "the angel of the hearth" could find maximum expression only within matrimonial bonds.

4

El ángel del hogar and the Bourgeois
Ideal of Domesticity

Parting from the premise that "the construction of women in terms of recognizable roles, images, models, and labels occurs in discourse in response to specific social imperatives," we must begin our analysis of the nineteenth-century model of domesticity by surveying the circumstances that propitiated its production and circulation (Sunder Rajan 129). The debate on the character and ideal of women in the second half of the nineteenth century must be considered in light of the country's changing political and socio-economic landscape, which was responsible for reconfiguring traditional gender roles. Although the effects of industrialization in Spain in the mid-nineteenth century were too insignificant to occasion women's active involvement in the state's productive sector or to give rise to an organized feminist movement, as was the case in England, the force of such change was palpable enough to warrant acknowledgments in countless manuals on female formation:

> [L]os autores de los manuales se daban cuenta de que las mujeres y jóvenes españolas, influidas en parte por el desarrollo en otros países, comenzaban a estar descontentas con su papel tradicional. Se alude frecuentemente a los nuevos conceptos de igualdad y emancipación así como a las consecuencias de adherirse a ellos, describiéndolas en términos apocalípticos: desorden, deuda, vicio, destrucción de la familia y—lo peor de todo—ostracismo social.
>
> J. Manjarrés advierte que el sentido común y la moral condenarán a aquellas jóvenes que se toman la libertad de quejarse de la condición de su sexo y que, de esta forma, 'no harán más que dar una prueba de su indiscreción y de su poco talento, no harán más que dar a conocer la crasa ignorancia en que se hallan sumidas acerca de sus obligaciones como mujeres.'
>
> ([T]he authors of the manuals realized that Spanish women and girls, influenced in part by development in other countries, began to be discontented with their traditional role. The new concepts of equality and emancipation are frequently alluded to, as are the consequences of following them. The latter are described in apocalyptic terms: disorder, debt, vice, destruction of the family and—worst of all—social ostracism.

J. Manjarrés warns that common sense and morals will condemn those young ladies who take the liberty of complaining about their sex's condition, thus 'solely demonstrating their indiscretion and little worth, solely showing the crass ignorance in which they are immersed regarding their obligations as women.')[1]

The burgeoning number of prescriptive texts on the role and ideal of women fomented the model that best embodied middle-class values, *el ángel del hogar,* or the angel of the hearth.[2] As the existing scholarship on the subject has convincingly argued,[3] the propagation of the aforementioned domestic ideal was concomitant with the emergence of bourgeois order:

> En la España de medio siglo, hombres y mujeres de la *inteligentsia* coinciden en el proyecto de la creación de la sociedad burguesa en cuyo centro se inscribía un nuevo tipo de mujer para el nuevo tipo de sociedad: la mujer virtuosa y doméstica, metaforizada—desde el siglo XIX—como 'ángel del hogar.'

> (In mid-century Spain, men and women of the *intelligentsia* joined in the project of creating bourgeois society, in the center of which was inscribed a new type of woman for the new type of society: the virtuous and domestic woman, metaphorized—since the nineteenth century—as 'the angel of the hearth.') (Blanco, "Escritora" 19)

Bourgeois claims for social and political ascendancy were legitimated on the grounds of merit, as opposed to birth or title. Virtue and morality, previously deemed as an exclusive privilege of the upper classes or as religious tenets for spiritual edification, were reconfigured as practical means to material ends. Still, in a country where Catholic values exercised a long-standing moral hegemony and shaped the cultural understanding of virtue, no purely lay or secular definition of merit was possible, at least not if it were to achieve social, political, and cultural legitimacy. The ensuing relationship between the rising bourgeoisie and the Church can best be described as symbiotic. In order to assert their own moral and social code, the middle classes had to take into account the pervasiveness of Catholic mores. A succession of liberal reforms

---

[1] J. Manjarrés, *Guía de señoritas en el gran mundo* (Barcelona, 1854). Qtd in Scanlon, *La polémica feminista* 20.

[2] María del Carmen Simón Palmer documents the existence of some two thousand texts on the subject. See "La mujer en el siglo XIX: notas bibliográficas" in *Cuadernos Bibliográficos* 31 (1974) 114–98; 32 (1975) 109–50; 37 (1978) 163–203 and 38 (1979). Qtd in Alda Blanco, *Escritoras virtuosas* (Granada: Granada, 2001) 54.

[3] See studies by Bridget Aldaraca, Alda Blanco, Lou Charnon-Deutsch, Guadalupe Gómez-Ferrer Morant, Catherine Jagoe, Susan Kirkpatrick, Geraldine Scanlon and María del Carmen Simón Palmer, among others.

that undermined the Church's institutional power had placed it in an unusually vulnerable position and consequently in need of reinforcing its authority. Feeding on each other's weaknesses and ambitions, the Church and the emerging middle classes formed an amalgam of traditionally conservative and economically liberal ideals, and an ostensibly seamless union of material and spiritual interests. Such a union is perhaps best illustrated in the bourgeois institution of family, and the two metonymically linked concepts of home and woman. A closer look at these categories reveals the differentiated and gendered basis for their harmonious co-existence within the new social order.

Central to our understanding of *el ángel del hogar* and how it came to embody both bourgeois and pseudo-Christian ideals is the conception of the individual in terms of public and private selves, which operate in two separate and corresponding spheres; in the words of Isabel Burdiel: "La construcción del 'hombre doméstico y sentimental' como el alter-ego del 'hombre económico y público' es un fenómeno crucial de la cultura burguesa sin cuya comprensión ni siquiera la actuación de ese supuesto hombre público y económico es entendible históricamente" ("The construction of the 'domestic and sentimental man' as the alter-ego of the 'economic and public man' is a crucial phenomenon of burgeouis culture, without an understanding of which not even the behavior of that supposed public and economic man is historically comprehensible") (6). The two spheres were conceived as different but complementary: one was reserved for making profit, the other for the exercise of virtue. Rid of the conflicts and uncertainties of the outside world, home was the one place where a man could enjoy material and spiritual bliss. It was at once a sign by which he could gauge his material success and a space to which he ascribed those qualities that only served to guarantee that success symbolically; that is, tenets which, while irreconcilable with man's public life, were passed off as its necessary precondition.[4] These included Christian

---

[4] The practice of regulating social and religious mores based on the two antagonistically conceived spheres of operation forms part of a process that Bridget Aldaraca deftly defines as bourgeois "privatization of virtue." The following aspects further attest to this process: "la apropiación de toda 'virtud' y su codificación como norma única del comportamiento social—es decir, la redefinición de la virtud como el decoro—por la burguesía, que será en adelante el único árbitro de lo que es o no es respetable (aceptable); . . . la ausencia de un concepto del decoro o de la respetabilidad como control sobre la acumulación y expansión del capital; . . . la sustitución del concepto de la virtud o el honor por una ética utilitaria en la esfera pública de la producción; y finalmente, el desarrollo dentro de la clase dominante de la idea del derecho a la intimidad: *the right to privacy*" ("the appropriation of all 'virtue' and its codification as the only rule of social behavior—that is to say, the redefinition of virtue as decorum—by the bourgeoisie, which will be from that point on the sole judge of what is and what is not respectable (acceptable); . . . the absence of a concept of decorum or of respectability as a control on the accumulation and expansion of capital; . . . the replacement of the concept of virtue or honor by a utilitarian ethic in the public sphere of production; and finally, the development within the dominant class of the idea of the right to intimacy: *the right to privacy*"). See "*Tormento*" in *Textos y sociedad* (Amsterdam: Rodopi, 1990) 221.

virtues conveniently embodied by the bourgeois ideal of domesticity, *el ángel del hogar*:

> Woman's selfless investment of her desires in the family was supposed to counteract the ruling principle of bourgeois society: self-interest. As Barbara Taylor points out, women became the repositories of the moral conscience of the bourgeoisie, for, 'having confined all those virtues inappropriate within the stockmarket or the boardroom to the hearts of their womenfolk, middle class men were then left free to indulge in all those unfortunate vices necessary for bourgeois enterprise.' (Jagoe, *Ambivalent Angels* 25)

Religiosity among women was particularly encouraged, as it ensured their virtuousness. A convincing argument can be made for the bourgeois com-modification of religious and pious practices, as well as of those precepts that, subsumed under the category of feminine virtue, came to stand for markers of social distinction.

The notion of irreconcilable yet complementary spheres was inscribed in the gender ideology of the time. Home, a refuge and sanctuary, became iden-tified with those emotive, unadulterated, and sacred practices that were embodied by women, men's indispensable and "asymmetrical companions" (Kirkpatrick, *Las Románticas* 289). If previously their domain was deter-mined by women's moral inferiority (by exposing their natural proclivity to vice, women were thought not only to jeopardize their own precarious defenses against sin, but also others' spiritual welfare), by the mid-nineteenth century they were regarded as pure, innocent beings in need of protection from the baseness and corruption of the outside world (bourgeois society saw in women's child-like inexperience and unadulterated existence a redemptive force). While Fray Luis had to command women to be virtuous, exposing the gap between the actual and the desired feminine practices, the nineteenth-century spokesmen of domesticity reduced this gap by inscribing prescription into description, that is, by making of their injunctions the very definition of womanhood: women *were* the angels of the hearth and as such, they dwelled at home and were subject to their own virtuousness (and sense of decorum). According to Catherine Jagoe:

> Part of the puritanical aspect of domestic ideology, which shows its humble social origins, was the emphasis placed on work and frugality. Thrift, understated elegance, and simplicity were constantly prescribed in the con-duct manuals, in opposition to the vice of *el lujo*, the gaudy display of luxury. . . . The angel of the nineteenth century was constantly employed in supervising household tasks . . . because she truly loved her role. . . . She was expected to be clean, frugal, hardworking, cheerful, and contented: 'hormiguita de la casa, es limpia como la plata, cantadora como los ruise-ñores, madrugadora como el gorrión' ("little ant of the house, she is clean

as silver, musical as the nightingales, and an early riser like the sparrow.")
(*Ambivalent Angels* 26)

With their predecessor, *la perfecta casada*, the angels of the hearth shared a
subjectivity founded on humility and modesty, vigilance and chastity, self-
sacrifice and abnegation, forbearance and restraint, submissiveness and the
desire to please. Idleness and intemperance were refuted by industriousness
and needlework. In this respect, the angels of the hearth were set apart from
their upper- and lower-class counterparts who, according to the moralists of
the time, adulterated their natural propensity to be virtuous by practices that
were deemed incompatible with true—that is, middle-class—feminine identity. Only in the case of extreme penury were domestic angels authorized to
engage in money-earning activity, a concession that took into account the
increasing social mobility and financial instability of middle-class constituents. Francisco Alonso y Rubio's 1863 treatise, *La mujer*, portrays lower-class
women engaged in physical labor as perversions of their sex and prone to
adversity. The following passage lays bare the kind of aberrations that await
women who take on manly duties and fall short of the institutionalized feminine ideal:

> Pierde la belleza de sus formas, la frescura de su tez, la suavidad de su col-
> orido: endurece su cuerpo, desarrolla sus músculos, aumenta sus fuerzas,
> pero a expensas de dejar sus rasgos característicos, de adquirir dureza en sus
> contornos, y de aproximarse por su configuración física y sus costumbres al
> hombre. Su inteligencia duerme en profundo sueño: no la cultiva con ningún
> género de trabajo de los que sirven para su desenvolvimiento: su corazón se
> endurece, y pierde ese rico caudal de sentimiento y de dulces afecciones que
> tanto la embellece y distingue. Apartada casi todo el día del hogar, del
> humilde caserío, donde se albergan sus hijos, no puede prestarles los tiernos
> y cariñosos cuidados de que tanto necesitan en sus primeros años. No puede
> ilustrar su inteligencia ni formar su corazón, ni dedicarse tranquilamente a
> las labores propias de su sexo, que para ella constituirían ocupación más
> grata.
>   En las ciudades industriales, la mujer concurre a las fábricas a ganar el pan
> para sus hijos, y emplea sus brazos en oficios mecánicos que la ocupan todo
> el día, quedándole sólo la noche para el reposo y para el arreglo de su hogar
> y el cuidado de la familia. Trabajando largas horas, respirando un aire
> impuro y recibiendo las nocivas influencias que resultan de la excesiva
> acumulación de personas en una misma localidad, deteriora su salud, que-
> branta sus fuerzas, contrae graves padecimientos, y hasta corrompe sus
> costumbres y se degrada, sintiendo los efectos de un maléfico contagio
> moral.

(She loses the beauty of her form, the freshness of her complexion, the soft-
ness of her coloring: her body hardens, her muscles develop, her strength

increases, but at the cost of losing her characteristic features, of acquiring sharpness in her contours, and of approximating a man in her physical configuration and habits. Her intelligence sleeps deeply: she does not cultivate it with any kind of work that serves to develop it: her heart hardens, and she loses that rich wealth of sentiment and sweet affections that so beautify and distinguish her. Removed almost all day from the home, from the humble dwelling where her children take shelter, she cannot give them the tender and affectionate care that they so need in their first years. She can neither enlighten their intelligence nor shape their hearts, nor tranquilly devote herself to the labors appropriate to her sex, that for her would constitute the most gratifying occupation.

In the industrial cities, the woman goes to the factories to win bread for her children, and employs her arms in mechanical tasks that keep her occupied all day, leaving her only the night to rest, tidy the house, and care for the family. Working long hours, breathing polluted air, and absorbing the noxious influences that result from too many people crowded into one place, her health deteriorates, her strength fails, she contracts grave illnesses, and even her habits are corrupted and she demeans herself, suffering from the effects of a harmful moral contagion.) (qtd in Jagoe et al., *La mujer* 69–70)

However, unlike Fray Luis' perfect wife, the bourgeois feminine ideal was conceived as man's equal so long as she remained within her own realm of influence. And while her realm was clearly home, her influence remained to be circumscribed. That is to say, although the functions of each sphere and those of the women within the private sphere were as visibly delineated as they were staunchly reiterated, the dividing line between the two became diffuse as the activities of one continued to seep into the other. Following Alda Blanco's allegation, it was the bourgeois woman's moral prerogative that propitiated broader interpretations of what this ideal was called to do and how she needed to go about doing it, all within the fringes of the dominant discourse.

Before concluding this brief survey of the *ángel del hogar*, we must turn our attention to the contradictions implicit in the discourse of domesticity, especially given their bearing on the nationalist configurations of womanhood almost a century later. "[The] tension between woman's ascribed power and powerlessness," contends Jagoe, "is variously inscribed in bourgeois domestic ideology" (*Ambivalent Angels* 35). In her exposition of women's writing at the backdrop of this ideology, Alda Blanco makes a similar observation when she states that "[t]anto el poder como la prohibición están presentes en estos textos, y dan lugar a múltiples ambigüedades que marcarán las narrativas. Se podría decir, por ejemplo, que el ángel del hogar ocupa un lugar paradójicamente ambiguo en la imaginación social de la época . . ." ("[b]oth power and prohibition are present in these texts, and they give rise to multiple ambiguities that mark the narratives. One could say, for example, that the angel of the hearth occupies a paradoxically ambiguous place in the social imagination of the period . . . ") (*Escritoras* 108). Following their line of argument, we may conclude that the nineteenth-century representations of the *ángel del hogar* were not univocal, yet they shared a prescriptive modality that consisted in "offering rules, opinions, and advice on how to behave as one should" in accordance with the bourgeois mores (Foucault 2: 12). Such a modality, as a rule, presupposes a system of representation in which the relationship between signifier and signified is clearly demarcated so as to ensure a desired, or correct interpretation of a given ideal. The internalization of these relationships—which translate into attitudes, actions, and expectations—guarantees the production and reproduction of the normative model. Yet even those signifying practices that achieve a high degree of interpretative determinacy can neither terminally preclude the production of alternative meanings nor prevent the adoption of available signs for their investment with second-order meanings (Barthes 114–15). Given this "constant sliding of meaning in all interpretation" (Hall 33), it is hardly surprising that some of the inconsistencies in the bourgeois discourse of domesticity should stem from a dual and antithetical function of a single female qualifier/sign: virtue. It can be argued that the primary and intended function of virtue within the discourse of domesticity was to regulate and guarantee normative behavior; its derivative and unintended application within the same discourse, however, gave rise to the legitimate transgressions of the prescribed norm.

Paradoxically then, it was through the straitjacket of benign sainthood that the angels of the hearth came to exercise a degree—albeit mediated and limited—of social agency.[5] One important consequence of female edification was that it conferred symbolic capital upon middle-class women. That is to say, within given discursive formations these angelic daughters, wives, and mothers enjoyed unprecedented prestige and respectability. Another is that it imbued feminine practices with didactic purpose. "Idealization," observes Aldaraca, "implies control within the imagination over the desired object" (*El Ángel* 83). As repositories of virtue, women had no choice but to be virtuous (lest they fall into disgrace), but they did have a right, if not an obligation, to instill these virtues in others. The two corollaries were indivisible given that the institution of women's moral prerogative was a necessary stipulation for its exercise. Be that as it may, neither the symbolic capital nor the didactic purpose that testified to the women's "position as the moral axis of contemporary society" (Blanco, "The Moral Imperative" 105) can be taken at face value if we consider that the obsession with conferred honor and social respectability merely exacerbated the need for compliance, while the right to predicate

---

[5] My use of the term here is limited to "influence" or "action" and is not intended to suggest either defiance or contention on behalf of the actors. *A Dictionary of Sociology* (3rd edn, Oxford: Oxford UP, 2005) 9.

the prescribed virtues ensured their practice and reproduction. What concerns us here is the process by which these tokens of consent are transformed into legitimate strategies of dissent; how within the very discursive formation that gives rise to the domestic ideal, women go from passively accepting the status quo to becoming its active proponents. The irony lies in the fact that to do so they have to transgress the established norm. The two cultural phenomena that enable us to examine how the angels of the hearth came to exert their influence beyond the boundaries of home, even as they remained within the discursive limits of domesticity, are the so-called professionalization of motherhood, or *la carrera de madres de familia*, and the legitimization of women's linguistic authority.

The redefinition of the gender differences that anticipated the production of the bourgeois ideal of domesticity had begun a century before, when "the emerging social forms and ways of thinking, in fact, produced a new concept of the self, a new kind of subjectivity" (Kirkpatrick, *Las Románticas* 3). Locke's notion of the mind as a *tabula rasa* called for the reappraisal of the mother's role in the child's education, and the changing views on feminine responsibilities elicited new debates about female formation.[6] The Enlightenment thinkers saw education as a means of social regeneration, but this idea gradually gave way to one of social control and reproduction.[7] This change was reflected in women's teaching and in their function as transmitters of dominant values. It was assumed that although women were virtuous by nature, they were also malleable and as such in need of a sound moral formation. Such a formation would prepare women for their mission, which—as the proponents of nineteenth-century domesticity saw it—consisted of marriage, motherhood, and the socialization of future citizens. In their role as wives, mothers, and ministers of virtue, a role that perpetuated their category of "others," women were portrayed as men's complementary and antithetical partners (Kirkpatrick, *Las Románticas* 289). What made them "equal" was their allegedly common purpose: to create a harmonious society where "harmony" stood for stability, order, and preservation of the existing status quo. Angela Grassi, who participated in the production and configuration of the domestic ideal through her own bestselling novels, wrote in "La misión de la mujer" (1857): "Si no son iguales los medios que emplean para llevar a cabo la gran obra de la regeneración humana, iguales son los resultados que con-

---

[6] The advances made in the second half of the eighteenth century with respect to female involvement in public life were curbed by the effects of the French Revolution, and by the beginning of the nineteenth century women were once again relegated to their traditional role as mothers and wives. See Sally-Ann Kitts, *The Debate on the Nature, Role and Influence of Woman in Eighteenth-Century Spain* (Lewiston, NY: Edwin Mellen, 1995).

[7] See Scanlon, "Revolución burguesa e instrucción femenina" in *Nuevas perspectivas sobre la mujer*, vol. 1 (Madrid: Universidad Autónoma, 1982) 163–73.

siguen" ("If the means that they employ to carry out the great work of human regeneration are not equal, the results that they achieve are") (qtd in Jagoe et al., *La mujer* 56). The disparity between them thus lay in how the members of the opposite sex went about achieving this nominally joint enterprise, of which both the disparity and the enterprise were taken to be at once divinely ordained and naturally predetermined.

This new varnish on the old role simultaneously prohibited and encouraged women's social involvement. By celebrating what the rhetoric of the time called the "raising" of a woman's dignity and the "elevating" of her position to the heights of her male counterparts, the bourgeois discourse of domesticity aligned itself with its object of representation, thereby producing an ideal of a woman content with her lot. But while the primary function of such representation was to generate compliance, its corollary was the formation of women's symbolic capital, which contributed to the gradual broadening of the range of her influence from the private to the public sphere. As Alda Blanco notes: "Aunque no se le permitía a la mujer formar parte de la esfera pública podía—y debía—incidir en ella a través de su 'poderoso ascendiente' sobre los sentimientos y la moralidad del hombre" ("Although women were not permitted to form part of the public sphere, they were able—and it was their duty—to impinge on it through their 'powerful influence' on the feelings and morality of men") (Blanco, *Escritoras* 61). The rhetorical practice that rendered feminine influence as beneficial and indispensable to the functioning of society therefore validated the transposability/utility of specifically feminine qualities to the public sphere. The expansion of feminine responsibilities at once propitiated and legitimized the need for female instruction, which until then consisted primarily of moral and religious formation. These practices gradually led to the redefinition of women's missions within the discourse of domesticity to include some public sites where the need for the exercise of benign feminine influence was perceived as being particularly high:

> La noción de la superioridad moral y afectiva de la mujer y de su correspondiente capacidad para desempeñar ciertos trabajos sociales mejor que el hombre se fue ensanchando a varias funciones sociales ligadas con el cuidado de los miembros de su familia, que en primer lugar fueron la enseñanza, la enfermería y la filantropía. Las mujeres fueron presionando poco a poco los límites de la esfera privada, escudándose precisamente en la ideología decimonónica sobre la superioridad femenina en el territorio moral afectivo para superar la esfera privada.
>
> (The notion of women's moral and emotional superiority, and their corresponding capacity to carry out certain social tasks better than men, gradually was broadened to include certain social functions linked to the care of family members, beginning with teaching, nursing and philanthropy. Little

by little—shielding themselves with the self-same nineteenth-century ideology of feminine superiority in emotional and moral territory—women
continued to stretch the boundaries of the private sphere so as to move
beyond them.) (Jagoe et al., *La mujer* 41)

Thus, fomenting a positive correlation between women's social valorization
and the range of their influence, the institution of women's moral prerogative
represented a significant aperture within the discourse of domesticity.

Finally, we must comment on the virtuous woman's acquisition and exercise of discursive authority (Lanser 6). What interests us here, in light of the
post-Civil War discourse on womanhood, is women writers' enunciative position (a position stemming from the reigning conception of literature as a
medium of social control, and the endorsed view of women as barometers of
virtue) and how this position provides space for expanding the limits of normative behavior for women (in other words, how it legitimates dissent within
the boundaries of normativity). According to Susan Kirkpatrick, the representation of the bourgeois feminine ideal as complementary rather than inferior
to men "permitted women a legitimate arena of self-expression and artistic
authority in place of the silence that the sexual hierarchy of an earlier social
formation had enjoined on them" (*Las Románticas* 287). Furthermore, it can
be argued that the discursive space claimed by women like Angela Grassi,
Faustina de Melgar, and Pilar Sinués, whose narratives participated in the
articulation of normative womanhood, was contingent upon, as well as
contributed to, the increase in women's cultural capital, and validated their
didactic function. Following Blanco's claims, they redefined the act of writing as an extension of the feminine mission, enabling those who practiced it
to predicate dominant values and reproduce prescribed models of conduct.
"As education became the preferred instrument of social control," it was
believed that "fiction could accomplish much the same purpose" (Armstrong
16).[8] Women's texts accordingly formed educational sites with an embedded
structure of exemplarity; they constructed models of female comportment
that the readers were expected to either emulate or reject based on the shared
system of values. Because writing was justified on the grounds of women's
moral privilege, female writers were obliged to write under the sign of a "virtuous woman" themselves, whereby the writing subject was perceived as
homologous to its narrative voice.[9] But despite these impositions and their

[8] Alicia Andreu elaborates this point with regard to the rise of the popular novel in mid-
nineteenth-century Spain. See *Galdós y la literatura popular* (Madrid: Sociedad General
Española de Librería, 1982).

[9] These observations draw on Alda Blanco's insightful studies on the relationship between
Spanish women writers' social role and their enunciative authority in the second half of the
nineteenth century. Among her other works on the subject, see "The Moral Imperative for
Women Writers," *Indiana Journal of Hispanic Literatures* 2.1 (Fall 1993): 91–110.

conformity, women's prescriptive texts presented an interesting deviation from their male-authored counterparts. As critics like Blanco attest, this difference stemmed primarily from the fact that women could not take their own act of writing for granted, and in justifying this practice they often became its proponents. As a result, not only did these officiators of domesticity manage to transgress the traditional and normative boundaries from within, but, sustained by their legitimate and legitimating didactic purpose, they also became advocates of female literacy.[10]

Bound with the figure of the *ángel del hogar*, the following are the aspects that we must bear in mind as we begin our discussion of the Falangist feminine ideal: first, the bourgeois doctrine of separate spheres and the ideology of complementary gender difference (which maintains that the roles of men and women are equal in importance but different in substance, and that women may publicly exert their influence, so long as it is not perceived to infringe upon males'); second, the institution of women's moral superiority, which elevates women's social standing and imbues them with didactic authority; and third, the practice of exemplarity as a normative model for female representation in women-authored texts.

[10] In addition to Blanco's "The Moral Imperative," see Chapter 3 of *Escritoras virtuosas*. For the statistics on female literacy in the second half of the nineteenth century, consider "La enseñanza femenina en la España decimonónica," in *La mujer* 105–32.

5

Female Formation and *la nueva mujer of* the Falange

The sacred mission of forming future wives and mothers was entrusted to the women's cadre of the Spanish Falange, otherwise known as *Sección Femenina* (1934–77). Its modest origins (not to be confused with its far less modest social and political underpinnings) can be traced to a group of seven women, mainly kin of male activists, who, a year after the launching of the party by José Antonio Primo de Rivera and two years before the breakout of the Civil War, coalesced under the leadership of José Antonio's sister, Pilar.[1] With the absorption of the Falange into Franco's National Movement,[2] *Sección Femenina* assumed the role of mediator between the state and its female constituents, thus forming a dominant cultural filter through which to interpret women's familial, social, and political obligations. Despite the Falange's waning prestige, that *Sección Femenina* remained one of its most active and staunch proponents for over four decades (nominally outlasting Franco's regime) was by and large due to Pilar's proselytizing zeal and unflagging devotion to her brother's pronouncedly fascist program of national-syndicalist revolution.[3] By a broad consensus, she was "both the link with the original truths of Falangism and the guarantor of their survival within the National Movement."[4]

The chapter first appeared in the form of the article as "The Right to be Selfless and Other Prerogatives of the Weak in the Rhetoric of *Sección Femenina*" in the Spring 2008 issue of *Romance Quarterly* (55:2): 109–127.

[1] The first women to become members of *Sección Femenina* were in charge of distributing propaganda, looking after the imprisoned Falangists and their families, and raising funds. See Luis Suárez Fernández, *Crónica de la Sección Femenina y su tiempo* (Madrid: C.I.R.S.A., 1993) 28–9.

[2] On the consolidation of the National Movement, see Sheelagh Ellwood, *Spanish Fascism* 42–4.

[3] Drawing on Roger Griffin's definition of generic fascism, Falange may be described as "a revolutionary form of nationalism, one which sets out to be a political, social and ethical revolution, welding the 'people' into a dynamic national community under new elites infused with new heroic values. The core myth which inspires this project is that only a populist, trans-class movement of purifying, cathartic national rebirth (palingenesis) can stem the tide of decadence." *The Nature of Fascism* (London: Routledge, 1991) xi.

[4] See Kathleen Richmond, *Women and Spanish Fascism* 9; Victoria L. Enders, "Nationalism and Feminism" 673; and Carmen Martín Gaite, *Usos amorosos* 56.

It was the war that gave the Falangist women the necessary impetus for mobilization, and by 1939 their cadres counted over a half a million adherents.[5] While not everyone chose to join the party, the members of the *Sección Femenina* were in charge of providing venues to all who wished to lend their assistance to the nationalist troops. Their activities ranged from distributing leaflets and other propagandistic materials, to attending to the prisoners, caring for the children, looking after the sick and the wounded, facilitating blood donations, organizing training centers for the nurses, founding orphanages, setting up diners and sewing workshops, making clothes, sending women as laundresses to the front, embroidering the Falangist insignia, and writing letters to unknown soldiers as expressions of moral support.[6] Among the rightwing women's most lasting wartime contributions was the creation of Social Aid (*Auxilio Social*) intended to address the nutritional and welfare needs of the civilian population and organize relief programs for the combatants.[7]

The underlying contradiction of the Falangist feminine ideal, as it oscillated between demure (traditional) and enterprising (modern), surfaced early on.[8] As the *Sección Femenina*'s first manifesto stated: "Nuestra misión no está en la dura lucha, pero sí en la predicación, en la divulgación y en el ejemplo" ("Our mission is not in the rigors of combat, but in preaching, spreading the word, and setting an example") (qtd in Gallego Méndez 212). In a similar fashion, the women involved in the program of *Auxilio Social* claimed that "no se trataba de un intento de confinar a la mujer en su prisión de viejos prejuicios; por el contrario, ahora se la necesitaba como 'madre de todos' en el 'gran hogar' del nacional-sindicalismo" ("it was not about attempting to confine woman to her prison of old prejudices; on the contrary, now she was needed as 'mother of all' in the 'great home' of national-syndicalism") (Scanlon 317). The two statements are homologous in that both present an attempt to redefine women's role in national life, while paying heed to the prevailing bourgeois model of different but complementary gender relations. As we shall see, this ostensibly incongruous stance (of change and intran-

---

[5] For the statistical data, see Geraldine Scanlon, *La polémica feminista* 317.

[6] See Aurora M[orcillo] Gómez, *True Catholic Womanhood* 24–5 and Gallego Méndez, *Mujer, falange y franquismo* 55–7.

[7] The *Auxilio Social* was eventually supplanted by *Servicio Social* under the aegis of *Sección Femenina*. On the conflict of interests between Mercedes Sanz Bachiller, the founder of *Auxilio Social*, and Pilar Primo de Rivera, see Gallego Méndez 59–61 and Richmond 17.

[8] The use of the terms "traditional" and "modern" can be problematic, among other reasons, for obscuring the distinction between the value judgments that are passed on specific historical circumstances and those proper to them. For the nationalist ideologues, "traditional" womanhood denoted authentic and intransient values threatened by the changing socio-economic conditions conducive to the emergence of new feminine types. These observations echo Bridget Aldaraca's comprehensive study of the nineteenth-century feminine ideal. See Aldaraca, *El Ángel del Hogar* 26.

sience) turned into *Sección Femenina*'s singular *modus operandi*, and may account for some of the challenges that its study poses to historians.[9]

Official recognition of *Sección Femenina*'s war effort illustrates one of many instances of fitting the organization's unconventional praxis into a familiar and unthreatening mold—a strategy that was to become commonplace in Pilar's own discourses. As the decree of September 28, 1939 averred:

> Ejemplar prestación guerrera y política que en nada ha disminuido las tradicionales virtudes de la mujer española, antes bien, las ha exaltado al calor de una profunda educación religiosa y patriótica, que ha constituido incesante preocupación para la Sección Femenina, en su anhelo hacia una total formación espiritual de la mujer.

> (Exemplary wartime and political effort has in no way diminished the traditional virtues of the Spanish woman, but rather has elevated these virtues in the heat of a profound religious and patriotic education, which has been a constant concern of *Sección Femenina* in its yearning for women's total spiritual formation.) (qtd in Gallego Méndez 209–10)

By presenting the organization's activities as an expression of traditional feminine virtues, the document suppressed any apparent conflict between the image of a publicly engaged wartime woman and the time-honored ideal of a devout housewife advocated by the regime. Furthermore, it precluded the possibility of interpreting the role played by women during the war as acceptable peacetime practice.

Accordingly, one of *Sección Femenina*'s primary tasks under the National Movement was restoring women to the hearth.[10] In her address to 11,000 affiliates gathered in honor of Franco and his troops, Pilar declared, "[e]stamos aquí reunidas solo para festejar vuestra victoria y honrar a vuestros

---

[9] Recent scholarship on the subject has tried to refute monolithic portrayals of the organization. While it may be argued that *Sección Femenina*'s activities were defined by the pursuit of doctrinally homogeneous formation, its ideal type—here studied under the label of *la nueva mujer*—constituted an ambiguous cultural sign. See Victoria Lorée Enders, "Problematic Portraits: The Ambiguous Historical Role of the *Sección Femenina* of the Falange," *Constructing Spanish Womanhood* (New York: State U of New York P, 1999) 375–97. That this valuable contribution to the debate is preceded by a quotation—"Understanding does not necessarily imply agreement"—is indicative of the overriding biases at work within the given field of inquiry.

[10] In addition to founding the "domestic schools" (*escuelas de hogar*), *Sección Femenina* was in charge of providing all women's schools, elementary and secondary, with qualified staff to teach the compulsory housecrafts. As Morcillo notes, "no girl could graduate without passing the courses in home economics, sewing, pattern design, arts and crafts, darning and mending, cooking, and music": *True Catholic Womanhood* 44. See also Richmond, *Women and Spanish Fascism* 17, 23, and Pastor i Homs, *La educación femenina en la postguerra* 59–61.

soldados. Porque la única misión que tienen asignada las mujeres en la tarea de la Patria, es el hogar" ("[w]e are gathered here solely to celebrate your victory and to honor your soldiers. Because the only mission assigned to women in the work of the Fatherland is the home") (*Escritos* 152–3). Article two of the aforementioned decree conferred upon *Sección Femenina* the exclusive right to oversee women's political and social formation with the latent stipulation that far from drawing women away from home, it was to enhance their performance as mothers and wives: "Tenéis que daros cuenta de que a las camaradas de las Secciones Femeninas hay que formarlas y enseñarles nuestra doctrina, sin apartarlas para nada de la misión colosal que como mujeres tienen en la vida" ("You have to understand that the comrades of the *Secciones Femeninas* must be formed and taught our doctrine without distancing them in any way from the tremendous mission that, as women, they have in life") (Primo de Rivera, *Discursos* 68). The challenge, as we may infer from the above quotation, lay in binding the new and the old expectations in a seamless feminine ideal.

"All women by nature were either private or social mothers" (Morcillo Gómez 138), and the *Sección Femenina*'s supreme task was to endow Spain with mothers conscious of their proselytizing mission, or, at the very least, with subjects disposed to impart the acquired values since, according to Pilar Primo de Rivera, "cada mujer que salga de nuestras escuelas, además de haber difundido por las Secciones Femeninas la luz de nuestra verdad falangista, tendrá después unos hijos a los que podrá llenar el corazón y el entendimiento con el gozo de estas enseñanzas" ("each woman who leaves our schools, in addition to having spread the light of our Falangist truth through the *Secciones Femeninas*, will later have children whose hearts and understanding she will be able to fill with the joy of these teachings") (*Escritos* 251). The pedagogic purpose ascribed to mothers as a consequence of their normative formation, and espoused by the members of the *Sección Femenina* by dint of their official commitment to the exigencies of the state, sought once again to affirm women's role as agents of continuity and permanence through the ostensibly timeless values that they were expected to embody and impart. However, as we saw in the previous section, by the second half of the nineteenth century women had already begun to articulate the need in society for purportedly feminine qualities, thus extending their moral and didactic prerogative from the private to the public domain. Assuming the role of surrogate mothers, accomplished care-takers and predicators of virtue, they established the grounds and set a precedent from which the leaders of the *Sección Femenina* could legitimate their own direct participation in the process of nation-building.

The power disputed by and bestowed upon the *Sección Femenina* represented a mixed blessing for a revolutionary movement. The very conditions that entitled the organization to extend its influence over a wide sector of the female population served to circumscribe the range and nature of its activities. The status of exemplary womanhood that the leaders of the *Sección Femenina* enjoyed as representatives of the state disciplinary apparatus demanded they not only disseminate but also adopt certain models of conduct and shun others; yet, as we shall see, their own lives were not easily reconcilable with either the image or the role they openly preached. Nevertheless, the visibility that the organization gained under the aegis of Franco's regime required that it align its activities with the interests of the new state even if the latter did not necessarily share *Sección Femenina*'s commitment to the Falangist doctrine.[11]

What Joseantonian fascism and Francoist authoritarianism had in common were their totalitarian ambitions, wherein the ascendancy of the state over personal welfare was just one manifestation. Another was the desire for homogeneity, which facilitated control over national practices through the imposition of common, Manichean belief systems. Hence the aggregate function of formation in post-war Spain was tantamount to training by inculcation. One of its immediate objectives, albeit of long-term consequence, was the purging of Republican and other lay models of socialization, and their expedient replacement with national-Catholic moral order. According to Mary Nash, along with the established ideal of *ángel del hogar*, the 1910s and the 1920s saw the emergence of the so-called *nueva mujer moderna*, which "accommodated more restrictive gender roles toward the new needs of the labor market and society" (*Constructing Spanish Womanhood* 31–2). Kathleen Richmond likewise remarks on the diversity of available feminine models in the first decades of the twentieth century from the standpoint of the developing urban culture: "With the growth of towns and cities came new opportunities for leisure. Women had increasingly taken advantage of opportunities to emerge from their homes into more public social spheres such as the tea salon, the club or the big hotel where they would drink, smoke and dress fashionably. Cinema stars, often American, were public role models and with them their fashions and social mores" (9). If we consider a plurality of models or possible realizations for women as a sign of modernity, then the 1940s represented a considerable setback not only from the short Republican tenure, but as the above examples demonstrate, from the first three decades of the century. The nationalist discourse on womanhood suppressed these modern and modern-

---

[11] On *Falange* and its absorption by the Nationalist Movement, see *Spanish Fascism in the Franco Era*. According to Ellwood: "Whilst the *Falange* acted in the areas of its control as a vehicle for the power of the Franco regime, it should not be considered that the party was unilaterally instrumentalised by the regime. The relationship was, rather, one of mutual support and belief. In the same way that, in return for political inhibition or para-military services, the pre-war *Falange* had continuously sought the patronage or numerical strength of forces outside its own ranks, it now accepted the patronage of the Franco regime in return for an active contribution to the latter's consolidation and perpetuation" (59).

izing representations in favor of traditional bourgeois and religious models of *ángel del hogar* and *la perfecta casada*, the most revolutionary hegemonic alternative being that of a Falangist "new woman." Even so, as novelist Carmen Martín Gaite notes, and as the study of contemporaneous women's narratives will demonstrate, the former models of conduct, thought, and cultural expectations were not so easily erased:

> Los chicos y chicas de postguerra, fuera cual fuera la ideología de sus padres, habían vivido una infancia de imágenes más movidas y heterogéneas, donde junto a la abuela con devocionario y mantilla de toda la vida, aparecían otra clase de mujeres, desde la miliciana hasta la 'vamp', pasando por la investigadora que sale con una beca al extranjero y la que da mítines. Las habían visto retratadas en revistas, fumando con las piernas cruzadas, conduciendo un coche o mirando bacterias por un microscopio. Habían oído hablar de huelgas, de disputas en el Parlamento, de emancipación, de enseñanza laica, de divorcio; sabían que no todos los periódicos decían lo mismo, que no todas las personas pensaban lo mismo y también, claro está, que a uno cuando fuera mayor le sería posible elegir entre aquellas teorías distintas que hacían discutir tanto a la gente, y entre aquellos tipos de mujer, para imitarlo, si se era una niña, o, para casarse con ella, si se era un niño. Ahora esos estilos 'viejos' se habían quedado para los países sin fe, donde soplaba, según expresión del Papa *un aire malsano de paganismo renacido*, que tendía a *engendrar e introducir una amplia paridad de las actividades de la mujer con las del hombre* [sic].
>
> (Post-war boys and girls, whatever the ideology of their parents, had lived a childhood of more lively, heterogeneous images, where, next to the grandmother with her prayer book and perpetual mantilla, appeared other types of women, from the female soldier to the 'vamp,' not to mention the researcher who goes abroad with a grant and the woman who leads rallies. They had seen their pictures in magazines, smoking with their legs crossed, driving a car or looking at bacteria through a microscope. They had heard talk of strikes, of disputes in Parliament, of emancipation, of lay education, of divorce; they knew that not all the newspapers said the same thing, that not all people thought the same things and, also, it was obvious, that when they grew older it would be possible for them to choose among those different theories that made people argue so much, and among those types of women whom one was to imitate, if one was a girl, or marry, if one was a boy. Now those 'old' types were only for the countries without faith, where, according to the Pope, *'an unhealthy air of reborn paganism'* blew, tending to *'engender and produce a broad parity between the activities of women and men.'*) (*Usos amorosos* 26)

The memories of a heterogeneous past and awareness of an alternative present were measured against the national-Catholic social enterprise, which rendered common wellbeing a consequence of a common outlook.

De esta manera, conseguida una uniformidad de educación en todos los mandos femeninos de la Falange, puede decirse que en todas las familias españolas habrá desde la próxima generación una unidad de criterio y una sola manera de entender a España como fiel cumplidora de una empresa en lo universal. A cuya empresa habrán de doblegar todos los españoles los intereses de grupo o de clase.

(In this way, with a uniform education in all feminine ranks of the Falange having been achieved, one can say that in all Spanish families from the next generation on there will be a unity of criteria and one single way of understanding Spain as a nation that faithfully fulfills her role in the universal enterprise. To which enterprise all Spaniards will have to cede the interests of any group or class.) (Primo de Rivera, *Escritos* 251)

The purpose of female formation, as predicated by the women's section of the Falange, was the forging of national-Catholic female consciousness. As such, it promoted a "system of (partially or totally identical) schemes of perception, thought, appreciation and action," which would ensure the consolidation and perpetuation of the established order (Bourdieu, *Reproduction* 35). It was assumed, not without foundation, that the acquisition of legitimate dispositions placed one in optimal conditions to feel, act, and think within the confines of the permissible. The near identical content of the following passages serves, at the very least, to advance Susan Suleiman's notion of redundancy from being an indelible mark of authoritarian fictions to broader prescriptive practices:

Ya no habrá más que juventudes de miradas claras, educadas con la doctrina de Cristo y a nuestro modo nacional-sindicalista, que sabrán en cada momento qué es lo que les debe gustar y qué es lo que deben repeler como perjudicial para la ambición colectiva de la Patria.

(From now on, there will be only young people with clear vision, educated according to the doctrine of Christ and our national-syndicalist method, who will know at every moment what is it that they should like and what they should reject as detrimental to the collective ambition of the Fatherland.) (Primo de Rivera, *Cuatro discursos* 21)

[A] las mujeres de España hay que proporcionarles revolucionariamente unos conocimientos que hasta ahora desconocían y formarles una conciencia basada en la doctrina de Cristo y en nuestras normas nacional-sindicalistas, para que, sin deformaciones, sepan distinguir claramente en cada momento el bien del mal, tanto en materia religiosa como en el conocimiento que han de tener de la Patria, del hogar y de los hijos.

(We must provide the women of Spain, in revolutionary fashion, with the knowledge they have lacked up to now. Their consciences must be shaped within the doctrine of Christ and our national-syndicalist tenets, so that,

without wavering, at every moment they are able to clearly distinguish good
from evil, both in religious matters and in the understanding they must have
of the Fatherland, of home, and of children.) (Primo de Rivera, *Discursos*
67)

No perder ni minuto, ni hora, ni día en esta complicada misión de enseñar,
que de toda esta prisa necesita la Patria para que ni una sola mujer escape a
nuestra influencia y para que todas ellas sepan después, en cualquier circun-
stancia, reaccionar según nuestro entendimiento falangista de la vida y de
la historia.

(We must not lose one minute, hour, or day in this complex mission of teaching; the Fatherland needs haste so that not a single woman escapes our
influence, and so that all women know, afterward, in any situation, how to
behave according to our Falangist understanding of life and history.) [12]

[L]o que hay que hacer con la juventud de hoy es procurar que adquiera,
como decía José Antonio, 'un sentido total claro en el alma que le dé las
soluciones para lo concreto.' Este claro sentido, basado, naturalmente, en
una auténtica formación religiosa y en este modo de ser que para nosotros
es la Falange. Es decir, poner a las chicas en condiciones de que ellas mismas se guarden, mediante una sólida formación moral. Y después dejar que
cada una desenvuelva su vida en el ambiente en que por su situación familiar le haya correspondido.

(What must be done with the young people of today is to insure that they
acquire, as José Antonio used to say, 'a complete clarity in the soul that
provides them with solutions for real problems.' This clarity [is] based,
naturally, on an authentic religious upbringing, and on this way of life that
is, for us, the Falange. In other words, we must create for girls conditions
in which they will protect themselves by way of a solid moral foundation.
Afterwards, let each young woman carry out her life in the environment that
corresponds to her family's station.) (Primo de Rivera, *Escritos* 258)

A widely exploited form of propagation was exemplarity. The *Sección
Femenina*'s first manifesto (1934) pronounced "'preaching, spreading the
word and setting an example'" common functions of the affiliates (qtd in
Richmond 34). All members were encouraged to serve as role models to those
immediately under their command. In her address to the future *mandos* (leaders), Pilar stated: "La buena marcha de las Secciones Femeninas solo depende
de vosotras, de la fe y la austeridad que las inculquéis con vuestro ejemplo. Si
vosotras sois disciplinadas, también lo serán ellas, y os seguirán sin titubeos
si ven que vuestra vida es exacta y justa" ("The progress of the *Secciones
Femeninas* depends solely on you, on the faith and austerity that you instill in

---

[12] From *Y*, the journal of *Sección Femenina*, April 1944. Qtd in Carmen Martín Gaite, *Usos
amorosos* 59.

them through your example. If you are disciplined, they will be too, and they will follow you without hesitation if they see that your life is fair and just") (*Discursos* 11). In a similar vein, the edifying literature (from pamphlets to textbooks), published under the auspices of *Sección Femenina*, abounds in hagiographic accounts of religious martyrs and national heroes.[13] Normative representations of Isabel the Catholic and St. Teresa of Avila were emblematic of this trend.[14] Since the 1930s, the two figures were employed as antidotes to the proliferating lay feminist movements. As Sunder Rajan contends elsewhere, the argument that "exceptional women of learning, or achievement, or military prowess" were not absent, in this case, from the valorized Spanish past, served to "undercut the need for an organized women's movement for achieving women's equality" (135). The consecration of given cultural figures as timeless role models of womanhood obfuscated the disparities between their historical and projected identities, thereby fomenting continuity between past and present on one hand, and encouraging emulation over change on the other.[15] It was in the interests of the *Sección Femenina* to ensure that in fact both role models could be followed without posing a threat to the dominant patriarchal order. Hence the abundance of references to the queen's and the mystic's domestic proclivities, epitomized by their fondness for needlework. According to Giuliana Di Febo: "la frecuente configuración de Teresa e Isabel dedicadas a los 'labores de su sexo' funciona como *understatement* frente al excepcional protagonismo de ambas, relativizando su alcance y subrayando su coexistencia con específicos roles femeninos" ("the frequent depiction of Teresa and Isabel devoted to the 'labors of their sex' functions as an understatement vis-à-vis the exceptional protagonism of both, relativizing their achievements and highlighting their coexistence with specific feminine roles") (*Ritos de Guerra* 105). The emphasis on Isabel and Teresa's domesticity, in lieu of their public persona, had as its obvious corollary the displacement of female agency from the public to the private sphere. The recasting of authoritative feminine figures into "tame protagonists" may be viewed as necessary for the legitimization of *Sección Femenina*'s own

---

[13] Such a climate was propitious for the production of reading formations understood as "a set of discursive and intertextual determinations that organize and animate the practice of reading, connecting texts and readers in specific relations to one another by constituting readers as reading subjects of particular types and texts as objects-to-be-read in particular ways." See Tony Bennett, "Texts in History: The Determinations of Readings and their Texts" in *Reception Study: From Literary Theory to Cultural Studies* (London: Routledge, 2001) 66, and the "Editor's introduction" to "Building the State and the Practice of Power 1940–1959," *Spanish Cultural Studies* 169.

[14] Their homologation dates back to the seventeenth-century bishop Juan de Palafox y Mendoza. See Giuliana Di Febo, *La santa de la raza* (Barcelona: Icaria, 1987) 97.

[15] See Giuliana Di Febo, *Ritos de Guerra y de Victoria* (Bilbao: Desclée de Brouwer, 2002) 94–5.

unconventional praxis.[16] After all, "the SF's cadres were single, economically independent women with an unusually self-sufficient life-style"—a fact that allows Helen Graham to rightly conclude that—"[t]he discrepancy between this and the message they disseminated—of the virtues of female submission, subservience, and joy through domesticity—was remarkable" (193). Yet without this message there would have been no normative alternative to the status quo. If their lives formed an exception to the norm, it was because they assumed the role of its predicators.

Pilar's symbolic link with the original teachings of the Falange through her brother, José Antonio, served to bolster her, and through her, the organization's claims of expertise on the role and ideal of womanhood under the new order. As there was very little that José Antonio wrote or said about women, the oft-quoted passage below comes from his only recorded address to the members of the *Sección Femenina*. In it, he outlines the party's relationship toward women as situated between the opposite poles of retrograde and ultra-liberal models. Women as hailed by the Falange were to be neither passive heroines bent on frivolity, nor militant feminists and perceived victims of uneven competition with men:[17]

> . . . acaso no sabéis toda la profunda afinidad que hay entre la mujer y la Falange. Ningún otro partido podréis entender mejor, precisamente porque en la Falange no acostumbramos a usar ni la galantería ni el feminismo.

[16] According to Gallego Méndez: " . . . en Falange se amaba lo difícil y se convertían en dogmas de fe la disciplina y el sacrificio. Y en ello no iba a la zaga la Sección Femenina, cuyo comportamiento, acorde con esos valores, se medía a veces con el de los hombres, aludiendo al lema isabelino de 'Tanto monta. . .' Un ejemplo claro se encuentra en las palabras de Rosario Pereda: '. . . como la vuestra, acaso mayor que la vuestra a veces la de nuestras secciones femeninas, orgullosas de su inferioridad, tanto como de vuestro mando (grandes aplausos). Y si de sacrificio se habla, ¡ah! Entonces, entonces roto queda a nuestro favor el equilibrio del "Tanto monta. . ." porque lo sacrificamos todo; y no una vida, no nuestra propia vida que tan poco vale, sino mil vidas, nuestras vidas, esas otras vidas de mujer que son vidas de hombre, vidas de hijos y de hermanos'" (". . . in the Falange, what was difficult was loved, and discipline and sacrifice became dogmas of faith. And in this the *Sección Femenina* was not left behind, as its behavior, according to those values, was measured at times against that of men, alluding to the Isabeline motto 'Tanto monta. . .' A clear example is found in the words of Rosario Pereda: '. . . like yours, at times perhaps greater than yours is that of our women's cadres, as proud of their inferiority, as of your leadership (loud applause). And if it is sacrifice that one speaks of, ah! Then, then the balance of "Tanto monta. . ." is in our favor because we sacrifice everything; and not merely one life, not our own life that is worth so little, but a thousand lives, our lives, those other lives of women that are men's lives, lives of sons and of brothers'"): *Mujer, falange y franquismo* 31.

[17] Since this passage is seldom quoted in its entirety (and using only part of the quotation alters its interpretation), I have chosen to reproduce it here almost in full, marking by asterisk the point from which it is commonly cited. A similar break with this obscuring trend may be found in Jo Labanyi's article, "Resemanticizing Feminine Surrender" 76.

La galantería no era otra cosa que una estafa para la mujer. Se la sobornaba con unos cuantos piropos, para arrinconarla en una privación de todas las consideraciones serias. Se la distraía con un jarabe de palabras, se la cultivaba una supuesta estúpida, para relegarla a un papel frívolo y decorativo. Nosotros sabemos hasta dónde cala la misión entrañable de la mujer, y nos guardaremos muy bien de tratarla nunca como tonta destinataria de piropos.
Tampoco somos feministas. *No entendemos que la manera de respetar a la mujer consista en sustraerla a su magnífico destino y entregarla a funciones varoniles. A mí siempre me ha dado tristeza ver a la mujer en ejercicios de hombre, toda afanada y desquiciada en una rivalidad donde lleva—entre la morbosa complacencia de los competidores masculinos—todas las de perder. El verdadero feminismo no debiera consistir en querer para las mujeres las funciones que hoy se estiman superiores, sino en rodear cada vez de mayor dignidad humana y social a las funciones femeninas.

(. . . perhaps you are not aware of the profound affinity that exists between women and the Falange. You will not be able to understand any other party better, precisely because in the Falange we recur neither to gallantry nor to feminism.
    Gallantry was nothing but a swindle for woman. She was bribed with a few compliments which were intended to marginalize her and deprive her of all serious consideration. She was distracted by a syrup of words, she was taught to appear stupid, in order to relegate her to a frivolous and decorative role. *We* know how far the true mission of woman extends, and we are very sure never to treat her as a foolish recipient of flattery.
    We are not feminists, either. *It is not our understanding that the way to respect woman consists in diverting her from her magnificent destiny and delivering her over to masculine functions. It has always saddened me to see a woman doing man's work, harried and at her wits' end in a rivalry that—to the morbid satisfaction of her male competitors—she is destined to lose. True feminism should not consist of wanting for women functions that are seen as superior today, but instead in giving ever more human and social dignity to feminine functions.)[18]

This speech provided the groundwork for the *Sección Femenina*'s self-representation as it strove to differentiate its own ideal of womanhood from romantic, liberal, religious, feminist, and intellectual types. It rejected the "ñoñería" or spinelessness of the first, the atheism and immorality of the second, the false piety, backwardness, and hypocrisy of the third, and the perceived sterility, androgyny, and disregard for paramount feminine virtues of the latter two.

---

[18] See "Palabras pronunciadas por José Antonio en Don Benito (Badajoz), después del mitin, a unas camaradas," *Obras completas de José Antonio Primo de Rivera* (N.p.: Delegación Nacional de Prensa y Propaganda de Falange Española Tradicionalista y de las J.O.N.S., n.d.) 167–8.

Instead, the organization fomented "an ideal of femininity that would place women above criticism, allowing them to be educationally and professionally fulfilled and yet not a challenge to male authority" (Richmond 10). The materialization of such an ideal required the production of a public field in which women could act without overt reference to men (Richmond 108), and for which the organization drew on the nineteenth-century bourgeois discourse of different and complementary gender relations—the foundational basis of its statutes.

Chapter one of the aforementioned document defined women's, and subsequently *Sección Femenina*'s, role in the following terms:

> El fin esencial de la mujer, en su función humana, es servir de perfecto complemento al hombre, formando con él, individual o colectivamente, una perfecta unidad social.
> Por lo tanto, la Sección Femenina de Falange Española de las J.O.N.S., al incorporarse con misión, sentido y estilo netamente femeninos a la obra viril de la Falange, lo hará para auxiliar, complementar y hacer total aquella obra.

> (The essential destiny of woman, in her human function, is to serve as a perfect complement to man, forming with him, individually or collectively, a perfect social union.
> Therefore, the *Sección Femenina* of the Spanish Falange of the J.O.N.S. will join in the virile work of the Falange through a purely feminine mission, sensibility and style, so as to help, complement and complete that work.)

Article 4 of this same chapter pronounced the women's task within the organization to be:

> la realización de todos los servicios que concuerden exactamente con el espíritu y facultades de sus masas, cumpliendo con ello en la Falange las funciones de la mujer en el hogar—arreglo material, aliento y cuidado—y de otra parte los servicios extraordinarios de participación en la obra sanitaria y desarrollo de la obra social benéfica . . .

> (carrying out all the services that conform exactly with the spirit and capabilities of its members, and thereby fulfilling in the Falange woman's domestic duties—material upkeep, support, and care—and in addition, the extraordinary services of participating in sanitary work and the development of charitable social work . . .)

Finally, article 6 promised to maintain the male–female division of roles through the observance of a distinct style and mode of conduct that was intended to denote Falangist women's inherent femininity: "Para cumplir todas sus fines, la Sección Femenina . . . fijará a la mujer en el íntegro y pleno sentido del ser femenina, según es por naturaleza inabdicable, apartándola en la conducta, la forma y el estilo de toda función o apariencia varonil" ("In order to achieve all of its goals, *Sección Femenina* . . . will confirm in women their full and integral femininity, which is by nature unrenounceable, by removing them in conduct, form, and style from all male functions or appearances") (qtd in Gallego Méndez 216).

The two channels through which the organization could legitimately assert its influence were education and welfare programs. Both demanded that the *mandos* or the heads of women's cadres lead a lifestyle that differed substantially from the one promoted by the organization. As Richmond observes, "they had to be flexible professionals, able to cope with varied responsibilities and prepared to live and work away from home. Most, although not all, stayed single, challenging the stereotype of the unmarried woman as an object of pity" (12). This apparent deviation from the norm nonetheless enjoyed a normative interpretation whereby the women in question were considered to be sacrificing their personal happiness for service to the Fatherland and for the good of society at large. As such, the Falangist women made a case for social rather than biological motherhood. Offering a homology with Catholic nuns, the Falangist women were wedded to the national-syndicalist vision of a new state, which it was their duty to serve and uphold.

Thus, contrary to what might be expected, women's leadership roles made available by the *Sección Femenina* were founded on the very discourse that relegated them to a separate and subordinate field of action. We may further contend that one of the *Sección Femenina*'s most striking accomplishments was the reconfiguring of difference from a disabling into an enabling category for women. Whether this was done in a spirit of defiance or compliance, the fact remains that:

> for its members and particularly the elites (*mandos*), SF gave opportunities for a way of life that was rare in the Franco regime before the 1960s, when the development of mass tourism heralded social and economic changes for Spanish women. Prior to that, for the majority of women, the goal of marriage, children and domesticity remained uncontested. . . . The activities of the *mandos*, on the other hand, allowed certain freedoms while remaining publicly acceptable. (Richmond 101)[19]

As we have seen, the underlying stipulation of women's changing life script was that it alleviate the material and welfare needs of the new state

---

[19] In her study on women under Italian fascism, Victoria De Grazia asserts that women were not passive subjects but protagonists who made choices, "although how they negotiated these choices is harder to document than the fact that they made them, for the preponderance of written sources echo male anxieties rather than voice women's concerns": *How Fascism Ruled Women* (Berkeley: U of California P, 1993) 11.

without in any way perturbing the established order, a stipulation that permeated *Sección Femenina*'s discourse at every level. The initial challenge of creating a space for female agency without undermining or threatening male authority came to define the organization's rhetoric and praxis. Because some practices were more useful than others in promoting the national-Catholic feminine ideal, and contained potential for "misinterpretation," their injunction as a rule came with a mandatory interpretation.[20]

As one compulsory text for future instructors of the *Sección Femenina*'s domestic schools averred, women's individual formation and professional initiation consisted "no en instruir intelectualmente a la mujer . . . sino en que aprenda en la escuela aquellos conocimientos que le son imprescindibles para su actuación en la familia" ("not in the intellectual instruction of women . . . but in ensuring that they learn in school all those things which are indispensable for their performance in the family"). Similarly, political formation to raise female awareness of national concerns and interests was intended "no para discutirlos, sino para poder infundirlos en el corazón de los hijos y hacer de este modo que un verdadero patriotismo informe toda la vida española" ("not to debate them, but to be able to instill them into the hearts of their children, and in this way ensure that true patriotism inform all Spanish life") (qtd in Pastor i Homs 60–1). The above use of the negative construction bespeaks the perceived need to limit the gap between desired and alternative ends of the endorsed training, which is in turn indicative of the organization's latent anxiety about the reception of its teachings both by the state (for whom the inclusion of normative interpretation into the injunction was a means of pre-empting criticism) and by their female addressees (in whom this same mechanism sought to curb the authority for making contesting interpretations). Implicit in these discursive practices were inconsistencies between realizations of prescribed tenets and their univocal rationalization. It was the latter that imbued given practices with a normative content, and it was in the ensuing gap between their authorized and censored interpretations where the institutional discourse was unsettled as an ultimate and unambiguous source of meaning.

What any new welfare, social or educational program needed as a precondition for its successful implementation was a command of legitimate and legitimating rhetoric and an observable compliance with the status quo. Rendered as subservient to state-sanctioned objectives, female formation—

---

[20] It is not incidental that the practice of inscribing meaning in the text to safeguard its "correct" interpretation (which Suleiman identifies as a distinctive feature of authoritarian fictions) is exercised when the discourse on womanhood treats functions that stand out for their potential multivalence and as such threaten the tight web of meanings that constitute Spanish womanhood. This may also account for sublimation as a recurrent strategy in women's writing (in either manuals and handbooks or narratives of female exemplarity).

whether it addressed the question of hygiene, morality, beauty, or learning—could not stand as an end entirely on its own. Among the potential points of contest were the *Sección Femenina*'s advocacy of female instruction, employment, and sports. In and of themselves, none of the above was considered indispensable for the fulfillment of the female mission of marrying, bearing and raising children. Instead, all three were endorsed and legitimized as means to this desired, hegemonic end. Consider the following passage from the "Discurso de la Excma. Sra. Dª Pilar Primo de Rivera y Saenz de Heredia" quoted by Morcillo Gómez:

> We are convinced that by protecting women's access to work and learning, we do not violate the laws. An educated, refined, and sensitive woman—precisely for that reason—is a better educator of her children and a better companion for her husband. In the Women's Section, we have thousands of cases of university women who are married and whose families are a model of compassion and harmony. According to José Antonio, a woman cannot limit herself to being a 'foolish recipient of compliments.' Abnegation, her essential virtue, is much more consciously and efficiently developed if she has an education." (*True Catholic Womanhood* 69)

But Pilar's argument did not stop here. An educated woman was able to play a greater role in the instruction of her children and enjoy the status of "amiga y mujer" ("friend and wife") rather than simply "mujer" (wife, or woman) so long as:

> no se trate de ponerse en un plan de igualdad con el hombre que eso es pedante, ridículo y camino seguro del fracaso como mujer. . . . Ahora, si la cultura se lleva hasta el punto de que la mujer se queda en un árido producto intelectual, sin una sola de las condiciones humanas que debe tener para alcanzar sus fines naturales, entonces la cultura es totalmente negativa; pero, gracias a Dios, en España no suele darse ese tipo de mujer puramente intelectual.

> (there is no question of putting her on an equal plane with man, since that is pompous, ridiculous and a sure road to failure as a woman. . . . Now, if the culture reaches a point in which woman is left as an arid intellectual product, without a single one of the human conditions that she must have to fulfill her natural destiny, then the culture is totally negative; but, thank God, in Spain that type of purely intellectual woman does not come about very often.) (Primo de Rivera, *Escritos* 259)

In a similar vein, while it helped restore women to their natural purview (jeopardized by the changing expectations of lay and materialist cultures), the *Sección Femenina* both acknowledged and sanctioned the need for feminine labor through its serial publications. According to one such publication, middle-class women "could aspire to become nurses, language teachers, secretaries, librarians, research assistants, opticians, tourist guides, and even international bureaucrats" whereas women from the working classes could become qualified "cooks, maids, nannies, or hairdressers" (Morcillo Gómez, *True Catholic Womanhood* 74). The legitimating basis for this institutionally unauthorized stance was what De Grazia calls "ideology of scarcity," an upshot of extreme penury and economic uncertainty wrought by the Civil and the Second World Wars. Consequently, work for women was permissible, but unlike for men, it was conceived as a temporary measure rather than a norm.[21] According to Richmond, the member of *Sección Femenina* gave labor a culturally accepted varnish of service. The wages were either non-existent or so low as to pass for tokens of appreciation rather than due recompense. Instead, much of the work was done on a voluntary basis, pre-empting charges of self-interest, greed, or feminism that were commonplace against female paid labor. Normative rationalization for a working woman was that she complied with her familial obligations by contributing to the waning domestic economy. Conversely, the *Sección Femenina*'s promotion of voluntary service afforded its leaders a kind of distinction in keeping with "bourgeois opinion which equated paid work with need and preferred to see middle-class women in voluntary activities for church and country" (Richmond 106–7).

As for sports, according to the official rhetoric of the time, a woman who engaged in them did so to enhance her femininity and strengthen her health, both of which had positive repercussions in her wifely and motherly duties. Following De Grazia:

> Pastimes such as skiing, tennis, swimming, horseback riding, or sailing were like piano playing for nineteenth-century bourgeois young women; they enhanced social grace, offered occasions to meet eligible young men, and were part of a common modern upper-class style of life, one shared by the royal young women of the House of Savoy as well as by the new fascist bourgeoisie. (220)

Feminization of sports or their incorporation into middle-class feminine aesthetics is manifest in popular romance novels of the time whose protagonists are at once agile and frail, spirited and vulnerable, tenacious and graceful, accomplished yet uncompetitive. The vigilance of the Church and the ensuing moral order ensured that women's dress code did not compromise the stringent sexual mores, even in the water. Competition was eliminated from sports as a "masculine element," just as certain careers remained inaccessible to women both in study and practice. Even so, for the clergy and moralists,

---

[21] Anyone interested to learn more about the subject should consult the cited works by Richmond and Morcillo Gómez. My own analysis is much indebted to their contribution.

physical education was a controversial practice,[22] as were the pursuits of higher education and career goals, which threatened to undermine the institution of marriage and to empower women intellectually, socially, and economically, thereby jeopardizing male supremacy in both the domestic and public realms. A woman who considered learning and employment a source of personal gain and fulfillment was ostensibly betraying her very nature, which exacted abnegation—"todo lo contrario del egoísmo, de la comodidad, de lo fácil" ("the complete opposite of selfishness, of comfort, of that which is easy") (Primo de Rivera, *Escritos* 249).

But for the representatives of more conservative circles, the gravest threat to the feminine psyche throughout the 1940s was the post-war climate itself (owing to the relaxation of the conservative status quo before the consolidation of the national-Catholic mores—a recurring motif in women's contemporaneous narratives). The imposition of order and discipline hailed by the Falange therefore was seen as a positive measure aimed, among other things, at securing resolve and restoring premises shaken by war and deprivation. In this respect, watching films and reading literature warranted particular caution, especially for those who were in want of a solid national-Catholic foundation.

As Richmond observes, the party's trans-class aspirations and bourgeois underpinnings were manifest in the organization's promotion of meritocracy; that is, while its leaders constituted a select minority (in line with Joseantonian dictum), in principle, acceptance of Falangist doctrine enabled anyone to excel in the spirit of service and sacrifice, regardless of his or her social provenance: "Tenemos que meterles tan dentro de sí este espíritu nuestro, que lleguen a olvidarse de su procedencia, que sientan el orgullo de ser españoles con la misma fuerza con que nosotros lo sentimos, y que ya entre sus hijos y los nuestros no perciban diferencia alguna" ("We have to instill our spirit in them so deeply, that they forget where they came from, that they feel the pride of being Spanish as strongly as we do, and that there be no perceptible difference between their children and ours") (Primo de Rivera, *Discursos* 21).

One way to a "classless," harmonious, and unified Spain was through homogeneous formation. Realization of a similar goal (totalizing formation) required a complex educational and propagandistic network comprised of

---

[22] According to one of the former affiliates: "when they [the members of *Sección Femenina*] introduced gymnastics for girls into the schools, it was considered very 'provocative; and the mothers of the girls wouldn't let them put on bloomers. . . . Now, you hear those bloomers being laughed at, and they say, 'How ridiculous' [they were].' At the time, however, these activities of the *Sección Femenina* ran counter to established Church norms. 'There were bishops who did not look at us with a kind eye; they would even say to us that we were perverting the youth. . . . Even I had to experience on one occasion that a priest, who had confessed me, said that if I did not leave the *Sección Femenina*, that my soul was in danger. . . . Certainly, I didn't ever return to confess with that man." Qtd in Lorée Enders, "Problematic Portraits," 384.

theoretical and practical training, specialized schools and literacy centers, camps and mobile institutes, and compulsory women's Social Service (*servicio social*). An equivalent of men's obligatory military service, it had been initiated as a wartime auxiliary measure and graduated into a form of social control and assistance (and, through Carmen Martín Gaite's prose, may be one of the *Sección Femenina*'s most popularized measures in the shaping of Spanish womanhood). Its two components, theory and practice, matched its twofold objective of providing the state's ailing economy with free labor, and of regulating the female sector of the population. "Every woman who desired state employment, a passport, a driver's license, or even a fishing license passed through the six months required social service of the SF: in fact, the Women's Section affected—negatively or positively—a large majority of two generations of Spanish females" (Enders 676). Social Service thus became a prime vehicle through which *Sección Femenina* carried out its mission of reeducating and preparing women for the New Spain.

A considerable role in the *Sección Femenina*'s self-representation was awarded to faith in the party's doctrine:

> La fe mueve los montes. Tened fe, y todo lo demás os dará por añadidura. Dice José Antonio que lo que hace falta es encontrar la verdad, creer en ella e imponerla como él nos decía también: alegremente, poéticamente, y quizá en buscar la dificultad del riesgo está en parte la poesía de la Falange y mucha de nuestra alegría.

> (Faith moves mountains. Have faith, and all the rest will be given to you. José Antonio says that what is needed is to find the truth, believe in it and impose it—as he also said to us—happily, poetically; and perhaps much of our happiness and part of the poetry of the Falange consists in seeking the challenge, taking the risk.)

Conceived as acts of faith, Falangist women's activities could inspire no considerable criticism, only an understandable degree of incomprehension: "En nuestra misma Sección Femenina vemos cómo la camarada divulgadora deja pasar todo lo que para ella signifique comodidad o agrado y voluntariamente se lanza a lo difícil, a lo que los sensatos llaman absurdo" ("In our own *Sección Femenina*, we see how the comrade-propagandist leaves behind all that for her means comfort or pleasure and voluntarily plunges into that which is difficult, into what sensible people call absurd") (Primo de Rivera, *Escritos* 249–50). One may find this same logic operating in the novels of Carmen de Icaza, an honorary member of the *Sección Femenina* whose protagonists are distinguished for their resolve and tenacity, qualities that as a rule have not been associated with the traditional patriarchal model of womanhood.

To complete our analysis of the Falangist feminine ideal, we must now turn to Emilio Gentile's notion of fascism as a political religion. The legitimating role played by the Catholic Church in the consolidation of the Francoist regime has precluded, in my view, the study of Falange as a civic religion in the vein of Italian fascism. According to Gentile:

> Se puede hablar de sacralización de la política cuando una entidad política, por ejemplo la Nación, el Estado, la Raza, la Clase, el Partido, el Movimiento, se transforma en una entidad sagrada, es decir, trascendente, indiscutible, intangible y, como tal, se convierte en el eje de un sistema, más o menos elaborado, de creencias, mitos, valores, mandamientos, ritos y símbolos, transformándose así en objeto de fe, de reverencia, de culto, de fidelidad y entrega para los ciudadanos hasta el sacrificio de la vida, si fuera necesario.

> (It is possible to talk of sacralization of politics when a political entity (e.g., the Nation, State, Race, Class, Party, Movement) is transformed into a sacred entity (i.e., transcendent, indisputable, intangible), and as such becomes the axis of a more or less complex system of beliefs, myths, values, commandments, rites and symbols, thus turning into an object of faith, reverence, worship, devotion and submission for citizens, even to the point of sacrificing their lives, should it be necessary.) (57)

The notion of the Falange as a civic religion provides an interesting angle for the study of the totalitarian and totalizing ambition of the party, which sought to imbue all human activity with a sense of cohesion and purpose in keeping with its own mandates. For a true Falangist there was no meaning outside of the Falange. Those who wished to join its ranks were considered to be at the brink of a new life. Predictably, such a life entailed surrender of one's will, renunciation of former ways, and tempering of all instincts that threatened to compromise the truths represented by the Falange: "Y al darnos cuenta de que habíamos encontrado la verdad amorosamente nos pusimos a servirla, dejando atrás y como olvidada nuestra inútil vida anterior" ("And realizing that we had found the truth, we lovingly dedicated ourselves to its service, leaving our useless previous life behind, as if forgotten") (Primo de Rivera, *Escritos* 247). In a pledge that marked the passage from an old and meaningless existence to one full of promise, the future affiliates of the *Sección Femenina* swore to display obedience, enthusiasm, zeal, patience, valor, silence, resilience, integrity, and dedication.[23] These were but some of the qualities that

---

[23] The following was the pledge taken upon initiation into the ranks of *Sección Femenina*: "Juro darme siempre al Servicio de Falange. Juro no tener otro orgullo que el de la Patria y el de la Falange y vivir siempre bajo la Falange en obediencia y alegría, ímpetu y paciencia, gallardía y silencio. Juro lealtad y sumisión a nuestros Jefes, honor a la memoria de nuestros muertos, implacable perseverancia en todas las vicisitudes. Juro dondequiera que esté para obedecer, o para mandar, respeto a nuestras Jerarquías, del primero al último cargo. Juro rechazar y dar por no oída toda voz del enemigo, que pueda debilitar el espíritu de Falange. Juro mantener sobre

constituted the Falangist ideal type. As José Antonio Primo de Rivera claimed, and Pilar Primo de Rivera liked to remind her followers, the Falange was, above all, a way of life:

> Dijo José Antonio el 29 de octubre: 'Que nuestro Movimiento no estaría del todo entendido si se creyera que era una manera de pensar tan solo; no es una manera de pensar, es una manera de ser. No debemos proponernos sólo la construcción, la arquitectura política. Tenemos que adoptar ante la vida entera, en cada uno de nuestros actos una actitud humana, profunda y completa. Esa actitud es el espíritu de servicio y de sacrificio, el sentido ascético y militar de la vida.'

> (José Antonio said on October 29: 'Our Movement would not be fully understood if one were to regard it as only a way of thinking; it is not a way of thinking, it is a way of being. We should not only aspire to construct the framework, the political architecture. We have to adopt in our entire life, in each one of our acts, a humane, profound, and complete attitude. That attitude is the spirit of service and sacrifice, the ascetic and military way of life.') (*Cuatro discursos* 31)

It was this attitude toward life that distinguished a true Falangist from a mere affiliate as well as from other normative types. Characterized by gravity of manner, defiance of obstacles, and unyielding optimism, it denoted faith in the party's transcendental purpose, in its dream of national revival. Its materialization was the task of a select few, who in José Antonio's words constituted "una minoría inasequible al desaliento" ("a minority impervious to despair");[24] hence, the optimism, or "alegría," that necessarily permeated all Falangist activities from service to sacrifice.

The acceptance of the Falange's palingenetic mission—which enabled the members of the party to live, serve, fight, and die in voluntary submission to its doctrine—therefore presupposed more than training, a conversion. The by-

---

todas las ideas de Unidad. Unidad entre las tierras de España. Unidad en el hombre y entre los hombres de España. Juro vivir en santa hermandad con todos los de la Falange y prestar todo auxilio y deponer toda diferencia, siempre que me sea invocada esta santa hermandad." ("I swear always to put myself at the service of the Falange. I swear not to have any other pride than that of the Fatherland and that of the Falange and to live always under the Falange in obedience and happiness, urgency and patience, magnanimity and silence. I swear loyalty and submission to our leaders, honor to the memory of our dead, implacable perseverance through all vicissitudes. Wherever I may be, whether to obey or to lead, I swear respect to our Hierarchies, from the highest to the lowest official. I swear to reject and turn a deaf ear to the enemy's voice, as that could debilitate the spirit of the Falange. I swear to maintain above all the idea of Unity. Unity among the lands of Spain. Unity in each man and among the men of Spain. I swear to live in holy brotherhood with all those of the Falange and lend all aid and put aside all differences, whenever this holy brotherhood is invoked."): Pilar Primo de Rivera, *Cuatro discursos* 14.

[24] Qtd in Pilar Primo de Rivera, *Cuatro discrusos* 20.

product of the party's belief system was a new man, who, according to Stanley Payne, "incorporated nearly all the qualities of the traditional Catholic hero, while fusing it with certain twentieth-century components" (*Franco* 58–9).[25] Yet unlike those of Catholic heroes and heroines, Falangist acts were not inspired so much by traditional Christian faith as by faith in a palingenetic vision of "the nation rising phoenix-like from the ashes of decadence" (Griffin xii). Hence, while there is no denying that as a nationalist movement, the Falange embraced Spanish Catholicism (as Payne further points out, many of its members were practicing Catholics (*Franco* 259)), I subscribe to Kathleen Richmond and Victoria De Grazia's view that the study of a Falangist ideal type, or at least that of an ideal Falangist woman, must take into account a "deep conflict within the fascist state between the demands of modernity and the desire to reimpose traditional authority" (De Grazia 2; Richmond 5). Even as they upheld conservative Catholic values and bourgeois mores, the leaders of the *Sección Femenina* rejected the role of passive bystander in favor of women's mobilization and incorporation into national life through the state political body.

We may thus conclude that the *Sección Femenina*'s task was to adapt the notion of the new 'Falangist man' "who is instinctively prepared to sacrifice himself to the higher needs of the nation" (Griffin 42) to Falangist women. By advocating heroic action, the leaders of the party legitimated their own non-conformist stance; in other words, by transposing the myth of 'new man' to 'new woman,' they produced at least theoretical grounds for female agency. However, such a practice was less of a rule than an exception, for despite the party's alleged populism, the revolution, in keeping with Joseantonian mandate, was the task of a select minority, and it was just such a minority that the leaders of *Sección Femenina* represented themselves to be. It was they who could identify with the otherwise incongruous symbols of St. Teresa and Queen Isabel. For the masses in need of reeducation, these models of far-from-submissive women were reinterpreted and "sanitized" to the point of becoming quaint icons of piety and domesticity (Graham 184–5).

Both the Falange and Francoism presented themselves as a panacea for the nation's ills. A woman's role in nation-building, as predicated by the moralists and ideologues of the time, was not an entirely novel one. In Di Febo's words, theirs was "la misión 'regeneradora' y 'recristianizadora' . . . en la reconstrucción de la trama de valores disgregados por la República y la Guerra civil y recuperados por el 'Nuevo Estado'" ("the 'regenerating' and 'rechristianiz-

---

[25] Although useful, such an assertion exacts further precision, for by subsuming the Falangist image of an ideal man under a Catholic model, it tends to reinforce Francoist emphasis on the Falange's traditionalism in lieu of its more revolutionary claims (a tendency that gained cultural and political legitimacy with the defeat of the Axis powers in the Second World War and the subsequent defascistization of the regime).

ing' mission . . . in the reconstruction of the set of values torn asunder by the
Republic and the Civil War and recovered by the 'New State'") (*La santa*
105). And yet it was through this mission that the leaders of the *Sección
Femenina*, akin to the example of the nineteenth-century "virtuous women
writers", found legitimate discursive authority from which to interpret their
own duties to the Fatherland.

We may thus conclude that much of the ambiguity behind the *Sección
Femenina*'s policies resulted from its own peculiar position as both a dominated (within the Falange and the state apparatus) and dominant (vis-à-vis the
female constituents) group. As such, its discourse (the rationale employed by
the organization to legitimate its activities) presents a constant balancing act
between power and subordination, claims and disclaimers, advances and
retractions, affirmation and effacement. What had to be avoided at all cost
was the notion that women could ever supplant men in any endeavor that was
not feminine by the ruling definition; in other words, the production and/or
delineation of a gendered public sphere was a precondition to any female
claim to action. In her address, "Fe y conducta de las mujeres" ("Faith and the
Conduct of Women"), Pilar Primo de Rivera reiterated the organization's
stance as it appeared in the original statutes:

> Lo que no haremos nunca es ponerlas [a las mujeres] en competencia con
> ellos [los hombres], porque jamás llegarán a igualarlos, y, en cambio,
> pierden toda la elegancia y toda la gracia indispensable para la convivencia.
> Y ya veréis como estas mujeres, formadas así con la doctrina cristiana y al
> estilo nacionalsindicalista, son útiles en la familia; en el municipio y en el
> sindicato.

> (What we will never do is put [women] in competition with [men], because
> [the women] will never match [the men], and instead they will lose all the
> elegance and grace indispensable to family life. And you will see how these
> women, formed according to Christian doctrine and in the national-syndi-
> calist mode, are useful in the family, in the municipality and in the syndi-
> cate.) (*Discursos* 14)

The difficulty in taking the organization's ostensibly anti-feminist stance at
face value resides in the simple yet often-neglected fact that "under an authoritarian government, people [even those in the position of power] were not free
to express their opinions" (De Grazia 13). What remains clear is that the advocacy of any apparent deviation from the norm (any practice that could potentially distract women from their mission), whether pursuit of higher education,
career, or sports, had to meet two stipulations: it had to be secondary to marriage and motherhood, and it could not be construed as grounds for parity
with men. To challenge the latter was not only deemed vain and untenable,
but also strategically flawed: "Pero no pretendáis poneros con ellos de igual a

igual, porque entonces, lejos de conseguir lo que pretendéis, os tendrán los hombres en desprecio infinito y jamás podréis influir sobre ellos" ("But do not attempt to put yourselves on equal terms with them, because if you do, far from achieving what you seek, men will hold you in infinite disdain and you will never be able to have any influence on them") (Primo de Rivera, *Escritos* 173). The peculiarity of this assertion lies not in its challenge of the status quo (which it does not offer), but in its rationalization of compliance as a means for circumventing male authority. In a similar vein, the first official address to future proselytizers of the Falangist doctrine by the head of the women's cadre opened with a disclaimer for female involvement in the party:

> El caso de las mujeres no puede ser de ninguna manera como el de los hombres. La mujer tiene un único fin que cumplir en la vida, y, por lo tanto, encaminadas a conseguir ese solo fin han de ir todas las normas que se le den para el desenvolvimiento de la misma. Así, pues el acoplamiento de la mujer dentro del Partido creo que debe de hacerse tomando como unidad su condición de mujer, y como cosa secundaria su profesión, trabajo, etc., ya que, por muy obrera, por muy estudiante y por muy maestra que sea, principalmente es mujer, con un fin determinado que cumplir, al que llega algunas veces pasando accidentalmente por la Universidad o por centros de trabajo.

> (The case of women can in no way be like that of men. Women have a unique role to play in life, and consequently, all the tenets guiding their development must be directed towards that one end. Therefore, I believe that the placement of women within the Party should take into primary consideration their condition as women, and on a secondary level their profession, work, etc., since no matter how much of a worker, student, or teacher they may be, principally they are women, with a pre-determined destiny to fulfill, at which some arrive after accidentally passing through the University or through work centers.) (*Escritos* 195)

The need for demarcating the difference between the acquisition of a skill and its application, between knowledge and its exercise, merely accentuates the concomitance in discourse of two diverging impulses: for the preservation of the status quo and for its contravention.

The Falangist new woman was above all selfless, disciplined, obedient, composed, poised, steadfast, joyous, dynamic, valiant, graceful, industrious, sensible, and thrifty. She was recognized by her integrity, immaculate bearing, and dignified—verging on triumphant—demeanor, a sign of her moral rectitude and affiliation with the victorious forces that stood for all that represented good in the prevailing black-and-white representational system. What set her apart from other feminine types was her attitude of defiance in the face of adversity. She welcomed challenges and sought difficulties as an occasion to display her characteristic optimism, condensed in a maxim— "La vida sonríe a quien le sonríe, no a quien le hace muecas" ("Life smiles upon those who smile at it, not upon those who scowl")—popularized by the protagonist of one of Carmen de Icaza's most widely read novels, *Cristina Guzmán, profesora de idiomas* (qtd in Martín Gaite, *Usos amorosos* 40). The Falangist woman's other distinguishing marker, her "good taste," was founded on the bourgeois definition of beauty as morality and on the party's ascetic sensibility, which were observable both in her appearance and surroundings (Mosse 246).

In addition, the members of *Sección Femenina* were marked by what was known as Falangist "style," which served to emphasize their femininity in lieu of their public persona. In keeping with Victoria De Grazia's observations on the politicization of fashion, any conspicuous display of wealth was considered distasteful and unpatriotic. By the same token, the Falangist women's engagement with national life demanded that their appearance convey solidarity with the times. The plain refinement advocated by the leaders of the organization—the tailored grey suits worn by the heroines of popular romance novels—had the dual function of making a female presence in the male-dominated world undisruptive and unthreatening, while underscoring her discreet personality, sensible character, and innate femininity (De Grazia 221–6).

Perhaps where the paradoxes and incongruities underlying the Falangist feminine ideal are most perceptible is in its normative representations, which sought to fuse more traditional (bourgeois and Catholic) mores with the fascist penchant for dynamism, youthfulness, enthusiasm, physical gracefulness, and resolve, not to mention a more progressive—however modest—emphasis on female education and employment. The new woman was to be at once politically conscious, yet domestically inclined; skilled, yet unemployed; well versed, yet quiet; subservient, yet enterprising; youthful, yet grave; meek, yet dignified; modest, yet accomplished; longsuffering, yet cheerful; staid, yet dynamic; simple, yet refined; austere, yet elegant, binding the ascetic with the aesthetic sensibility.

PART II
READING ROMANCE: QUESTIONING THE NORM

6

Post-War Conventions of Representing Women: Gender and Genre Constraints

As our previous discussion has shown, the two doctrines that, during the years immediately following the Spanish Civil War, offered legitimate ways of structuring, understanding, and evaluating "always already" gendered national practices and individual experiences, belonged to the Church and the Falange. Accordingly, the normative models of womanhood were based on a constellation of the sixteenth-century Catholic model of *la perfecta casada*, the nineteenth-century bourgeois ideal of *el ángel del hogar*, and the regime's contemporary *la nueva mujer* of the Falange, promoted seamlessly through a range of educational, political, juridical, and familial policies. Constant among them was the insistence on marriage and motherhood as a woman's paramount objective and a matrix of female subjectivity.

Although the Falangist and Catholic discourses did not always agree in their interpretations of desired feminine conduct (the Church disapproved of the *Sección Femenina*'s modernizing zeal),[1] both those who summoned women to the relinquishing of personal ambitions, embracing difficulties and triumphing over challenges, and those who promoted the Christian rhetoric of humility, resignation, and suffering sought to exalt women's capacity for abnegation: "Acostúmbrate a lo arduo, a superar lo difícil, a la lima de lo áspero, a la poda de la mortificación de los sentidos, al ejercicio de la negación de los caprichos, al vencimiento del *yo* [sic]" ("Accustom yourself to what is arduous, to overcoming what is difficult, to smoothing out what is rough, to pruning and mortifying your senses, to practicing the denial of your whims, to conquering of the *self* [sic]"), counseled bishop Enciso Viana (109). Thus, renunciation and suffering were to feminine essence what marriage and motherhood were to female destiny: two sides of the same coin, complementing and completing post-war representations of ideal womanhood.

---

[1] See Victoria Lorée Enders' essay "Problematic Portraits: The Ambiguous Historical Role of the *Sección Femenina* of the Falange" in *Constructing Spanish Womanhood*, and Kathleen Richmond's chapter entitled "Modernity and reaction: SF and religion" in *Women and Spanish Fascism.*

"En la obediencia que imponemos a los ciudadanos" ("Regarding the obedience which we impose upon the citizens"), wrote Cayuela, an influential intellectual and literary critic of the time, "no se han de contentar con ejecutar la voluntad de los Superiores, sino que han de llegar a reverenciarlos y amarlos" ("they must not be contented merely to follow the will of their Superiors, but instead they must come to revere and love them") (qtd in Valls 94). This attitude of loving deference that subordinates owed to their superiors found its epitome in the patriarchal family unit, namely in the overpowering desire for surrender that women presumably experienced vis-à-vis men.

> Se daba por supuesto, que ninguna mujer podía acariciar sueño más hermoso que el de la sumisión a un hombre, y que si decía lo contrario estaba mintiendo: 'La vida de toda mujer a pesar de cuanto ella quiera simular—o disimular—, no es más que un continuo deseo de encontrar a quien someterse. La dependencia voluntaria, la ofrenda de todos los minutos, de todos los deseos e ilusiones es lo más hermoso porque es la absorción de todos los malos gérmenes—vanidad, egoísmo, frivolidad—por el amor.'

> (It was a given that no woman could cherish a more beautiful dream than submission to a man, and if she said anything to the contrary, she was lying: 'The life of all women, however much they want to pretend—or dissemble—is no more than a continuous desire to find someone to whom to submit themselves. Voluntary dependence, the offering made each and every minute, is the most beautiful of all desires and dreams because it allows love to absorb all the bad germs—vanity, egotism, frivolity.') (Martín Gaite, *Usos amorosos* 45)

Hence, to speak of romance in the early years of Franco's rule—at least from a feminine perspective—is to speak of love's coercive power.

Arguably the most dangerous period in a woman's life corresponded to the passage from girlhood to womanhood, which was believed to be exacerbated by the secularizing tendencies of the modern world, the remnants of liberal education, and the still-palpable effects of the chaos and immorality that allegedly preceded the nationalist victory. "¡S.O.S.! muchacha. Peligro a la vista. Unos golpes de remo y llegas a un paso difícil lleno de escollos y remolinos" ("S.O.S., young lady! Danger in sight. A few strokes of the oar and you will arrive at a treacherous pass full of obstacles and whirlpools") (Enciso Viana 8). The dangers to which Enciso Viana alerts his female audiences—the dangers wrought by contact with the opposite sex at a time when parents' custody had lessened and that of a husband had yet to take effect—lie in the path of every maiden desirous of fulfilling her expressly feminine mission.

El noviazgo, or engagement, and romance as its literary counterpart, thus constituted a period of trial and apprenticeship, and it is in this officially sanctioned sense, as conduits to marriage—or as "*la escuela de matrimonio*" ("the school of matrimony") (qtd in Martín Gaite, *Usos amorosos* 162)—that they gained valence in the normative renderings of feminine experience. The pervasiveness of romance (here understood as the triad of love, marriage, and happiness) in so-called "women's literature" should therefore come as no surprise, especially if we keep in mind that "plotting" is not an autonomous literary device but rather a historically and culturally conditioned practice (Franco 266).[2] In this respect, any reading of women's post-war narratives that does not acknowledge the constraints operating on these texts—the limits of what can and cannot be represented—is likely to be partial or anachronistic.[3] Conversely, to neglect an entire body of work on account of its strictly regulated conditions of emergence is to deny these texts and their readers any agency, engaging instead in a kind of determinism that is ultimately reductionist.

The fact, however obscured, remains that 1940s saw a burgeoning of women writers. Those who have delved into the matter may remark, like Carmen Servén, that: "los oscuros años cuarenta, años de postguerra en que la retórica oficial insiste en situar a la mujer en el reducto del hogar, son también los años en que se asiste a una 'eclosión . . . de la literatura femenina' . . ." ("the dark years of the forties, post-war years in which the official rhetoric insists on situating the woman within the fortress of the home, are also the years which witness an 'emergence of feminine literature' . . ."). Furthermore, "[e]sa eclosión de la literatura femenina, no sólo se ha de entender como aparición de numerosas nuevas firmas femeninas, sino también como renovado interés por la mujer como objeto narrativo y como destinataria del producto literario" ("[t]his emergence of feminine literature should not only be understood as the appearance of many new female authors, but also as renewed interest in the woman as a narrative object and recipient of the liter-

---

[2] Nancy Miller similarly argues that the plots of women's literature are about "the constraints the maxim places on rendering a female life in fiction" wherein the term "maxim" refers to approved codes of behavior. *Subject to Change* (New York: Columbia UP, 1988) 26, 43.

[3] The need for historically and culturally grounded criticism, especially when dealing with women's literary production, has elicited considerable attention in recent years. Ellen Mayock notes that "at the conference of the Modern Language Association in 2001 (and subsequently in *ALEC* 28:1 [2003]), several well-known Hispanists appealed to their colleagues in Hispanic Studies to begin to focus more on specific cultural context as they undertake the study of texts from Spain. They insisted that too many critical works base themselves within Anglo-American and French theoretical frameworks without attempting to peel apart the complex layers of Spanish history, politics, and culture as they relate to the texts at hand. Likewise, at the 2002 conference of the *Asociación Internacional de Literatura Femenina Hispánica*, many panelists emphasized the need to initiate more projects that specifically address the role of women in Spain and (and *versus*) in Latin America, acknowledging that political idiosyncrasies and cultural traditions create a unique atmosphere in which women develop in multifarious ways according to the manner in which they shape and are shaped by the specific cultures of which they are a part." *The 'Strange Girl' in Twentieth-Century Spanish Novels Written by Women* 3.

ary product") (92). The state-identity politics couched in the rhetoric of domesticity and the proliferation of written discourses on and by women may be viewed as two related phenomena. The socializing power of the printed word was employed towards fomenting new forms of subjectivity and models of conduct. Predictably, the task of defining (and thereby delimiting) women's participation in national life to the interests of new Spain[4] gave rise to a body of prescriptive texts on the nature and role of ideal Spanish womanhood (not all of which were produced by men, while nearly all were intended for female readership).

In this respect, the post-war "restructuring" of gender relations (De Grazia 3) and the bourgeois "privatization of virtue" (Aldaraca, *Tormento* 221) offer some interesting parallels. In both cases, the polemic on women is employed by individual or small clusters of female constituents as legitimate and hence legitimating grounds for accessing the public sphere. Not unlike "virtuous women writers" (Blanco)—whose discursive authority,[5] ironically, rested on the espousal of domesticity—for many women writing in post-war Spain, subscription to the officially sanctioned gender roles became at once a means to and a stipulation for public involvement.[6] As with their predecessors, the weight of propriety fell more heavily on women, a consequence of a moral double standard that found its justification in religious and scientific

---

[4] See De Grazia's chapter on the "nationalization" of women. Her study of *How Fascism Ruled Women* in Mussolini's Italy offers valuable insights into the complexities of Francoist gender politics. According to De Grazia: "how fascism ruled Italian women is also the story of how Italian women experienced fascist rule. At one level, the ways in which Italian women related to their families, to their society, and to each other were the outcome of the myriad policies which shaped family planning, the labor market, educational opportunities, and public attitudes. At another level, they were the result of women's own actions: in particular, how they responded collectively and individually to enticing new habits of mass consumption, to changing standards of family and child care, and to the novel occasions of sociability offered by the fascist auxiliaries, as well as by Catholic women's groups, informal neighborhood networks, and the several surviving feminist clubs. As we come to see how Italian women shared information among themselves—about sentiments, sexuality, family, and work—their responses to fascist rule appear more complex than the attitudes commonly ascribed to them, namely, passive subordination or delirious enthusiasm. Among Italian women there was disquiet, rebelliousness, dissimulation, and shrewd manipulation, together with a newly arising consciousness of their rights as women and as citizens of Italy" (11–12).

[5] I adopt Susan Lanser's definition of "discursive authority" by which term she refers to "the intellectual credibility, ideological validity, and aesthetic value claimed by or conferred upon a work, author, narrator, character, or textual practice." *Fictions of Authority: Women Writers and Narrative Voice* 6.

[6] For the vast majority, however, partnership in nation-building was mediated by family life, and when they did engage in public activity, middle-class conventions upheld by the regime demanded that it be done as an extension of their familial duties (man's assistants/secretaries, care-takers/nurses or social workers, educators/teachers) or as a manifestation of innately feminine sensibilities (fashion, cosmetics, film, art, poetry, homecrafts).

discourses.[7] Moralists, educators, and novelists alike subscribed to the view that women were naturally pious and drawn to beauty as a manifestation of virtue.

On the level of literary analysis, familiarity with the then-prevailing attitudes towards women and their place in society facilitates an understanding of a number of operating constraints in their fictions, especially if these fictions are about women. For instance, a heroine's transgressions could have led to charges against the author's own morality, if and when the author was a woman.[8] To quote Patricia O'Byrne, "since women were perceived as moral, innately religious and sublime creatures, it was unacceptable that their literature should portray wayward or deviant members of the species or that it should in any way challenge the role assigned them by the Church and society." Hence, the study of women-authored texts must take into account "shared perceptions among critics and censors alike regarding appropriate themes and style for women writers" (O'Byrne 200). In such a climate, romance, namely the *novela rosa*, presented itself as an apposite mode of expression and diversion for women, not to mention a convenient vehicle for indoctrination. As the authors of "The Romance Novel, or, the Generalísimo's Control of the Popular Imagination" affirm, "[t]he *novela rosa* contributed to the government's post-Civil War reconstruction of Spain. Fictional texts were presented as reflecting the lives of the most virtuous among Spaniards, and those who wished to 'attain virtue' had to adapt their experiences to the guidelines established by the approved government formula" (49). The socializing

---

[7] See Geraldine Scanlon, "Fuentes de autoridad del antifeminismo," in *La polémica feminista*, and the first three studies published under the heading "Los Modelos de género y su difusión" in *Mujeres y hombres en la España franquista: Sociedad, economía, política, cultura* edited by Gloria Nielfa Cristóbal.

[8] On the discussion of the intricate relationship between cultural expectations, gender norms, modes of expression and interpretative conventions, see Susan Lanser, *Fictions of Authority*. "Given the precarious position of women in patriarchal societies," writes Lanser, "woman novelists may have avoided personal voice when they feared their work would be taken for autobiography" (20). An interesting example of how hegemonic models of selfhood structure self-representation is Luisa-María Linares' autobiographical sketch for the editorial *Juventud*, which published all of her works. After falling in love and marrying the man of her dreams, with whom she shares three unforgettable years of bliss, Luisa-María is forced to confront a life alone with two children. The war deprives her of her husband, and as a consequence, to make ends meet, she takes up writing for the public (a distinction she is keen to draw). Since her spirits remain high, events take a fortunate turn, and she is promptly rewarded for her efforts. However, her blurb suggests that it would be wrong to understand Luisa-María's success in terms of her career alone; instead, it ought to be understood as the success of a mother who delights in the company of her two daughters and of a wife who has remained forever faithful to the memory of her husband. At the end, the readers are left with the impression that Luisa-María has led a full life and is not afraid to look the future in the eye for, like the protagonists of her own novels, she has managed to triumph in the face of adversity. See http://www.editorialjuventud. es/LMLinares.htm

function of post-war popular romance novels is also stressed by María Elena Soliño, according to whom "women's literature" served as a worthy successor of fairy tales for little girls:

> As they mature, girls abandon their fictional 'friends,' but what these characters teach them about being female remains. And this 'angel in the house' type of femininity continued to be reinforced as girls 'advanced' from children's literature to 'women's literature.' . . . Unfortunately, once the values of the patriarchal bourgeoisie were internalized, women themselves started producing this type of work. Up until the middle of the twentieth century, for many women who wished to write, the fairy tale or the romance novel was the only literary model available to them, and for which they could find a more receptive market. After girls outgrew fiction for children, they 'progressed' to the romance novel, or the *novela rosa*, characterized as sentimental, predictable love stories, usually written by women. (60)

While Soliño proposes to view the *novela rosa* in terms of prescribed models of selfhood, Benjamín Manzano Badía underscores the primordial role that popular romance novels assign to the creation of the traditional, patriarchal, family unit:

> Habría que empezar a definir la novela rosa desde la familia, bien como punto de llegada (el noviazgo), bien como punto neurálgico de cualquier problema (el matrimonio). Es la familia vista desde una óptica muy concreta, la pequeño-burguesa, y desde un rol determinado, la mujer. Todo el discurso de la novela rosa atiende a la mujer, como novia, como esposa, como madre. Luego la mujer siempre en función del otro, la búsqueda, su búsqueda, pasa necesariamente por el otro, el novio, el marido, el hijo.

> (One would have to begin to define the *novela rosa* from the family, be it as a point of arrival (engagement), or as a neuralgic point of any problem (marriage). It is the family seen from a very specific view, that of the petit-bourgeoisie, and from a particular role, that of the woman. The entire discourse of *novela rosa* focuses on the woman, as fiancée, as wife, as mother. Thus the woman always depends on the 'other,' the search, her search, necessarily warrants the other, the suitor, the husband, the son.) (109)

The importance of family in the Francoist discourse is well known. Conceived as the basis of the national-Catholic state, it replicated the state's vertical ordering (Graham) and fomented the view of national unity and homogeneity. In this respect, Badía's study raises the possibility of considering post-war popular romance novels as foundational fictions.[9]

[9] See "Carmen de Icaza, una apología pequeño-burguesa y conservadora de la familia" in *Mujeres novelistas en el panorama literario del siglo XX* (Cuenca (Sp.): Universidad de Castilla-La Mancha, 2000) 107–21.

For further illustration of how prevailing gender conventions, on the one hand, induced women to adopt certain literary conventions and, on the other, affected the reception of their work, we must consider the following fragment from a 1945 interview with writer and journalist Rosa María Aranda (contributor to such magazines as *La moda en España, Fotos, Letras* and *Medina*):

—Rosa María, ¿estás contenta de tu obra?
—Muy poco, me horroriza quedarme donde estoy. Mis obras son aún pocas y escasamente profundas. Aspiro a escribir algo muy original y bueno. No estoy conforme con lo escrito.
Le pregunto sobre las novelas rosa y se asusta. No quiere decirme nada, luego la llamarían petulante y vanidosa. . . . Sin embargo, me dice, yo no escribo novelas rosa. Jamás he intentado hacerlo, mis novelas no son crudas y violentas, porque me retirarían el saludo mis amistades, porque no me comprenderían; pero nada más lejos de mí que la novela cursi, sentimentalmente solterona, estereotipada en una colección. . . . En fin, prefiero callarme. . . .
—Y aquí quien tiene que disculparse soy yo. Sí, sí, yo te he llamado novelista rosa, perdón.
—No, no es eso. Es que parece que una mujer no puede escribir más que cosas de las llamadas rosas—un niño calavera millonario, una aristócrata arruinada, metida a señorita de compañía. . . la boda. Y eso no es la realidad. Yo quisiera escribir una novela cruda, real y psicológica. . . .

(—Rosa María, are you pleased with your work?
—Not really, the thought of remaining where I am horrifies me. My works are still few and far from profound. I aspire to write something very original and good. I am not satisfied with what I have written.
I ask her about *novelas rosa* and she becomes frightened. She does not want to tell me anything, for fear people will say she is petulant and vain. . . . However, she tells me, I do not write *novelas rosa*. I have never attempted to do so, my novels are not crude and violent, because my friends would turn their backs on me, because they would not understand me; but there is nothing more distant from me than the trite, sentimentally spinsterish, stereotyped genre novel. . . . In short, I prefer to remain silent. . . .
—And in that case, I am the one who should apologize. Yes, yes, I've called you a romance novelist, excuse me.
—No, it's not that. It's just that it seems a woman can only write these so-called rose-tinted things—a guy who is a reckless young millionaire, a girl who is a ruined aristocrat, stuck as a lady-in-waiting . . . the wedding. And that is not reality. I would like to write a raw, real, psychological novel. . .)

Regrettably for Rosa María, the interview appeared as part of a two-page survey with six other women novelists under an eye-catching title, in large, bold print: "María Pilar, María Teresa, Paloma, Carolina, María, May y María escriben novelas rosa" ("María Pilar, María Teresa, Paloma, Carolina, María, May y María write *novelas rosa*") (16–17). The fact that Rosa María's novels were regarded as *novelas rosa* may be as much a consequence of what she wrote as of what she was expected to write, and hence what her novels came to signify.[10] As Fredric Jameson points out, our readings tend to draw less on the actual texts than on ready-made valuations of them.[11] In Jameson's words,

> [T]exts come before us as the always-already-read; we apprehend them through sedimented layers of previous interpretations or—if the text is brand-new—through the sedimented reading habits and categories devel-

[10] By dint of socially and culturally conditioned normative expectations, many women novelists found themselves in a double bind: if they wrote what was expected of them (works emanating purity, innocence, love, virtue, even lyricism), the most to which they could aspire was the status of best among the writers of "second-rate" literature (for this was the position that corresponded to "women's literature"—from popular romance novels to children's fictions—within the field of literary production). If they went against these expectations, they ran the risk of not being published or read, in addition to being criticized for betraying their feminine nature (either by falling short on moral grounds or succumbing to vanity by venturing into male-dominated genres). This bind was ameliorated by the possession of what Bourdieu calls different forms of capital, whether economic (independent means for survival), social (relations—inherited or otherwise—with the reputable members of the industry or valorized literary currents), and/or political (affiliation with and backing from the established order).

[11] It is to counter this tendency of interpreting texts in terms of preconceived notions or set expectations that George Bernard Shaw writes an afterward to *Pygmalion*: "The rest of the story need not be shown in action, and indeed, would hardly need telling if our imaginations were not so enfeebled by their lazy dependence on the ready-mades and reach-me-downs of the ragshop in which Romance keeps its stock of 'happy endings' to misfit all stories" (101). For Shaw, the play's didactic purpose is irreconcilable with the impulse to romanticize its ending, which as Everding points out, "began with the play's London premiere when its Higgins tossed a bouquet of flowers from his balcony to the departing Eliza," a practice that continued "despite Shaw's protestations, clarifications and textual revisions" (315). However, in contrast to *Pygmalion*, whose romance, as Shaw claimed, consisted not in Eliza's marriage, but in her transformation from a poor girl into a lady, in the selected novels, the protagonists' transformations are corollary to the novel's marital teleology. In this sense, romance and the text's didactic purpose (endorsement of prescribed models of female conduct) are intertwined. In other words, romance functions as a coercive force that effectuates normative transformations, where becoming a heroine entails becoming a wife, and love is a sugar coating that makes conformity with the conventional gender roles not just palatable but desirable. And yet, contrary to the ready-made interpretations of this particular plotline, I will argue that the conventional happy ending/marriage can also function as a legitimating seal of approval for alternative models of female conduct. See Robert Everding, "Shaw and the Popular Context" in *The Cambridge Companion to George Bernard Shaw* (Cambridge: Cambridge UP, 1998); Ana Rueda, "Lecciones de sociedad para Galatea" in *Pigmalión y Galatea: Refracciones modernas de un mito* (Madrid: Fundamentos, 1998); and Linda K. Christian-Smith, *Becoming a Woman through Romance* (London: Routledge, 1990).

oped by those inherited interpretative traditions. This presupposition then dictates the use of a method . . . according to which our object of study is less the text itself than the interpretations through which we attempt to confront and to appropriate it. (*Political* 9–10)

Although the recent studies of women's post-war literary production are almost invariably prefaced by remarks about the oblivion to which these narratives have been relegated, the steps taken towards the recovery of this vast corpus remain provisional. The obvious exceptions present some rare and valuable insights into both the field of inquiry and the course of future investigations.[12] While a survey of existing scholarship would attest to the canonical status of Carmen Laforet, Ana María Matute and Carmen Martín Gaite,[13] the names of Concha Alós, Mercedes Ballesteros, Teresa Barbero, Rosa María Cajal, Concha Castroviejo, Paulina Crusat, Concha Espina, Mercedes Fórmica, Luisa Forrelad, Elena Galvarriato, Carmen García Bellver, Carmen Kurtz, Susana March, Eva Martínez Carmona, Liberata Masoliver, Dolores Medio, Elena Quiroga, Mercedes Sáenz Alonso, Mercedes Salisachs, Elena Soriano, Angeles Villarta—whose works garnered considerable recognition upon their appearance—are being subjected to a significant, albeit slow, process of recovery (Montejo Gurruchaga 153–4). Among the women writers who have received scant, if any, critical attention but originally enjoyed a far wider readership are Corín Tellado,[14] Concepción Castellá de Zavala, Estrella López Obregón, Trini de Figueroa, María del Pilar Carré, María Teresa Sesé, Matilde Redón Chirona, María de las Nieves Grajales, May Carré, María Adela Durango, María Luisa Fillias de Beckér, Marisa Villardefrancos, Patricia Montes, María Luisa Alberca, Elizabeth Maulder, Carmen de Icaza, Luisa-María Linares, María Mercedes Ortoll, and Concha Linares-Becerra (Charlo 206, 214–21).

Parting from Emilie Bergmann's view that when "the canonical texts that lend resonance and significance to the narration of women's lives no longer correspond to the experience they were meant to explain, women authors must seek narrative strategies to express what has not been expressed before"

---

[12] Martín Gaite's work remains instrumental in this respect, especially *Usos amorosos* and *Desde la ventana.* Among more recent contributions, see studies by Andreu, Castillo, Labanyi, López, O'Byrne, and Sérven Díez.

[13] A cursory look at the existing scholarship will suffice to substantiate this view; however, statistical evidence may be found in Joan Brown and Crista Johnson's article "Women Writers in the Hispanic Novel Canon in the United States" in *Hers Ancient and Modern* (Manchester: U of Manchester P, 1997).

[14] Perhaps the only figure, other than Carmen de Icaza, who has elicited critical scholarship (more as a sociological than a literary phenomenon). See Blanca Alvarez, "Corín Tellado: mantilla y matrimonio" in *La novela popular en España* (Madrid: Robel, 2000), and María Teresa Gonzales, *Corín Tellado medio siglo de novela de amor (1946–1996)* (Oviedo (Sp.): Pentalfa, 1998).

(154), we may hypothesize that the existence of a vast corpus of neglected works by women is not necessarily an index of some inherent inadequacy of the texts that makes them unreadable, but rather a possible failure of existing interpretative models to account for them. In identifying the Falangist "Sección Femenina" as "a cultural correlative of women's fiction," Brownlow and Kronik point out that:

> Few academic readers of Spanish narrative would recognize Castillo's subject, Mercedes Salisachs, as an author of canonical stature, although she has written at least twenty-five books and is the winner of numerous Spanish literary awards. Fewer still will know how to read and think about the implications of Salisachs's apparently undemanding fictions. (17)

According to these critics, many of the works in question are "neither low enough to appeal to popular culture studies nor literary enough to be considered high art" (17). In this regard, I share Francisca López's postulate that "las escritoras españolas de posguerra deben su fracaso, al menos parcialmente, a la dificultad que supone para la crítica el integrar sus obras en las diversas clasificaciones elaboradas por y para la producción masculina. Al no saber dónde encajarlas, mediante un acto de 'Denial by False Categorizing,' simplemente se ignoran" ("Post-war Spanish women writers owe their failure, at least partially, to the difficulty critics have in fitting their works into the various classifications invented by and for masculine production. Due to not knowing where to place them, they are simply ignored through an act of 'Denial by False Categorizing') (16). As an example of "false," or rather nonexistent categorizing, López mentions female *bildung*, which, despite its application to women's post-war novelistic production, is only recently being used as a viable model for reading.[15]

Two other approaches to the study of the aforementioned corpus follow the course outlined in Carmen Martín Gaite's writings. One adopts as its basis the category of *la chica rara* (*the strange girl*), a type of female representation—popularized by Carmen Laforet's 1944 novel *Nada*—that is at odds with both the official and popular models of womanhood.[16] The other pursues the notion of the "modernidad moderada" ("moderated modernity") (*El cuarto* 141) of selected women-authored texts, underscoring the contradictions latent in the

---

[15] See Chapter 4 of María del Carmen Riddel's *La escritura femenina en la postguerra española* (New York: Peter Lang, 1995) 67–121, and María Pilar Rodríguez's introduction to her *Vidas Im/Propias: Transformaciones del sujeto femenino en la narrativa española contemporánea* (West Lafayette, IN: Purdue UP, 2000) 1–20.

[16] For the elaboration of this category by Carmen Martín Gaite, see *Desde la ventana.* For its ensuing application to women's post-war fictions, see Ellen C. Mayock, *The 'Strange Girl' in Twentieth Century Spanish Novels Written by Women* and Nuria Cruz-Cámara's "'Chicas raras' en dos novelas de Carmen Martín Gaite y Carmen Laforet."

Falangist ideal of *la nueva mujer* ("the new woman"). All three approaches presuppose the socializing role of post-war gender representations, echoing yet another notion advanced by Martín Gaite, here discussed under the label of "exemplarity."

Although the reactionary and propagandistic nature of post-Civil War cultural practices has been widely studied, their exemplary modality merits further consideration. The consolidation of the nationalist order was contingent upon "government efforts to control the production of meaning" (Castillo 97). The ensuing national-Catholic signifying system, which the 1938 Law of the Press helped to implement,[17] demanded that the members of the new Spain become "culturally competent readers", able not only to correctly decode messages but to generate corresponding meanings as well, a practice that, according to Labanyi and Graham, bore also the converse effect of making Spaniards adept in the so-called 'art of resignification' (169).

A privileged form of hegemonic expression was "la presentación alternativa del bien y el mal de la forma más clara y precisa" ("the alternative presentation of good and evil in the most clear and precise way") (Roca i Girona 7). But even as "good" and "bad" role models abounded in the political, religious, and literary discourses of the time, "[l]os jóvenes de postguerra sabíamos muy bien" ("[w]e, the young people of the post-war era were well aware"), writes Martín Gaite,

> que una película española o nos iba a contar una historia heroica de las que venían en los libros de texto o nos iba a ensalzar las delicias de un amor sacrificado y decente. . . . La maldad o la frivolidad que pudieran darse en algunos personajes de película española se justificaban siempre en nombre del redoblado brillo de ejemplaridad que adquiría, por contraste, la conducta contraria.

> (that a Spanish film was either going to tell us a heroic story of the sort found in the textbooks or extol the joys of self-sacrificing and honorable love. . . . The wickedness or frivolity that could be seen in some Spanish film characters was always justified by the redoubled glow of exemplary behaviour they brought out in the contrasting character.) (*Usos amorosos* 33–4)

---

[17] On censorship, see M.L. Abellán, *Censura y creación literaria en España (1939–1976)* (Barcelona: Península, 1980). On censorship and popular culture, see Jo Labanyi, "Censorship or the Fear of Mass Culture" in *Cultural Studies*. On censorship and women writers, see Patricia O'Byrne, "Spanish Women Novelists and the Censor (1945–1965)." Censored passages from women-authored texts can be found in Lucía Montejo Gurruchaga's study *Las mujeres escritoras en la historia de la literatura española* (Madrid: UNED, 2002).

In other words, to argue that the state monopolized meaning-producing practices is not the same as to contend that its constituents were the passive recipients of those meanings.

But whether we choose to focus on the regime's authoritarian politics or the ensuing forms of resistance, the fact remains that in the early 1940s, "exemplarity" was ubiquitous both as a representational modality and an interpretative convention. Underlying this notion of "exemplarity" is a belief in the power of fictional works to influence the conduct of their readers, thereby molding their character and impelling them toward either good or evil: "the notion—somewhat disreputable in the West—that literature, and particularly fiction, must be held accountable, since it encodes messages which affect not only the subjective world view of readers, but their attitudes and actions" (Beaujour 325). Such a conception of literature entails a hierarchical relationship between text and reader, precipitating a teacher–disciple relationship that assigns to reading a formative function. [18]

As Fernando Valls' illuminating study on the post-war uses of literary texts avers, "[l]o que interesaba de la literatura . . . era su 'potencia educadora'. Sus mejores virtudes eran debidas a que" ("it was the 'educational potential' of literature that was of interest. Its highest virtues were due to the fact that"), and here Valls quotes a 1951 article from the literary journal *Atenas*, "'contribuye poderosamente a mejor recordar, forma la imaginación, afina la sensibilidad, desenvuelve el juicio, enseña a odiar el vicio y a amar la virtud'" ("it 'contributes powerfully to one's ability to remember, shapes the imagination, refines sensibilities, develops judgement, teaches one to hate vice and to love virtue'") (98). In a similar vein, the contemporaneous women's magazine *Medina* claimed that the novels' objective was "levantar el ser a definitivos propósitos" ("to raise the self to a clear sense of purpose") (qtd in Martín Gaite, *Usos amorosos* 148). In other words, the novels had to prod readers toward a particular course of action, always in consonance with their state-approved objectives. As we have seen, for women, such a course was tantamount to marriage and motherhood. But while ubiquity of marriage in women's post-war romance fictions would suggest their consonance with the hegemonic gender norms, a closer reading of selected texts proves that female representations are often at odds with the univocal readings that their happy endings suggest.

---

[18] See *Reader in the Text,* especially the aforementioned article by Beaujour (Princeton: Princeton UP, 1980) 329–49, as well as Susan Suleiman's discussion of *roman à thèse* in *Authoritarian Fictions*. According to Suleiman, the so-called "culture of exemplarity" is symptomatic of drastic socio-political changes wherein the new models of conduct are actively disseminated until the prescribed value systems become sufficiently naturalized and ingrained to perpetuate themselves.

As a rule, the disparities that arise in the selected texts are suppressed by one of the two interpretative conventions, denunciative and emancipatory, that dominate the critical practice in the field. That is, on the rare occasion of being examined, they are either listed as mouthpieces of hegemonic discourse, or singled out for counter-hegemonic readings. The advantage of reading romance fictions in terms of exemplarity is that it allows us to consider simultaneously the ways in which given texts at once "reinforce" and "deviate" from the norm, instead of limiting our choice and interpretation of post-war novels to one or the other category.[19] It is in light of these observations that I would like to extend the application of what Suleiman calls "the structure of apprenticeship" from *bildungsroman* to popular romance novels, always keeping in mind that the writing and reading of romance in post-war Spain bore a potentially formative function. While legitimate accounts of romance, as a rule, lead to the production of an ideal type (models to be emulated), the very transformation that the heroine undergoes on the way to matrimony presupposes a departure from the norm—a disruption, error, defiance—that must be eliminated, corrected or redeemed as a precondition for the narrative's happy end.

For critics, the happy endings that characterize women's post-war romance novels have become unmistakable signs of the text's ideological complicity with the hegemonic order. Conversely, the "unhappy" endings, which characterize women's canonical texts from the period, have come to stand for ideological dissent. Such a paradigm, while not groundless, tends to lead to facile categorizations based solely on the dénouement. In other words, the privileging of the selected novels' endings as an ultimate place of position-taking, a place that articulates the novels' relationship to the complex web of social, gender, and political relations that are enmeshed in them, perpetuates "the always-already read interpretations" (Jameson) of these texts, thereby precluding the possibilities for reading them in their own right, bringing to the fore alternative, if not always subversive interpretations. Thus, even when we make a conscious choice to read these resolutions as univocal signs of the texts' ideological loyalties, we must not forget their compulsory nature; we must keep in mind that these were the obligatory resolutions, both according to prescribed gender and genre conventions. For this reason, it may be more useful to read them as markers of legitimacy and therefore as legitimating markers corresponding to the dominant representational system.

---

[19] Examining the role of popular culture in *El cuarto de atrás,* Stephanie Sieburth remarks: "In this context, mass culture divides into two categories: texts which attempt to buttress Francoist ideology, and texts which allude to *real* [sic] emotions, dreams, or situations that belie the false, anesthetized world of the postwar period. Some texts, then, reinforce the norm; others suggest the exception, the deviation from the norm." See *Inventing High and Low* (Durham, NC: Duke UP, 1994) 192.

Finally, if the mass-produced novels' resolutions are uniform by dint of being prescriptive, what happens before the heroine succumbs to this inevitable bliss merits closer reading. "I shall not suggest that the romances studied here contain a feminist subtext," writes Labanyi,

> for they virtually end with the heroine's capitulation to the hero's embrace, resulting in the loss of her previous independence. But I am interested in looking at the plot twists that occur along the road to love, since there are some fairly extraordinary things going on—and the end *is* [sic] seen as a capitulation. ("Romancing" 4)

Although Labanyi's study situates these novels in the context of continuing modernity, implicit in her statement is the idea that the normative transformation in the protagonist, and her final "capitulation," is a consequence of falling in love. Since love is considered the foundation of marriage, and marriage is a normative outcome in these novels, then the very act of falling in love, or the love itself, takes on a coercive role.[20] Another inference to be made from the above-cited passage is a notable disjunction between narrative events ("the fairly extraordinary things") and their predictable outcome ("capitulation"). While the latter affirms the hegemonic norm, the former constitutes its breach. It is the concomitance of these two impulses, the "conformist–contestatory ambivalence" noted elsewhere by Labanyi and Graham (170), that binds the study of selected novels.[21]

Given the scope of this project, and after careful consideration of more than fifty novels by twenty-odd novelists, ranging temporally from the early 1930s to the early 1960s,[22] I have decided to limit the present discussion to

---

[20] Enciso Viana, a clergyman and a prolific writer of women's handbooks, author of *¡Muchacha!*, *La muchacha en el noviazgo*, and *La muchacha en el hogar*, defined love in the following sobering terms: "Amar es soportar. Soportar las intemperancias, las genialidades, las particularidades, las rarezas de él" ("To love is to endure. Endure his moods, his tempers, his idiosyncrasies, his oddities") (*La muchacha en el noviazgo* 105).

[21] According to Suleiman, these contradictions, present even in the so-called "readerly" or "overdetermined" texts, distinguish the novel (namely, the "ideological novel" or *roman à thèse*) as a genre from parables or exempla unencumbered by the obligatory length and subsidiary character development to make their point.

[22] Concha Alós, *Los cien pájaros* (1963); María Dolores Boixadós, *Aguas muertas* (1945); Rosa María Cajal, *Un paso más* (1956); Carmen Conde Abellán, *Cobre* (1953) and *Las oscuras raíces* (1953); Rosa Chacel, *Memorias de Leticia Valle* (1945); Concha Espina, *Un valle en el mar* (1949); Mercedes Fórmica, *A instancia de parte* (1954); Eulalia Galvarriato, *Cinco sombras* (1947); Carmen de Icaza, *Cristina Guzmán, profesora de idiomas* (1936), *La fuente enterrada* (1947), *Las horas contadas* (1953), *¡Quién sabe...!* (1940), *Soñar la vida* (1941), *Vestida de tul* (1942), and *Yo, la Reina* (1950); Carmen Kurtz, *Al lado del hombre* (1961), *El desconocido* (1956), *Duermen bajo las aguas* (1954), and *La vieja ley* (1956); Carmen Laforet, *Nada* (1945), *La isla y los demonios* (1952), and *La mujer nueva* (1955); Luisa-María Linares, *En poder de Barba Azul* (1939), *Un marido a precio fijo* (1940), *Esta noche volveré tarde* (1958), and

four renowned authors of *novelas rosa*: Luisa-María Linares, Concha Linares-Becerra, Carmen de Icaza, and María Mercedes Ortoll. Here, a compendium of existing taxonomies elicited by their works may prove useful in view of the scarcity of information and the dearth of scholarship available on the subject. Three of the novelists—Luisa-María Linares, Concha Linares-Becerra, and Carmen de Icaza—appear under the label of "novelistas con el Imperio" ("novelists with the Empire") in Rodríguez-Puértolas' *Literatura Fascista Española* (492), and all four are listed as "grandes autoras" ("great female authors") in Ramón Charlo's comprehensive study of "La novela sentimental" (*La novela popular* 2/218). They themselves claim common ground as authors of *novelas blancas* (Servén Díaz 94), and, to use Manzano Badía's words, belong to "una serie de autoras que marcan el imaginario de toda una época" ("a group of female authors who mark the social imaginary of a whole period") (107).

Implicit in the first categorization, which places them among "novelistas con el Imperio" ("novelists with the Empire"), is an affinity between the aforementioned novelists and the reactionary politics of post-war Spain. The main drawback of such tagging is not that it invites a reader to regard given cultural products in terms of dominant ideologies, but that such an invitation is often reduced to facile homologations, resulting in the dismissal of the entire corpus as a mere mouthpiece of the regime.[23] It is this notion of unproblematic and univocal subscription to the hegemonic norms that by and large has precluded the study of the selected texts in their own right.

The second of the aforementioned classifications, that of "grandes autoras" ("great female authors") of *novelas rosa*, draws on a system of distinc-

---

Imposible para una solterona (1959); Concha Linares-Becerra, *Cita en el paraíso* (1940), *Diez días millonaria* (1934), *Maridos de lujo* (1934), *Sanatorio de amor* (1945), *El matrimonio es asunto de dos* (1949), and *Como los hombres nos quieren* (1944); Cecilia Mantua, *Ave de paso* (1944); Susana March, *Algo muere cada día* (1955), and *Nina* (1949); Carmen Martín Gaite, *El balneario* (1954) and *Entre visillos* (1958), Ana María Matute, *Primera memoria* (1959), Julia Maura, *Ventolera* (1943), and *¡Quién supiera escribir!* (1945); Dolores Medio, *Nosotros los Rivero* (1952), *El pez sigue flotando* (1959), and *Diario de una maestra* (1961); Elizabeth Mulder de Daumer, *Alba Grey* (1947); María Teresa Olán, *Rumbo a lo desconocido* (1944); María Mercedes Ortoll, *Asilo de huérfanas* (1942), *¡Ella es así!* (1942), *La casa de los Guzmán* (1947), *En pos de la ilusión* (1940), and *El pecado de Lida Verona* (1953); Elena Quiroga, *Algo pasa en la calle* (1954), *La enferma* (1955), and *Tristura* (1960); Mercè Rodoreda, *La Plaza del Diamante* (1962); Mercedes Salisachs, *Una mujer llega al pueblo* (1956); Elena Soriano, *La playa de los locos* (1955); María Luisa Villardefrancos, *Días de niebla* (1952); and Angeles Villarta, *Una mujer fea* (1953).

[23] According to Debra Castillo, "[t]he romance novel, or 'la novela rosa,' is a frequent literary correlative of the falangist women's section, since it shares with the social movement a profound, if covert, conservative ideology and a severely limited social agenda" (100). While drawing an otherwise indispensable connection between the values promoted by *novela rosa* and those endorsed by the *Sección Femenina*, the above statement fails to account for inconsistencies and complexities that underline both popular and Falangist female representations.

tion operating within the realm of popular romance novels (the distinctions frequently obscured by the dearth of nuanced studies on the post-war publishing industry of mass cultural texts to which the two volumes dedicated to *la novela popular* are a welcome addition). Not all *novelas rosa* were considered as having the same value (monetary or literary), nor did they all enjoy the same distribution or readership (while some were accessible to all, others sought primarily middle-class audiences). "[L]as pobres empleaditas modestas, muchachas que tienen todas mis simpatías . . ." ("[T]he poor little modest employees, girls that have all my sympathy . . .") wrote Luisa-María Linares, "difícilmente pueden gastarse las 10, 15, 20 o 30 pesetas" ("can hardly afford to spend 10, 15, 20, or 30 pesetas"), which, according to this popular author, was the price of novels by Carmen de Icaza, Linares-Becerra, Julia Maura, Rafael Pérez y Pérez, and herself. She vindicates these novels' main plotline through their middle-class audiences, arguing that:

> en nuestra vida de mujeres burguesas . . . es corrientísimo y normal entre el noventa y nueve por ciento . . . que tengamos novio a los diez y ocho años, nos casemos a los veinte y a los veinticinco nos encontremos rodeadas de un agradable surtido de pequeñines. El reflejar estos ambientes ¿puede ser calificado de ñoño, intrascendente y poco humano?

> (in our life as bourgeois women . . . it is very common and normal for ninety to ninety-nine percent . . . to become engaged at eighteen, get married at twenty and at twenty-five find ourselves surrounded by a charming cluster of little ones. Can depicting these circumstances be classified as silly, pedestrian, and unkind?)[24]

Together with the label of "grandes autoras" ("great female authors"), Luisa-María's words allude to the privileged position that the selected novelists held among the authors of *novelas rosa*. Such a position may in part be explained by these novelists' social and cultural capital. In addition to being one of the leading members of *Sección Femenina,* Carmen de Icaza was the daughter of a poet and diplomat; and, although little is known about María Mercedes Ortoll, both Luisa-María Linares and Concha Linares-Becerra were daughters of accomplished figures of the publishing world.[25]

---

[24] See "Hablemos también de las novelas grises," *La estafeta literaria* 38 (Dec. 15, 1945).

[25] There are reasons to suppose that Luisa and Concha were sisters; however, as Labanyi observes, the available sources are scare and contradictory: "A January 1944 interview with them both in the falangist film magazine *Primer Plano* (Garcia Viñolas) states categorically that they were sisters and within the interview they refer to each other as such. But the publisher's blurb facing the title page of Concha's first novel, *Por qué me case con él* (1933), gives her father as Luis Linares Becerra (1887–1931), author of popular comedies, melodramas, zarzuelas, operettas, and 'dramas líricos'; while the website of their publisher (www.editorialjuventud.es)

The third grouping, offered by Servén Diez, is founded on a stand taken by Carmen de Icaza and the Linares sisters[26] with regard to their own works, which they classify as "*novela blanca*" ("*white novel*").[27] In a series of interviews published in the first issue of *La estafeta literaria* (March 5, 1944), both Icaza and Linares-Becerra affirm that what they write are *novelas blancas y modernas* ("white, modern novels"). Their interviews appear under the respective headings of "La 'rosa' no existe y es inocua" ("'*Rosa*' does not exist and is innocuous") (Icaza) and "No existe novela rosa. Yo escribo novelas modernas" ("The *rosa* novel does not exist. I write modern novels") (Linares-Becerra). By way of definition, Icaza simply offers her own two novels: *Cristina Guzmán* and *Soñar la vida*. Linares-Becerra is more expressive on the subject. For her, literature dedicated to the feminine public is

> literatura blanca, tan distante de la que aquí llaman . . . 'rosa', como pueda estarlo un apunte rural a lápiz de la acabada obra pictórica que reproduzca un dilatado horizonte. La novela blanca existe entre nosotros como en todos los climas, en ninguno de los cuales se la ataca, por la sencilla razón de que es necesaria para el entrenamiento de una juventud a la que otros temas desmoralizan.

> (white literature, as distant from what here is called . . . 'rosa,' as a rustic pencil sketch may be from a finished work of art depicting an expansive horizon. The white novel exists among us as it does in all places, and nowhere is it attacked, for the simple reason that it is necessary for the formation of youth, whereas other subjects are demoralizing.) (7)

But she claims that her novels are more complex than that, as their protagonists are not flawless embodiments of ideals, but "seres humanos; por lo tanto imperfectos" ("human beings; and as such, imperfect"). As can be glimpsed through these passages, both novelists are eager to distinguish their novelistic production from the "mainstream" of novels known as "rosa." Hence, rather than attempt to trace the production of *novela blanca* as a separate genre (Servén's study being a case in point) or dismiss it as redundant to *novela rosa* (an attitude adopted by Martín Gaite), I shall examine the novelists' claim here in terms of position-taking.

gives Luisa-María's father as the prolific dramatist Manuel Linares Rivas y Astray, President of the sociedad de autores Españoles (1867–1938)." See "Romancing the Early Franco Regime."

[26] See note above.

[27] Qtd in Servén Diez (94) and Martín Gaite (148). Interestingly, the term appears in both Icaza and Ortoll's novels: in the first, to describe the works of the protagonist, Teresa Sandoval, who is also an author of bestselling novels (*Soñar la vida*, 1941), and in the second, to denote the type of novels read by a young woman who dreams of getting married (*En pos de la ilusión*, 1940).

As we have mentioned above, Icaza, together with Luisa-María Linares, Concha Linares-Becerra, and María Mercedes Ortoll, occupied a "privileged" position among the rapidly proliferating authors of *novelas rosa*. Given that the novels' popularity was in negative proportion to their valuation, Icaza's preference for the label "*blanca*" over "*rosa*" may be viewed as a strategy of increasing her works' cultural capital by distancing them from *novelas rosa*. Furthermore, the penchant for the term can be regarded as a way of eschewing the criticism that charged *novelas rosa* with being "escapist," "illusory," "deceptive," and, consequently, "menacing" to women's valorized domestic and social responsibilities. In contrast, the *novela blanca*, through its evocation of "purity," "virginity," and "innocence," was likely to ingratiate itself with the moralists of the time who were also the prime advocates of "realism" (understood as conformity to the dominant values), and staunch proponents of "*noviazgos blancos*" ("white courtships"). This "realism" must not be confused with the "social realism" that was slowly gaining currency within the literary circles, and had as its end social criticism. In fact, as far as the latter circles were concerned, *novela rosa*'s very subject was a betrayal of reality. It is in light of this tension that we must consider the following passage from Luisa-María Linares' aforementioned article:

> Cierta tarde me dió Carmen de Icaza una inteligente definición de la novela rosa, bajo el punto de vista de sus atacantes. Según éstos, un argumento rosa era el siguiente: 'Una muchachita pobre, joven y guapa, conseguía después de muchas vicisitudes, colocarse en una oficina. El jefe se enamoraba de ella. Tras de vencer unas cuantas dificultades, se casaban por fin.' Y un argumento trascendental y humano era éste, según dichos señores: 'Una muchacha pobre, joven y guapa, conseguía, después de muchas vicisitudes, colocarse en una oficina. El jefe se enamoraba de ella. Tras de vencer unas cuantas dificultades. . ., él se decidía a ponerle un piso.' Han dado en calificar de rosa a todas las novelas, películas o comedias de temas modernos y normales. ¿O es que no son normales los noviazgos y las bodas? Todos sabemos que existen muchas lacras y horrores en este mundo desquiciado en que habitamos. Pero, ¿debamos ser criticados unos cuantos porque no nos gusta ponerlos de relieve, prefiriendo describir ambientes menos desagradables y mucho más familiares porque en ellos nos desenvolvemos?
>
> . . . No era Henry Ardel el puntal en el que se fundamentaba la sociedad francesa, naturalmente. Pero en cambio, sí es un puntal, en todas las sociedades cristianas y civilizadas el sentido moral de la mujer. Y tratar de inculcar a las muchachas jóvenes, como se viene haciendo insistentemente, que sólo está la Verdad en las novelas que no acaban en boda, me parece un error gravísimo, mucho más grave que la supuesta creencia de que los jefes se casan siempre con las mecanógrafas y de que hay una colección de duques esperando su turno para pedir la mano de cualquier maniquí de una casa de modas.

(One afternoon Carmen de Icaza gave me a clever definition of the *novela rosa*, from the point of view of their attackers. According to them, a *rosa* plot was the following: 'An impoverished, young, pretty girl is able, after many vicissitudes, to get a job in an office. The boss falls in love with her. After overcoming a few difficulties, they finally marry.' And a transcendental and human plot was this, according to the aforementioned gentlemen: 'An impoverished, young, pretty girl is able, after many vicissitudes, to get a job in an office. The boss falls in love with her. After overcoming a few difficulties, he decides to get her an apartment.' They have taken to qualifying as *rosa* all novels, movies, or plays with modern and normal themes. Or by chance are courtships and weddings not normal? We all know that many stains and horrors exist in this mad world which we inhabit. But, should some of us be criticized because we do not like to emphasize them, preferring to describe less disagreeable and much more familiar environments because those are the ones we live in?
. . . Henry Ardel was not the base upon which French society was founded, naturally. But on the other hand, the moral sense of woman *is* a base, in all Christian and civilized societies. And to try to convince young girls, as is repeatedly done, that the Truth is only in novels that do not end in a wedding, seems to me to be a terribly grave error, much graver than the supposed belief that the bosses always marry the typists and that there is a group of dukes waiting their turn to ask for the hand of any fashion-house model.)[28]

In light of the above considerations, we may conclude that for the authors of *novelas rosa* and the moralists of the time, verisimilitude ("the quality of a text resulting from its degree of conformity to a set of 'truth' norms that are external to it" (Prince 102)) was subordinated to or equated with the text's moral imperative.

Lastly, the authors' public claim that their novels were *blancas* and not *rosa* may be taken as an invitation to read their works for their differences, instead of what they had in common with the others—namely, the mandatory happy endings. This difference may be said to reside in their aforementioned "modernidad moderada" ("moderated modernity")—the at once traditional and revolutionary femininity advocated by *Sección Femenina* (which imbued their heroines with greater dynamism). Furthermore, if in a typical *novela rosa* a protagonist, usually an outsider owing to formation, penury, or some unjust and often mysterious circumstances, which invariably work in her favor (as markers of her distinction), must overcome a hurdle or two prior to graduating into marriage, in the works of these novelists, the obstacle to be surmounted often resides in the heroine herself, whether in the form of ambition, desire, character, or career. In other words, the heroine is at once a site of

---

[28] See *La estafeta literaria* 38 (Dec. 15, 1945) 29.

conflict and an impediment to her own happiness (anticipated by the gender and genre conventions).

This notion that marriage presupposes a woman's overcoming of her self is present in a considerable number of the works in question. What makes them so interesting is their parallel espousal of the normative precepts of the time—the "vencimiento del propio yo" ("conquering of the self")[29] advocated by women's conduct manuals—and exposure of the constructed nature of femininity that provided the basis for the aforementioned precepts. The very process by which the heroine assumes her normative gender identity threatens the novel's normative subtext, for often the contrast between the heroine's character and the one that she must adopt as an ideal wife is so great as to betray the performative nature of her "essence." As Modleski observes:

> [T]he heroine of the novels can achieve happiness only by undergoing a complex process of self-subversion, during which she sacrifices her aggressive instincts, her 'pride,' and—nearly—her life. And a close analysis of the dynamics of the reading process will show that the reader is encouraged to participate in and actively desire feminine self-betrayal. (37)

Thus, the coercive power of romance extends from the protagonist to the reader through the realm of desire and imagination. As the heroine's success is contingent upon her transformation into a docile subject to the norm, the reader, in her parallel desire for the protagonist's deferred victory and the narrative's ensuing happy ending, becomes tacitly complicit with the external forces that demand the heroine's surrender or with that which in the text represents the voice of authority. As a result, the heroine's happiness, and perhaps the reader's as well, come to depend on the espousal of the prescribed gender roles rehearsed in the novels.

Finally, Manzano Badía's allegation that post-war women novelists were instrumental in the shaping of female subjectivity serves to underscore once more the socializing power of literature enhanced by the incidence of exemplarity as a standard representational and hermeneutic practice in the early years of Franco's rule. In this respect, Martín Gaite's reflections on the way given reading habits mediate our relationship to ourselves and our immediate surroundings, and on the potential of normative and popular representations to generate (or detract from) certain attitudes and models of being, remain the most persuasive argument to date for the vindication of the corpus in question.

Before embarking on the analysis of selected novels, we must devote a few more paragraphs to their happy endings, since it is this identification of the narrative's "resolution"—the sealing of matrimonial bonds—with its appar-

---

[29] See Enciso Viana on p. 71 of this text.

ent "purpose," or the reinforcement of the patriarchal order through the reproduction of normative gender roles, that, in my view, has conditioned, or in
many cases obstructed, the reading of women's post-war romance fictions as
anything other than repetitive, predictable, and homogeneous. Instead, I
would like to posit that together these novels present an interesting spin on
the maxim "the end justifies the means"—a narrative law[30] frequently
obscured by the linear representation of events. Our need for "coherence" is
such that we tend to interpret what follows in terms of what precedes, apply-
ing the logic of causation where we merely have consecution (Barthes, qtd in
Porter 266). This practice, also known as an interpretative fallacy, "*post hoc
ergo propter hoc*" or "after this, therefore because of this," not only limits our
interpretations to that which "makes sense," or to what is familiar, but furthermore requires that we provide explanations where none can be found (Porter
37–40). To use an Iserian term, it induces us to fill in (or rather gloss over) the
narrative gaps by the same token of "common sense" that is neither universal
nor subjective, but rather culturally and historically determined.

While we may contend that everything in a selected narrative is subordinated to or is a function of the dénouement,[31] that any disorder or breaking of
the norm in the course of the narrative may be seen as yielding to its final
restoration (a restoration made all the more significant by the overcoming of,
or to use the rhetoric of the time, triumphing over any potentially destabilizing factors), it may similarly be argued that it is the function of the dénouement to allow for and thereby legitimate the narrative representation of those
very deviations or departures from the norm that would otherwise be censurable. That is, owing to this legitimate and legitimating unraveling of the plot
(when not the ending or resolution), what until this point could have been
deemed transgressive or potentially censurable material becomes, in retro-
spect, a *felix culpa* or a "fortunate fault" (Genette 180)—a bone of contention
redeemed by its didactic or normative function. This may in part explain what
until now has been attributed to the censors' arbitrariness: namely, why some
novels got away with taboo topics and others did not. Illustrative of this tendency is a censor's report on Carmen Laforet's *La mujer nueva*:

> La protagonista Paulina es una licenciada en Ciencias Exactas, estudiosa y
> atractiva hija de padre hipócrita y bestial y de una madre débil, asustadiza y
> llorosa, que había contribuido a alejarse de toda creencia religiosa. Enamorada
> de Antonio, casado y primo de Eulogio, su marido oficial, huye de este doble

[30] See Gérard Genette, "Plausibility and Motivation" in *The Princess of Clèves* (New York:
Norton, 1994) 179. On the level of interpretation, such a law demands that narratives be seen as
having a function or an "end," and that their constituent elements not be considered independently,
for their own sake, but in terms of this overarching purpose.

[31] An argument that has been the penchant of critical practice and whose validity is not
contested here so long as it is recognized as a plausible rather than the overriding interpretation.

adulterio que la hace verse tan sucia e insincera como su padre. Súbitamente en el tren contemplando un amanecer castellano, se siente iluminada por la gracia y tras luchas y recaídas encuentra el verdadero camino de Dios. Como puede verse en este extracto del argumento, la intención doctrinal de la obra es ejemplarizadora. A juicio del lector puede autorizarse.

(The protagonist Paulina, with a degree in Hard Sciences, is the studious and attractive daughter of a hypocritical and bestial father and a weak, frightened, and tearful mother, which contributed to her distancing herself from any religious belief. In love with Antonio, the married cousin of Eulogio, her official husband, she flees from this double adultery that makes her feel as dirty and insincere as her father. Suddenly, while on a train witnessing a Castilian dawn, she feels illuminated by grace, and after struggles and relapses, finds the true path of God. As can be seen in this summary, the doctrinal intention of the work is exemplary. The reader's judgment is that it may be authorized.) (qtd in O'Byrne 207)

We may therefore contend that even as they are bound to control narrative possibilities, such obligatory endings are not always in consonance with the narratives' internal logic, which is to say, they do not always result from the narrative as a "logical" consequence. In none of the selected novels, save for one, do the protagonists "set out" to get married; in fact, their actions suggest the contrary. When an independent society girl (*Un marido a precio fijo*, 1940), an enterprising young woman (*Como los hombres nos quieren*, 1944), and a renowned writer (*Soñar la vida*, 1941) marry, it is by relinquishing what distinguishes them as women. Ironically, in the only novel where this pattern is slightly altered (*En pos de la ilusión*, 1940), the protagonist's "rebellion," her breach of the existing courtship practices, is rooted precisely in her zeal to marry. The fact that despite their differences all four novels share an identical end, at the cost of narrative coherence,[32] speaks more of the force of prescribed social and generic conventions and anxiety about the novels' reception, than of the texts' ideological "allegiances."

---

[32] On narrative incoherences ensuing from the censors' notations, see Patricia O'Byrne.

7

"La imperfecta casada" or the Making of an Ideal Wife in Luisa-María Linares' *Un marido a precio fijo*

According to post-war novelist and playwright Julia Maura, one of the short-comings of the *novela rosa*'s rendering of feminine experience is that it ends where "real" life for a woman begins: in marriage.[1] What the arbiters of femi-nine mores, authors of *novelas rosa*, and novelists like Maura agree on is that female representation is inconceivable without reference to men. Most pre-scriptive texts divide women's life experience into three phases: *el noviazgo* (courtship or engagement), *el matrimonio* (marriage), and *la maternidad* (motherhood). In keeping with Maura's assertion, the popular romance novels see the first phase as their legitimate domain and, in contrast to narratives like Maura's own *Ventolera* (1943)—which situate the male–female dynamic within matrimonial bonds—use the allure of love to disguise the complex, hierarchical nature of gender relations. Luisa-María Linares' 1941 romance novel, *Un marido a precio fijo,* manages to inhabit two of the aforementioned domains through the taming-of-the-shrew masterplot that characterizes many of her novels (Galerstein 178). While the "taming" in Linares' novels iterates and reinforces patriarchal authority, the very nature of the confrontation that underlies these narratives (the necessary disruption of the traditional order) lends itself to multiple readings, and substantiates the earlier hypothesis that any reading of dissent in the selected texts is grounded in their conformity (epitomized by the novels' conventional prefiguring of marriage and mother-hood). If "the internal composition of a given text is nothing more or less than the history of its struggle with contrary forms of representation for the author-ity to control semiosis" (Armstrong 23), then even those narratives, which seem to be interested in promoting a single point of view, are neither univocal nor impervious to internal contestations.

---

[1] "La novela rosa acaba siempre en donde comienza la vida, en el matrimonio. La gracia está en sacar cosas bonitas de la realidad. El momento de arranque de la novela debe ser el matrimonio, cuando empieza de verdad la vida de mujer" ("The *novela rosa* always ends where life begins, in marriage. Its appeal derives from selecting pleasant aspects of reality. The novel should start with marriage, where woman's life really begins.") See *La estafeta literaria* 1 (March 5, 1944) 7.

Ingeniously conceived as a charade of marriage, *Un marido a precio fijo* is a story of apprenticeship. Estrella Vilar, the adoptive daughter and heiress of tycoon Nicolás Mendoza, is prey to her own self-centeredness and frivolity. Her flawed character, we are told, is a consequence of her upbringing and the reason she is unfit to assume the role of domestic angel. She could be Bishop Enciso Viana's direct addressee when he writes:

> Muchacha, ya lo sabes: uno de los entrenamientos a que has de someterte durante el noviazgo es el dominio de tu genio, la conquista de la mansedumbre. Entrenamiento difícil y largo, sobre todo si en la educación infantil y de la primera juventud se ha abandonado, defecto muy corriente en nuestros tiempos.

> (Young lady, as you already know, one of the disciplines to which you must submit yourself during courtship is the taming of your temper and the attainment of meekness. A long and difficult discipline, above all if it has been neglected in childhood and early adolescence, a very common defect in our times.) (105)

As the novel makes amply clear, what Estrella lacks is not formal education (as she herself observes, "mi padrino se gastó una millonada en educarme" ("my godfather spent a million on educating me"), a comment that elicits an allusive "'¿Dices que . . . 'malgastó'?" ("You say that . . . 'he wasted it'?") from her putative husband [130]), but the specifically feminine formation advocated in the *escuelas del hogar* of the *Sección Femenina*.

Predictably, the traditional distinction between female education and instruction was still valid in the early Franco years. The former was intended to prepare women for the fulfillment of their responsibilities as wives and mothers. The latter referred to its subsidiary—formal education. A liberal-leaning, nineteenth-century authority on women's social role and responsibilities, Severo Catalina, warned in his classic treatise, *La mujer* (1858), that: "La mayor parte de las gentes confunde la educación con la instrucción. Es un error gravísimo. . . . La *educación* es de más importancia que la *instrucción* [sic]. La primera se dirige principalmente al corazón; la segunda a la inteligencia. Eduquemos a las mujeres, e instruyámoslas después, si queda tiempo" ("The majority of people confuse education with instruction. It is a very grave error. . . . *Education* is of greater importance than *instruction*. The first is principally directed to the heart; the second to the intelligence. Let us educate women, and instruct them later, if time allows") (26). In keeping with this distinction, if a woman were to reap the benefits of higher education or university training, it was to enhance her performance at home by making her an amenable conversationalist or, better yet, a sympathetic listener.

Instead, willful, unruly, independent-minded and "modern," Estrella smokes, drives a car, plays sports, enjoys flirting, and has friends with names

like Fifí and Cuchi. Financially secure, she is the antithesis of the ideal marriageable type, save for her age, beauty, and uprightness. However, as the
novel progresses, her erroneous dispositions are corrected and redeemed as
the novel's happy ending exacts the heroine's transformation from "la imperfecta casada" ("the imperfect wife") to "la perfecta reina de su hogar" ("the
perfect queen of her hearth"). This transformation is founded on three premises: recognition of male authority; internalization of femininity defined by
sacrifice and renunciation; and the primacy of middle-class mores.

Estrella's first appearance is marked by one of her many frustrated attempts
to "vivir su vida" ("to lead her own life") (7, 11), a term that ran counter to
hegemonic norms and was reserved for condemning what in women were
perceived as modern, rebellious, and selfish practices incompatible with
women's transcendental mission.[2] Vexed by her old suitor and godfather's
cohort, Julito, whom she had unofficially consented to marry (out of tedium
rather than love), Estrella leaves the two men behind, instead following her
own will (depicted as a whim). Keen to assert her autonomy—another sign of
her unbridled character—Estrella spends a month traveling alone through
Europe's most fashionable hotels, displaying her youth, beauty, and wealth
and thereby defying a number of "common sense" notions of the time such as
"una chiquilla inexperta . . . no debiera andar sola por el mundo sin la protec-
ción de sus papás" ("an inexperienced little girl . . . should not walk alone in
the world without the protection of her parents") and "las ricas herederas
deberían ser más cautas" ("rich heiresses should be more cautious"), not to
mention that displays of any sort in a woman, save for humility and abstemi-
ousness, were considered reprehensible (10).

During one of her hotel stays, she meets Eric, the supposed heir of an
Austrian baron, who appears to share her extravagant taste and habits, and the
two decide to marry. The wedding takes place in an obscure village court-
house prior to their departure for Paris, where Estrella plans to present her
stately husband to don Nico and Julito. However, events take a different turn
as the train leaves the station and Estrella learns that the man she took for a
husband is a swindler and a bigamist whose sole purpose in marrying her had
been to avail himself of her money and possessions. But for Estrella, even
starker than the revelation of Eric's true identity, is the sensation of having
been toyed with and disposed of as the wife of a runaway spouse.

---

[2] According to Martín Gaite: "la muchacha que soñara con 'vivir su vida' en seguida se daba
cuenta de que le resultaba más prudente conservar encerrado aquel propósito en la zona de los
anhelos inconfesables, como un tesoro que se convertiría en bazofia al exponerlo a la luz" ("any
girl that dreamed of 'leading her own life' soon realized that she was better served keeping this
dream safely in the realm of inadmissable desires, like a treasure that would become pig swill
when exposed to light") (*Usos amorosos* 49–50).

At this point Estrella meets Miguel Rivera, her second putative husband. Apprehensive about the upcoming encounter with her guardian and former suitor, she nearly overlooks the complete stranger traveling in her spacious quarters. His furtive presence, scruffy appearance and her own recent experience suggest to her that Miguel might be a thief. Instead, he is a former war correspondent and accomplished journalist who has followed Estrella into her car in pursuit of a story (although she does not learn this until the very end). Intrigued by her all-too-apparent dismay, Miguel accepts Estrella's accusations with sardonic complacency, offering in return his assistance as "un compatriota dispuesto a ayudar a una joven que viaja sola por un país extraño" ("a compatriot willing to help a young woman traveling alone in a foreign country") (15). For her part, Estrella, intent on sparing herself the added humiliation of coming clean to her uncle and former admirer, convinces Miguel—a perfect stranger whose true motives and identity remain unknown to her—to impersonate her husband for one month, in exchange for a tidy sum of money. And thus begins a rehearsal for a marriage in which Estrella's role, in contrast to the price she is willing to pay, is not negotiable.

The novel opens with the pronouncement of Estrella's first nuptials in the form of her two missives—intended symbols of her successful choices as an independent woman—addressed to don Nico and Julio. Almost immediately, the mystery of a romance that begins with a wedding starts to unravel by way of a challenge to the normative definition of marriage. For any reader familiar with the prevailing cultural codes, the wedding of a woman whose character defies the very foundation of her conjugal responsibilities (that is, a woman who represents the very opposite of self-denial) can only be an illusion or a disaster, or both, and is in no way the wedding so meticulously forestalled, desired, anticipated, and at last celebrated at the end of the novel.

Moreover, what by normative standards is just as unthinkable as the reconciling of a spoiled and pampered young woman with conjugal bliss—"[e]ra asombroso pensar que ella, Estrella Vilar, la niña mimada, acababa de casarse" ("it was astonishing to think that she, Estrella Vilar, the over-indulged child, had just gotten married") (6)—is the nonchalance with which Estrella approaches the single most "transcendental" event in the life of a woman: "Rió, divertida, ante el pensamiento de la mala pasada que jugaba a su padrino y a Julito" ("She laughed, amused, at the thought of the wicked trick that she was playing on her godfather and Julito") (6). But this apparent discrepancy between the lightheartedness with which she marries and the gravity of the matter is not lost on Estrella: "parecía imposible que hubiese tanta facilidad para hacer una cosa tan importante" ("it seemed impossible that a thing of such importance should be so easy to perform") (8). Here Estrella refers to the civil ceremony by which she marries Eric, but which by Francoist standards was merely perfunctory:

Claro que aún no estaban completamente casados. Su matrimonio civil, celebrado media hora antes . . . debería ratificarse en la Embajada española y celebrar luego, ante Julito y el padrino, la ceremonia religiosa, al día siguiente. Estrella era católica, y Eric también. Por tanto, hasta que su unión no hubiese sido bendecida por el sacerdote, no se consideraría casada.

(Of course, they were not yet fully married. Her civil marriage, which had taken place half an hour earlier . . . had to be ratified in the Spanish Embassy, while the religious ceremony would be carried out the following day, in the presence of Julito and her godfather. Estrella was Catholic, and so was Eric. As such, until their union had been blessed by the priest, she would not consider herself married.) (8)

For the unlikely "malpensado," or rather a "malpensada" reading the novel ("a man [or a woman] given to thinking ill"), Estrella's intimate thoughts are offered as proof that in the half-hour between the wedding ceremony and the departure of the train, she and Eric had not consummated their marriage; this reassurance is meant to eliminate doubt as to her physical and moral integrity in light of his desertion: "Menos mal—se dijo entre sollozos—que no consiguió otra cosa de mí. Cierto que él tampoco me pidió nada. Lo achacaba a corrección. Pero es que yo sólo era un 'objetivo metálico'. ¡De no haber sido así, me moriría ahora de vergüenza!" ("At least—she told herself between sobs—he did not get anything else from me. Of course he did not ask for anything else, either. He passed himself off as a gentleman. But I was just a means to an end for him. If it had not been so, I would die from shame now!") (12). These reiterations and "reading interludes" function as indices of how a given text "ostensibl[y] wants to be read and a cue to the kind of program it considers most useful for its decoding, and as a factor determining to some extent the response of any reader other than itself" (Prince, *Reader in the Text* 237). Estrella's thwarted romance in the beginning of the novel suggests that she is not yet fit for marriage, but that to fall in love and found a proper family, she must still be a virgin.

The final proof that their marital contract is ineffective comes from Eric. In a letter disclosing his true motives and identity to Estrella, Eric admits to having a wife. What is perhaps equally significant about this epistle—part exculpation of his deed, part indictment of her actions—is that it contains Eric's assessment of Estrella, intimating why, despite her two prospective marriages, she is not ready for conjugal bliss: "Me consta que no sufrirás con este desengaño. Sufrirá únicamente tu amor propio. No creo que quieras a nadie que no seas tú misma" ("I am certain you will not suffer from this deception. Only your pride will suffer. I don't think you love anyone but yourself") (10). Such an attitude on the part of a young woman preparing to marry presents a stark contrast to the one prescribed by the arbiters of feminine mores: "Atiéndeme, muchacha: ¿Eres novia? Pues antes de casarte vence el genio. El carácter violento incapacita a una chica para el matrimonio. La que no sabe frenar su amor propio y pisarlo, si es preciso, lleva muchas probabilidades de ser desgraciada en su casamiento" ("Listen to me, young lady: Are you engaged? Well, before marrying, tame your temper. A violent character incapacitates a girl for marriage. She who does not know how to curb her pride and trample it, if necessary, is likely to be unhappy in her marriage") (Enciso Viana 104).

Eric's judgment is further substantiated by Miguel, the voice of moral authority, who without going so far as to justify the former's wrongdoing, believes not only that Estrella brought such treatment upon herself—"Eric le ha dado su merecido . . . ¿a quién se le ocurre casarse con un desconocido?" ("Eric has given you what you deserve. . . who would possibly think of marrying a stranger?")—but that given her obstinacy and lack of remorse, she has yet to learn from her error: "Es usted una niña mal criada. Merecería una tanda de azotes" ("You are a spoiled child. You deserve a spanking") (21). Thus when Miguel eventually accepts Estrella's proposition to be her stand-in husband, it is to teach her a lesson: "¡Esta adorable princesita . . . merece una lección y a fe que voy a dársela" ("This adorable little princess . . . needs a lesson and I swear that I am going to give it to her") (26). This resolution is reiterated throughout the course of the narrative. However, even when Estrella is being criticized, the narrator is careful not to tip the balance between the heroine's lawlessness and her integrity. Though her plan may be reckless— "una locura" ("a folly"), "una atrocidad" ("an atrocity"), as Miguel labels it—the reader is assured that no sexual boundaries are breached. Estrella insists: "Debo advertirle que, en la intimidad, nuestro trato será estrictamente correcto. No le consentiré que me roce un dedo" ("I should warn you that, in terms of intimacy, our interactions will be strictly proper. I won't allow you to touch so much as my finger") (25).

One of the major sources of conflict in Estrella and Miguel's charade of marriage is their alleged incompatibility. As a rule, women were counseled to look for husbands within their own class:

> Dos personas nacidas en el seno de familias iguales, con padres del mismo estilo, educadas en escuelas o colegios paralelos, con influencias económicosociales parecidas, serán dos almas gemelas que vibrarán con los mismos sentimientos, experimentarán las mismas reacciones y tendrán criterios parejos que les permitan ver la vida a través del mismo prisma, soñar con los mismos ideales y lanzarse por los mismos derroteros.
>
> (Two people born into compatible families, of like-minded parents, educated in similar institutions, with common socio-economic backgrounds, will be two soul mates stirred by the same feelings, reacting the same way, sharing the same principles that will allow them to see the world through the same lens, dream of the same ideals and embark upon the same paths.) (Enciso Viana 74)

In the absence of such ideal parity, most conduct manuals champion bourgeois values that seemingly transcend barriers of class, thereby buttressing both the Falangist revolutionary ambitions of a classless society and the Francoist hierarchy of values that privileged moral reserves over material riches.[3] Estrella's upper-class world, made up of *parvenus* like her adoptive father and stagnant members of the aristocracy (like her admirer Julito, who also is rehabilitated by Miguel in the end), is criticized for its frivolity and idleness, which make its members particularly susceptible to "los malos vientos modernistas" ("harmful modernist currents") (Morales 12). The result is the confrontation of two worlds—that of Estrella, constituted by what she calls "élite internacional" ("international elite"), and Miguel's, who until the end of the novel is represented not in terms of his class, but rather in terms of his merits (a commonplace in bourgeois auto-representation)—that culminates in the final and unmistakable triumph of middle-class values. Accordingly, for Estrella, becoming an ideal wife presupposes a transformation into a bourgeois angel of the hearth, a transformation that in turn requires the concentration of power in Miguel's hands.

As we have seen, the chapter on conjugal rights and responsibilities of the then-operating 1889 Civil Code left little room for speculation with regard to its patriarchal nature. By the pronouncement of Article 57, a husband had the obligation to protect his wife, and she to obey her husband.[4] For this reason, it was incumbent on a woman to maintain an inferior self-image and be willing to recognize her husband as her superior in everything. In "El noviazgo, importancia y trascendencia del mismo" ("Courtship, its importance and transcendence"), María Pilar Morales counsels her readers not to forget that "[el novio] ha de ser superior en todo a nosotras para que encaje en su papel de cabeza de familia. Para que pueda constantemente hacernos ofrenda de su valer y nosotras podamos sentirnos protegidas y dignificadas a su lado" ("[the betrothed] must be superior to us in all things so that he may fulfill his role as head of the family. So that he can constantly make us an offering of his worthiness and so that we can feel protected and dignified at his side") (103). Thus, Estrella and Miguel's relationship presents the reversal of the established hierarchy, which, true to time and genre-induced expectations, will have to be restored before their union takes a legitimate and a happy turn.

The stated cause of Estrella's atypically dominant manner is her erroneous upbringing, aggravated by her upper-class milieu and ignorance of Miguel's true identity (whom she continues to regard as a thief despite the glaring evidence of his noble character). Uninitiated in the normative criteria for assessing

---

[3] Significantly, the type of reading that was promoted as ideal beyond national literature was none other than Victorian (José Pemartín, qtd in Valls 110).

[4] "El marido debe proteger a la mujer, y ésta obedecer al marido" (qtd in Nash, *Mujer, familia y trabajo* 160).

women's merit, Estrella's sense of prerogative is based on her privileged socio-economic condition rather than properly feminine virtues. Her sizeable fortune and its drawbacks are made patent from the novel's opening lines: "Era su costumbre viajar así, a todo lujo, derrochando el oro a manos llenas. ¿Para qué quería el dinero que su padrino tan pródigamente le entregaba, sino para gastarlo como se le antojase?" ("It was her custom to travel thus, in luxury, scattering gold by the handful. Why else would she want the money that her godfather so generously gave to her, if not to spend it as she pleased?") (9). Here we must not forget that Estrella's profligate habits defy the post-war ideal of a thrifty woman. Most conduct manuals are unanimous in their reprimand of frivolous spending. A parsimonious approach to money had to be instilled from an early age since it was believed that women who were accustomed to liberal spending would find it difficult to moderate their impulses once they became wives and mothers, thereby threatening the household economy and affronting the very essence of womanhood, defined as it was by self-restraint and abnegation:

> Aun cuando tu posición económica sea muy desahogada y te sepas heredera de un bonito capital, acostúmbrate a la sobriedad y a la economía, murallas defensoras de la virtud y elementos muy valiosos para la buena marcha de un hogar. . . . La falta de freno en los gastos lleva insensiblemente a la vanidad, frivolidad, molicie y a una carrera vertiginosa de apetencias imposibles de saciar, enemigos todos del equilibrio hogareño. Desengáñate; no puedes gastar lo que quieres, sino lo que debes.

> (Even if you are very well-to-do and know you will inherit a tidy sum of money, accustom yourself to sobriety and thrift, walls which will defend your virtue and invaluable resources for good home management. . . . Lack of restraint in spending leads imperceptibly to vanity, frivolity, indolence, and a giddy pursuit of appetites impossible to sate, all enemies of balance and tranquility in the home. Open your eyes; you cannot spend however much you may want, but only as much as you ought.) (Enciso Viana 112–13)

According to Narciso Malo Segura, the so-called "mal de orgullo femenino" ("vice of feminine pride") was particularly common among women of affluence and could only be redeemed by "el obrar digno del hombre, que prefiere una vida de medianía a una riqueza y lujo puestos al servicio de la indignidad, la vanidad o el capricho" ("the honorable activity of the man, who prefers a modest life to one of riches and luxury put in the service of unworthiness, vanity or caprice") (68). But before Miguel has a chance to exercise his corrective influence, Estrella applies her unrestricted capital instead to hire Miguel and command him as his superior.

In what may be perceived as a scandalous complicity, the readers are invited to partake of Estrella's short-lived ascendancy with full knowledge that this will not only be superseded, but that when all is said and done, Estrella will at last enjoy much-coveted and celebrated conjugal bliss. Until then, however, Estrella continues to openly dictate the terms and conditions of their self-styled marriage, flaunting her upper hand, and publically undermining Miguel's authority in the relationship. It is she who at the beginning of their arrangement exacts obedience, suggesting that Miguel conform his conduct to her will: "Tiene usted un carácter indomable. Chocaremos si no me obedece" ("You have an untamable personality. We will clash if you do not obey me") (31). For a reader who is reluctant to recognize Estrella's disposition as deviant, the narrator makes it plain that:

> El comportamiento de Estrella . . . era bastante molesto para un 'marido verdadero.' Desde la mañana cogía su coche y desaparecía. Ni comía ni cenaba en 'Los Almendros.' A nadie le daba la menor explicación de su conducta. Pasaban los días enteros sin verla, ya que solía llegar cuando todos se habían retirado a descansar. Aquello sumía a Miguel en un desasosiego inexplicable.

> (Estrella's behavior . . . was annoying enough for a 'real husband.' In the morning she would take her car and disappear. She ate neither lunch nor dinner in 'Los Almendros.' She did not give anyone the slightest explanation of her conduct. Days passed without anyone seeing her, since it was her habit to return after everyone had retired for the evening. That left Miguel in a state of inexplicable unease.) (92)

Estrella's godfather, who willingly assumes responsibility for her flaws, counsels Miguel to use his prerogative as a husband so as to avoid being trampled by her: "Te voy a dar un consejo, Miguel. A esa chiquilla tienes que atarla corto. Se ha vuelto demasiado independiente. Procura dominarla, si no quieres que ella te domine a ti" ("I am going to give you some advice, Miguel. Keep that little girl on a short rein. She has become too independent. Dominate her, if you don't want her to dominate you") (92). And in the end, male authority, which has been "always already" at Miguel's disposition, takes precedence over Estrella's capital.

The inevitable shift in power takes place in mid-air, as Miguel flies Estrella, against her will, to a remote cabin in the Pyrenees. Estrella's values, which until then subscribed to the worldly order of things, are superseded by Miguel's, whose elevated principles are accordingly asserted in the heavens:

> —¡Aterrice! ¿Me oye? ¡Le ordeno que aterrice!
> —¿Quién es usted para darme órdenes?
> —La persona que paga sus servicios.
> —¡Ba! Eso es en tierra. En el cielo rigen otros sistemas. Ahora soy yo él que manda.

(—Land! Do you hear me? I order you to land!
—Who are you to give me orders?
—The person who pays for your services.
—Bah! That is on land. The sky is governed by different rules. Now I am
the one in charge.) (107)

Faced with the fallacy of money's absolute power, Estrella is forced to
recognize the imprudence of her actions, the precarious nature of her feminine honor, and her sheer physical vulnerability. Once back on land and in the
cabin, she discovers that her room has no lock and that she is in no position to
defy Miguel's authority without jeopardizing her virtue. However, by then it
is only Estrella who can harbor any doubts about his irreproachable character
and her fears reflect her own errors, rather than any danger posed by Miguel.
As he soon makes clear, Miguel's intentions are far nobler than she suspects:
"Te he traído aquí, sencillamente, para darte una lección. Vas a hacer unas
cuantas cosas que no soñaste en tu vida. Vas a aprender a ser mujercita de tu
casa" ("I have brought you here, simply, to teach you a lesson. You will do a
few things that you have never in your life dreamed of doing. You are going
to learn to be a proper little housewife") (116). True to his word, in a chapter
evocatively titled "La imperfecta casada" ("The imperfect wife"), Miguel
presents Estrella with a set of written guidelines on the duties and responsibilities of an ideal housewife. These she finds nailed to the kitchen door on
her first morning in the cabin:

> *Manual de la perfecta mujercita de su casa*
>   Plan para el día de hoy:
> 9 de la mañana: *Toilette*. Preparación del desayuno. A saber: café con leche.
> (Y seguía una explicación detallada de cómo tenía que hacerlo.)
> 10 de la mañana: Faenas caseras: barrer, limpiar el polvo, hacer las
> camas.
> 12 de la mañana: Paseo con el maridito.
> 1 de la tarde: Preparación del almuerzo. Dos platos variados y un postre.
> 2 de la tarde: Fregar cacharros . . .
>
> (*Guide for the perfect little housewife*
>   Plan for today:
> 9 in the morning: *Toilette*. Preparation of breakfast. FYI: coffee with milk.
> (And this was followed by a detailed explanation of how to make it.)
> 10 in the morning: Household chores: sweep, dust, make the beds.
> 12 noon: A stroll with the hubby.
> 1 in the afternoon: Preparation of lunch. Two courses and dessert.
> 2 in the afternoon: Wash the dishes . . .) (124–5)

By the time she reaches the end of the list, Estrella is livid. However, her
resolve to meet Miguel's neatly charted expectations with a show of contempt

is challenged by cold, hunger, isolation, and fear, which make his masculine presence seem indispensable.

As their stay in the mountains continues, and as Estrella (however reluctantly) rehearses her role of *la perfecta casada*, the cabin undergoes a transformation from prison to safe haven, a transformation prompted by Estrella's unsuccessful attempt to free herself from Miguel's tutelage. A skilled skier, she decides to flee the cabin to seek help at a nearby shelter. But the shelter never materializes, the cabin disappears from sight and, to complicate matters further, she has to trudge through a snowstorm as day turns to night and wolves howl nearby. In this time, Estrella goes from placing the blame for her misfortune on Miguel—"por su culpa iba a padecer. El la había traído a aquel inhospitalario paraje" ("it was his fault that she was going to perish. He had brought her to this inhospitable spot") (137)—to placing it on to herself—"¡Qué insensata había sido! Tontamente se expuso a morir . . . Y estaba exponiendo la vida de aquel hombre" ("How senseless she had been! She had foolishly exposed herself to death . . . and now she was exposing that man's life as well") (140)—all in a silent promise to "apreciar mejor, en adelante, las pequeñas felicidades de la vida: una taza de té, un sillón acogedor, un interlocutor interesante" ("better appreciate, from now on, the little things in life: a cup of tea, a cozy armchair, someone interesting to talk to") (137). But even at this moment of realization, in seeing Miguel as her conversation partner, Estrella strays from the mark. None of the things she misses about their cohabitation intimates wifely virtue, except perhaps for the very fact that she comes to think of their life together in loving terms, the terms abated by absence and omission.

In the meantime, Miguel, overcome by remorse and angst, spends many tempestuous hours looking for Estrella (who eventually manages to reach the cabin on her own), but the incident leaves him severely ill. His long-term convalescence marks Estrella's true initiation into womanhood, understood as "una vida de ininterrumpido sacrificio" ("a life of uninterrupted sacrifice") (Enciso Viana 109). For the first time Estrella neglects her own wants in order to dedicate herself entirely to another's well-being: "La millonaria que ignoraba la parte amarga de la existencia no tenía la menor relación con la sufrida y abnegada muchacha a la que las duras pruebas marcaron profundas ojeras. Todas las cosas anteriores y presentes, enfocábalas desde un distinto punto de vista" ("The millionaire who was oblivious to the bitter side of life had nothing in common with this long-suffering and self-abnegating girl, beneath whose eyes the difficult trials had inscribed dark circles. She now looked at all things past and present from a different point of view") (144). All the previous events in the story may be perceived as leading to this particular perspective, which Estrella must attain prior to, and as a stipulation for, the novel's happy ending, a perspective that in the course of the narrative has become the object of the readers' desire. Thus suffering and deprivation bring Estrella an awareness of her until-now "dormant" femininity, inseparable from her acceptance of Miguel's superiority (at the time when he is weakest): "Ningún hombre de cuantos había conocido supo despertar en ella aquella sensación de . . . feminidad. . . . Sentíase más mujer que nunca y se daba cuenta de su superioridad masculina. No era un muñeco con el cual podía divertirse. Bien lo había demostrado. Era un hombre íntegro" ("No man she had ever known was able to awaken in her that feeling of . . . femininity . . . She felt more like a woman than ever and she was aware of his masculine superiority. He was not a puppet for her to play with. He had proven that. He was a man of integrity") (150).

Yet the novel doesn't end here. Estrella's readiness to accept Miguel's primacy in a secluded cabin is no guarantee that once in a familiar environment her newfound virtues will not be overcome by old habits. In a letter never sent, Miguel—wracked by anxiety over her economic ascendancy—manifests his true feelings for Estrella:

> Y ahora te repetiré, amor mío, que te quiero tanto que deseo ser de verdad tu marido. He meditado mucho antes de dar este paso. Tu conducta de las últimas semanas me hace concebir esperanzas.
>
> ¿Sería amor aquella maravillosa expresión que tenían tus ojos al decirme adiós esta mañana, o una simple sugestión que se habrá disipado al encontrarte entre los tuyos?
>
> El tiempo lo dirá. . . . He querido esperar a que pudieras leer dentro de ti. . . . Mi vida es clara y limpia. No soy el temible ladrón que despreciabas, sino un hombre trabajador y sin complicaciones.
>
> Estrella, adorada mujercita. Tengo un modesto medio de vida, suficiente para cubrir tus necesidades. Si correspondes a mi cariño, ¿será un egoísmo excesivo el pedirte que dejemos al buen padrino el disfrute de su fortuna, excesiva y un poco agobiante, para que vivas simplemente de mi trabajo?
>
> (And now I will repeat to you, my darling, that I love you so much that I truly want to be your husband. I have thought it over well before taking this step. Your conduct in recent weeks has given me hope.
>
> Could that marvelous expression in your eyes when you told me good-bye this morning be love, or is it just an illusion that will dissipate once you find yourself among your family and friends?
>
> Time will tell. . . . I wanted to wait until you could read inside yourself . . . My life is clear and pure. I am not the terrible thief that you despised, but an uncomplicated, hard-working man.
>
> Estrella, my adored one. I have a modest way of life, sufficient to provide for your needs. If you share my feelings, would it be too selfish to ask that we let your good godfather enjoy his excessive and slightly overwhelming fortune so that you may live simply off of my work?) (161–2)

Conveniently, Miguel's petition is rendered unnecessary by don Nico himself, whose unexpected death names Miguel (instead of Estrella) the sole benefactor of the tycoon's entire fortune. Convinced that don Nico's change of heart, manifest in the change of his will, was instigated by her putative husband, Estrella is averse to following the only course remaining to her if she is to keep poverty and disgrace at bay (i.e., to marry Miguel):

> Te creía mi marido y te deja su fortuna, creyendo que tú la administrarás mejor que yo. ¡Tú le sugeriste semejante idea! ¡Tú te aprovechaste de la situación para ganarte su confianza! Le hiciste creer que yo era una chiquilla insensata, derrochadora y pródiga! Y, claro, seguramente le insinuarías que, como marido, debería darte plenos poderes para refrenarme.

> (He thought that you were my husband and has left you his fortune, thinking that you would administer it better than I. You put that idea in his head! You took advantage of the situation to gain his trust! You made him think that I was a senseless little girl, wasteful and prodigal! And, of course, you suggested to him that, as my husband, you should be given full powers to control me.) (167)

When at last their ties are sealed by the only legitimate ceremony—religious sacrament—it is not Miguel who enters marriage under the suspicion of being a "cazador de dotes" ("fortune hunter"), but the disinherited and crestfallen Estrella. Instead of taking up her husband's residence, a necessary stipulation by law, Estrella settles in with her maid and the couple keeps in touch only by correspondence. Predictably, their separation lasts barely long enough to make Estrella succumb to the power of love. At the end of the novel, she is eager to leave behind her former extravagant existence for Miguel's protective, albeit modest roof, where happiness is indistinguishable from the espousal of all the prescribed tenets of ideal womanhood: "unirse al hombre, concebir y criar a los hijos. Trabajar junto al esposo y someterse mansamente, cristianamente a su autoridad indiscutible" ("uniting oneself with the man, conceiving and raising children. Working beside one's husband and submitting one's self meekly, in a Christian way, to his indisputable authority") (Morales 17). It is this final and hegemonic transformation of Estrella into "la perfecta mujercita de su casa" ("the perfect little housewife") that redeems and legitimates all her earlier errors. And it is through these errors, which constitute narrative infractions, that she comes to exemplify what, in keeping with the prevailing norms, would constitute a "positive" apprenticeship.

   In the face of all her flaws, what keeps Estrella on the "right side of law" is the split maintained between her "nature" and her "formation" (ironically revealing the arbitrariness of prescribed tenets in lieu of their purportedly inherent nature). "Estrella había sido una de las niñas que más juguetes, más diversiones y más caprichos había tenido en el mundo. Si no se convirtió en una criatura insoportable debíase a su natural encantador que, a despecho de sus defectos, hacíala ser querida por todos los que la trataban" ("Estrella had been one of those girls who had the most toys, games, and fancies in the world. If she did not become an insufferable creature, it was due to her charming nature that, in spite of her defects, made everyone who knew her, love her") (33–4). Thus, even when Estrella is deemed to be the sole architect of her misfortunes, her "errors" are constantly attenuated by repeated allusions to her deficient upbringing. First her uncle, then Miguel, reiterate this judgment. "¡Yo tengo la culpa! Yo, que he hecho de ella una niña mal criada" ("I am the one to blame! I, who have made her into a spoiled girl") (7), is don Nico's response to the news of Estrella's clandestine engagement. "No crea que le echo toda la culpa. Me la imagino desde muy niña haciendo siempre su voluntad, sin encontrar, tras las peores travesuras, más que el aplauso de todos" ("Don't think that I blame you entirely. I can picture you from the time you were a small child, always getting your way, and even after the worst behavior, encountering only everyone's applause") (22), is Miguel's assessment of the same situation. Similarly, the latter's resolve to "escarmentarla para toda la vida" ("teach her a life-long lesson") (88) is premised by his belief that beneath Estrella's "surface" depravity lies an "inner" goodness. Accused of breaching the distance imposed by Estrella's self-perceived superiority, Miguel thus retorts:

> En efecto. Olvido lo presumida y vacía que eres, Alteza; olvido tu mala educación y frivolidad. Olvido que no mereces ni el menor céntimo que se gasta en ti tu padrino, a quien tiranizas egoístamente. Lo olvido todo. ¿Sabes por qué? Porque quiero hacer una experiencia contigo. Tengo la absurda creencia de que dentro de ti hay algo dormido que merece la pena ser despertado. Algo menos malo que lo demás.

> (Indeed. I will forget how conceited and shallow you are, your Highness; I will forget your bad manners and frivolity. I will forget that you do not deserve even a cent of what your godfather, whom you selfishly tyrannize, spends on you. I will forget it all. Do you know why? Because I want to conduct an experiment. I have the absurd belief that there is something dormant within you that is worth awakening. Something not as bad as the rest. (114)

The awakening of this "innate" femininity, that is, the prescribed female subjectivity, is presented as a consequence of love. It is love that ultimately reconciles Estrella with her duties as an ideal wife.

If narrative redundancy is a "system of repetitions designed to ensure the optimum reception of a message" (Suleiman, *Reader* 16), and hence a measure of authority that a given text exercises over its own interpretation, then *Un marido a precio fijo* is markedly "authoritarian." However, if we note what is being reiterated—Estrella's formation or lack thereof and Miguel's resolve to teach her a lesson—then rather than eliminate narrative ambiguity, these redundancies merely amplify the rift between Estrella's "natural" and "acquired" dispositions. Let us now turn to Concha Linares-Becerra's 1944 novel, *Como los hombres nos quieren,* which explores the performative nature of "femininity," by positing that existing models of womanhood are but female representations of male constructs.

8

Interpreting 'Surrender' in Concha Linares-Becerra's *Como los hombres nos quieren*

Vying for their audiences' attention, women's conduct manuals, especially those authored by clergymen, were quick to denounce the pitfalls to which *novela rosa* exposed its readers. Not only did marriage mean sacrifice and renunciation—*not* perpetual bliss, as these novels would have them believe— but the irresistible good looks and fortune of the male protagonists were likely to foster unrealistic expectations and an unseemly view of marriage as a conse- quence of "un flechazo" (love at first sight) or, still worse, of convenience. Nevertheless, it was agreed that the most effective way to steer women toward their officially sanctioned end with their virtue intact was through idealism and ignorance. For this reason, the Francoist ideologues considered *la novela rosa* "un mal menor" ("a lesser evil"), if not an expedient means of distraction and indoctrination. Commenting on the relationship between women's prescriptive guides to socialization and popular romance novels, Martín Gaite remarks:

> era una retórica opuesta a la del sacrificio y el mérito, pero tan alevosa como ella. Y entre las dos contribuían a acentuar el desconocimiento de las cosas tal como eran. La primera por la vía de la ilusión y del refugio en los sueños; la segunda por el abandono de aquellos sueños en el nombre del acat- amiento a unas normas que tampoco se adaptaban de un modo flexible a la realidad.

> (It was a rhetoric opposite to that of sacrifice and merit, but just as treacher- ous. And between the two, they contributed to increasing the ignorance of things as they were. The first by way of illusion and of taking refuge in dreams; the second through abandoning those dreams in the name of com- pliance to rules that likewise failed to adapt themselves in a flexible way to reality.) (*Usos amorosos* 159)

The road to marriage was thus paved with innocent dreams and limited knowl- edge, which the reading of *novelas rosa*, far from challenging, was meant to buttress.

The extent to which representations of marriageable women, suffused by romantic fantasies and bourgeois sensibilities, upheld the status quo may also be glimpsed through the pages of contemporaneous women's magazines.

According to one such source, a woman robbed of her illusions (founded on legitimate dreams and desires) was a threat to the established order: "si la mujer desciende de su pedestal de sueños, delicadezas y espiritualidades al terreno crudo, brutal, de la vida . . . ¿en qué se convierte lo bueno del mundo?" ("if woman descends from her pedestal of dreams, delicacies and spiritual musings to the harsh, brutal soil of life . . . what will become of all that is good in the world?").[1] What happens when a woman, however briefly, ceases to dream about love (always the legitimate variety, always a conduit to marriage), is one of the most compelling questions raised by Concha Linares-Becerra's 1944 novel, *Como los hombres nos quieren.*

A first-person narrative, *Como los hombres nos quieren* is reticent about its own meaning, in defiance of the "always-already-read" text of *novela rosa* or, what amounts to being the same, of the ready-made interpretations of a conventional marriage plot. As befits the heroine of a romance novel, Eva's tale constitutes a literal and figurative journey to love, but her narrative describes the ideology of love understood as "persuasion by seduction" (Elam 146). Stripped of the "ilusión de enamorada" ("the dreams of one in love") (151) that renders the compulsory submission to male authority voluntary, the narrator-protagonist must convince herself, and thus the reader, of the desirability of marriage/surrender.

Though the novel adopts a modality of *bildung* or positive exemplarity, Eva's espousal of the normative doctrine entails the unlearning of her experience and the experiences of other women that figure in her narrative. In other words, her passage from "ignorance" to "knowledge" is concomitantly a passage from unauthorized and illicit "knowledge" to endorsed "ignorance." The view that Eva upholds at the end of the narrative—that surrender to male authority is compatible with a feminine quest for self-realization—supersedes the awareness she gains as a consequence of her own thwarted dreams, or loss of innocence: that subjected to male authority, women are what men want them to be (hence the title, *como los hombres nos quieren*). If on the level of the story Eva's reconciliation with the normative attitude (her professed love for Federico Villena and their anticipated marriage) endorses its reading as a reproduction of hegemonic gender norms, on the level of discourse the novel seems to suggest that womanhood, understood as a set of prescribed conventions, is a performative category.

The novel begins behind the scenes of a small theater, the Astoria, as Eva Carlés, an "improvised" chorus girl who is the daughter of a deceased colonel, prepares to meet her cohort and admirer Julio Aguilera. An aspiring composer without the means to launch his own production, Julio convinces Eva to leave the Astoria, and together with Rita, her roommate and a professional

---

[1] See *Chicas* (23, March 1952), qtd in *Usos amorosos* 158.

dancer, to sign an independent contract under the auspices of Gines Moyano, a wealthy businessman. This contract, as he explains to Eva, will serve to ensure their joint success and collaboration. However, the night she is summoned to Moyano's house to discover the terms of their agreement, also the night of her 24th birthday, Eva learns that her part in the production is not limited to performance on stage and that both Julio and Moyano, in exchange for their impending success, expect her to assume the role of the latter's mistress. This incident serves to introduce the novel's thesis, both remonstrative and conciliatory, that women's life scripts are authored by men, and as such, womanhood is a role to be performed or a condition to be enacted (Culler 103):

> Todo en la vida de la mujer—díjome en cierta ocasión Gracia Dorado mientras le hacía las uñas—depende de la voluntad del varón, señor del mundo, y nuestro talento estriba en amoldarnos a esa ley sin que lo parezca. ¿Quién ignora que yo soy una loca, una coqueta y hasta una amoral? Juego con los hombres como si esto me divirtiera, y la verdad es que a ellos les gusto así y que represento el papel que me han destinado, igual que a otras les reparten el de casadas, el de cuerdas o locas, el de esclavas o reinas. . . . Tanto presumir de personalidad y somos sencillamente, hija mía, como los hombres nos quieren.

> (Everything in the life of a woman—Gracia Dorado once told me while I was doing her nails—depends on the will of the man, master of the world. Our talent lies in molding ourselves to that law without appearing to do so. Everyone knows that I am a crazy, flirtatious, and even amoral woman. I toy with men as if I enjoyed it, but the truth is that they like me that way. They like me to play the role they assign me, just as they dole out to others the roles of married women, of sensible or crazy women, of slaves or queens. . . . We think we have so much personality, my child, but we are just the way men want us.) (25)

Eva's encounter with Moyano and subsequent resolve to break with Julio's expectations endow Gracia Dorado's words with a truth value that extends beyond the backstage of a substandard theater: "[A]l recordar hoy la frase íntegra, a punto estuve de protestar a gritos: '¡No! ¡Yo nunca seré como Julio quiso!' Y casi en el acto me burlé de mí misma. . . . ¿No debería a Julio mi eterna decepción, mi eterno rencor, mi eterna amargura?" ("Remembering her exact words, I nearly protested out loud, 'No! I will never be the way Julio wanted.' And almost in the same instant I made fun of myself. . . . Didn't I owe Julio my eternal deception, my eternal rancor, my eternal bitterness?") (25). Her final and irremediable surrender, a literary and ideological imperative, may be read as a consequence of love, as a sign of capitulation, or as lip service to the normative expectations. But irrespective of the interpretation one may choose, the fact that surrender is presented as a plight in need of rationalization remains noteworthy. Following this incident, Eva reevaluates her present condition—in fact her entire adult life—as a reaction to and a consequence of a man she knew when she was younger, Ignacio Escobar, and whose influence is later supplanted by yet another man, this time the angelic Federico Villena.

Back in the boarding house, Eva is greeted by her aunt, Lina, a renowned doctor to whom she has an uncanny resemblance and who, after breaking a year's silence, asks Eva to take her place in Estoril, in an extraordinary contest organized by the exclusive "Club de los silenciosos" ("Club of the silent ones"). There she must compete with nine other distinguished members in a game that requires of its participants 50,000 escudos and seven days of silence. The winner, who in the course of the week will have spoken no more than twice, will receive nine times the entry fee. If she agrees to play, Eva must ensure that the two representatives of the club who are acquainted with her aunt—Lina's former suitor, Ignacio Escobar, and the Portuguese diva Catharina de Prata—do not suspect the substitution. Without better prospects, eager to forget her grief, and keen on helping her aunt, Eva accepts the proposition, and after a brief but arduous preparation (she must be made to look older than she is), she departs for Portugal. Despite her determination to win, Eva soon discovers that the game is not only challenging, but also morally compromising. Her scruples are in the end relieved by the presence of Federico Villena, who unmasks the founders of the Club as members of an international criminal organization dealing with contraband. The guilty parties are arrested and the novel closes with a final embrace akin to "los finales de película" ("movie endings") (173).

According to Susan Lanser, "a female personal [autodiegetic] narrator risks the reader's resistance if the act of telling, the story she tells, or the self she constructs through telling it transgresses the limits of the acceptably feminine" (19). There are several ways in which Eva—a chorus girl posing as an eminent doctor—succeeds in creating a sympathetic audience partial to her rather unconventional cause of impersonating a woman who—without being the "vampiresa" ("vamp") or "femme fatale"—is reluctant to submit herself to male authority. Given that "self-interpretation," or the process by which Eva constructs and assigns meaning to her experiences, entails "engagement with the fictive [and endorsed] stories of selfhood" (Smith 47), Eva's initial task consists in overcoming what by normative standards represents a contradiction in terms: a chorus girl with high moral principles. In other words, the narrator-protagonist's task is to reconcile an irreputable and hence unauthoritative position with the respect and authority that she claims as a narrator, or with the project of self-authorization that every act of telling entails (Lanser 7). She does this by means of contrast/juxtaposition, and by inscribing the scrutiny and criticism of herself—the anticipated cultural responses to her position—into the narration.

¡Qué pesadas a veces mis compañeras! No me querían. Distinta a ellas en los gustos y ambiciones, teníanme por un bicho raro, por una especie de censor que se permitía arriesgar consejos sin invitación previa; . . . ¿Por qué declararles mi intención de abandonarlas en cuanto, al ser retirada del cartel *Rosa de Versalles*—la opereta de moda—, desapareciesen los complicados miriñaques para cederles el puesto a la ropa ligerísima? . . . ¿Por qué hacerlas caer en las muestras de respeto que, tanto en Madrid como en nuestra jira por provincias, me prodigaron los 'pelmazos' que mendigan o compran sonrisas de corista? ¿Por qué, en fin, exagerarles mi superioridad moral y física? ¿Para que me odiasen?

(What a pain my colleagues sometimes were! They didn't like me. Since my taste and ambitions were different, they saw me as a rare bird, as a kind of censor who presumed to offer unsolicited advice; . . . Why tell them my plan to abandon them as soon as the billboard for 'Rosa de Versalles'—the musical of the moment—came down, and the extravagant crinolines disappeared to be replaced with skimpy garments? . . . Why make them aware of the demonstrations of respect that, both in Madrid and in our tour of the provinces, were showered on me by the pests who beg or buy chorus girls' smiles? Why, after all, emphasize to them my moral and physical superiority? So that they would hate me?) (11)

For her companions at work and at doña Carmen's boarding house, Eva is "doña Melindres" ("Miss Fastidious"), "colegiala" ("schoolgirl"), "una muchacha desprovista de ambición" ("a girl devoid of ambition"), "un bicho raro" ("a rare bird"), and "la mosquita" ("the hypocrite"). However, through this self-presentation as a target for others' insults, the narrator-protagonist succeeds in underscoring her superior qualities (she is scrupulous, timid, unassuming . . . in short, unlike other chorus girls—a compliment, given their reputation). Furthermore, Eva—the narrator—enlists the readers as her allies by placing them in the unique position to judge and appreciate her alleged faults for the virtues they "truly" are, so they understand the criticism directed at her to be libel. "¿Qué opinarán de una fulana bella y tal, pudibunda y tal, y . . . corista?" ("What will they make of someone so pretty and all, so prudish and all—and a chorus girl?")—her colleagues demand to know as they contemplate the possibility (or implausibility) of Eva being introduced to Julio's parents. The parents, they seem to imply, would scarcely approve of a girl whose moral scruples could be no more than affectation, given her trade. "Corista. No se me olvidaba. Y antes, manicura. Y antes . . ., fracasada bachillera. Y antes aún, niña mimada de un padre coronel . . ." ("Chorus girl. I could not forget it. And before that, manicurist. And before that, a high school dropout. And before that, a colonel's pampered daughter . . .") (10). Through these initial descriptions, Eva paints a world hostile to her, a place where she doesn't belong, and conditions that she must overcome. In so doing, she vindicates her dubious experiences as a manicurist and a dancer, and exposes the adverse

circumstances that confront women lacking the protection of a family, an education or professional training when they attempt to attain a respectable position: "Un año más . . ., ¿y cuántas ilusiones menos?" ("One year more . . . and
how many dreams less?") she tells Julio even before his designs for her future
are revealed to her through Moyano. In response to her question, Julio
inquires:

> —¿Te he decepcionado ya . . .?
> —Tú no, El teatro . . .
> —El "Astoria"—corrigió el muchacho.
> —Bueno, pues el "Astoria"—accedí no muy convencida—No entré en él
> por afición, sino por casualidad, y un empleo de corista me satisface
> poquísimo, francamente. . . . Pero ¡estaba tan harta de mis veinticinco meses
> de manicura, que mi 'suerte' me deslumbró al principio! Y ya ves: salvo en
> el deslumbramiento—que se desvaneció—, continúo como entonces: tres
> pasos a la derecha, una vuelta; tres pasos a la izquierda, otra vuelta; dos
> pasos adelante, una reverencia. . .

> ("Have I disappointed you . . .?"
> "Not you, the theater . . . "
> "The 'Astoria,'" the young man corrected.
> "Fine, then the 'Astoria,'" I conceded, unconvinced. "I did not join it by
> inclination, but by chance, and frankly, working as a chorus girl does not
> satisfy me very much. . . . But I was so sick of my twenty-five months as a
> manicurist that my 'luck' blinded me at first! And now you see: except for
> the blindness—that disappeared—it's just the same old thing: three steps to
> the right, a turn; three steps to the left, another turn; two steps forward, a
> curtsy. . .") (14)

Yet even as the other chorus girls serve merely to accentuate Eva's superior qualities, the fact that someone as virtuous as she is a member of a theater
troupe shows the preconceived notions about women of her occupation to be
less than infallible. Conscious of the prejudices against her profession, which,
as she doesn't fail to point out, is not a consequence of vocation, but of
"improvisation" (as was her previous performance as a manicurist), and
which nonetheless elicits disapproval from her family, Eva is torn between
interpreting her circumstances in light of existing conventions and acting
upon what she considers to be her moral obligation (even if this entails dissent from the norm). That the two should be in conflict is telling in and of
itself. Prior to departing for Moyano's house, Eva invites the other lodgers to
a celebration of her birthday, not because she feels festive, nor because she
likes her housemates, but because she wants to exercise control over how others (within and outside the diegesis) perceive her; basically, she wants to
prove that she doesn't spend her free nights in unseemly diversions: "Deseaba
testigos para mi regreso" ("I wanted witnesses for my return") (24). When her

return is delayed because she and another lodger, Ino Galván (alias Federico Villena), are stuck in the elevator, Eva laments: "Aspiraban a sorprenderme en alguna escapatoria propia de corista, y . . . los he complacido" ("They hoped to catch me in some escapade fit for a chorus girl, and . . . I've given them that satisfaction") (31).

The scene in the elevator advances yet another of Eva's questionable views regarding the constraints inherent in the feminine condition, namely, that for a woman, the alternative to following the prescribed mold is just as menacing as the scripted passage itself. One allows for no agency, the other offers no security. In narrative terms, it's the difference between closure and indeterminacy. The time spent in the elevator is thus construed as a metaphor for Eva's yet undecided future, even if the suggested uncertainty is provisional: "No sé lo que haré mañana. Me siento como colgada en el aire" ("I don't know what I will do tomorrow. I feel suspended in mid-air") (34). Arguably, Eva's voice gives the narrative the illusion of openness that the plot, in keeping with its marital teleology, is bound to curtail (Lanser 32). On the other hand, the dissent from the norm, perceived as a reaction rather than a choice, is likewise confining. In this respect, Eva and her aunt Lina's distinct "formations" offer two sides of the same impasse that precludes women from forging their own destiny—possibilities that prove limiting, and limitations that can only be construed as choices by misrecognition.

If Estrella's exemplarity entails the mending of her flaws, Eva's demands the reconciliation of dissenting views. Accordingly, while in *Un marido a precio fijo*, the transformation from "negative" to "positive" model is embodied by a single character, *Como los hombres nos quieren* presents a "double structure" or "a cluster of apprenticeships," wherein the meaning of each one emerges through contrast with the others (Suleiman 84). Of the three—Eva, her aunt Lina, and her roommate Rita—only the latter is presented as an unambiguously negative model. An accomplished dancer, Rita lacks Eva's sense of propriety and is revealed as spiteful, dishonest, and morally inferior. She conspires behind Eva's back and later accepts Moyano's proposition herself. Her hands are greasy, her voice is unmodulated, her words are brazen, her behavior is scandalous, and her appearance is compared to an exotic bird out of its natural habitat. Lina, on the other hand, presents a "negative" role model only insofar as her life's story does not lead to the conventional happy end. Because Lina's choices are not crowned by happiness, and because they anticipate those that Eva has to make, the narrator-protagonist can both sympathize with and learn from Lina. Given that they share the same name (<u>Evange</u>lina, suggesting an angel suspended between them), are physically almost identical and are courted by the same man (Ignacio Escobar), their stories may be read as alternative representations of a single character, or as a continuum, since Eva's transformation entails the integration (to a point) of Lina's experiences.

Still in the elevator, which remains suspended for the better half of the night, Eva recounts the story of her and her aunt's thwarted dreams to the only other character in the story that merits her approval, Inocencio Galván (whose true identity as Federico Villena is concealed until the near-end).

> ¿Qué pensaría de lo ocurrido esta noche mi tía Lina, la generosa mujer que sacrificara al bienestar de su madre y hermanas sus íntimos anhelos? Como yo, tan sólo conoció del amor lo que en él hay de amargo. . . . Pudo casarse con un compañero . . . pero no evitaron el desacuerdo. . . . Ella se aferraba a Neila, e Ignacio Escobar, que paró en Neila seis meses, acariciaba proyectos ambiciosos. . .

> (What would my aunt Lina, the generous woman who sacrificed her own longings for her mother's and sisters' well-being, think about what happened tonight? Like me, all she knew of love was its bitter side. . . . She could have married[2] a colleague . . . but they couldn't agree. . . . She clung to [the town of] Neila, while Ignacio Escobar, who stayed in Neila for six months, harbored ambitious projects. . .) (35)

Through this digression, the reader learns how, unable or unwilling to abandon her mother and two sisters, Lina tried to persuade Ignacio to stay with her; how since both were doctors, she hoped their relationship would grow into a collaboration that combined family life with work, and how, despite her efforts, he left. In his absence, Lina became a co-proprietor of one of the world's leading spas, but her professional accomplishments failed to assuage her unsuccessful attempt to reconcile marriage and a career. To Ino's inquiry, "¿Y duda usted de la suerte de esa señora?" ("And do you doubt that lady's luck?") Eva responds with a staple: "¿Cree, Ino, que un balneario basta para hacer feliz a una mujer?" ("Do you think, Ino, that a spa is enough to make a woman happy?"). But what begins as a cultural given ends with a criticism directed at the curtailing of female education to socialization: "Tan feliz se consideraba mi tía, que a ello le debo la suspensión de mis estudios. . . . No me quiso sabia . . ., y me convertí en vicetiple. . ." ("Such was my aunt's happiness that she kept me from completing my studies. . . . She didn't want me to be learned . . ., and so I became a chorus girl") (35). However, it is not her aunt that Eva blames for her subsequent hurdles, but Ignacio Escobar—a man who, while courting Lina, makes a pass at her niece. Thus the final vindication of Eva's unseemly employment is her devotion to Lina (for it is to remove herself as an obstacle to her aunt's already precarious chance for happiness that Eva settles in Madrid). By the same token, the primary cause of her trials is Escobar's treachery.

When the two women finally meet again, on the night following Eva's encounter with Moyano and three years after her flight from Neila, each tries to

---

[2] Although the choice of "pudo" in the original suggests that Lina marries Ignacio Escobar, there is no evidence prior to or after this point in the narrative to substantiate such an interpretation.

make amends for any inadvertent harm done to the other. Lina reproaches her-self for her niece's tumultuous present, saying, "con mi oposición a que con-cluyeras el Bachillerato y estudiases carrera te arrebaté los medios de labrarte una situación" ("with my opposition to your completing high school and pursu-ing a career, I took away your means of carving out a future for yourself") (47), while Eva feels accountable for her aunt's spinsterhood: "Si nada admití de lo que mi tía ofrecióme al separarnos fue sencillamente porque los remordimien-tos me lo impidieron. . . . ¡Ya había despojado a la infeliz de algo de más valor que el dinero" ("If I didn't accept anything my aunt offered me when we sepa-rated, it was simply because I was prevented by remorse. . . . I had already taken from her something worth more than money") (43). But the more they scruti-nize the intentions behind their actions and the opposite consequences that these brought, the more apparent the narrow range of their possibilities becomes and the more obvious are the power relations implicit in gendered codes of behav-ior. Thus, in laying bare her motives for suspending Eva's studies—to ensure her niece's happiness—Lina reproduces the judgments attributed to the *vedette*, Gracia Dorado, whose validity has now been espoused by the protagonist:

> Apenas pude atenderte en los seis años que en casa pasaste. . . . Pero, eso sí: te he querido siempre, tal vez por egoísmo . . . ¿No posees mis ojos, y mi pelo, y mi voz, y mis facciones? ¿Cómo no aspirar a verte feliz? En Neila no lo hubieras sido, y de doctora en Medicina, ni en Neila ni en parte alguna. . . . Te preferí casada, rodeada de niños. . . . Y para esta profesión, el excesivo talento estorba. . . . ¿Qué ilusión resiste a nuestra manía de pensar y pesar? La mujer, cuanto menos ilustrada, menos complicada tam-bién, más primitiva y, por tanto, más dichosa. Cumple sin rechistar ni dol-erse esa ley natural que la decreta arcilla para el escultor Hombre. . .
> ¡Con diferentes palabras, la madura doctora Carlés expresaba la misma idea que Gracia Dorado, la 'estrella' de 'Astoria'!
> —Sí, tía—aprobé—. Nos rebelemos o no, somos como ellos nos qui-eren.

> ("I could barely attend to you in the six years that you spent at home. . . . But there is one thing of which I am sure: I have always loved you, perhaps out of selfishness. . . . Don't you have my eyes, my hair, my voice, and my features? How could I not hope to see you happy? In Neila you would not have been happy, nor would you have been happy as a medical doctor, whether in Neila or anywhere else. . . . I thought you would be better off mar-ried, surrounded by children. . . . And for that profession, excessive talent gets in the way. . . . What dreams can withstand our mania for thinking and weighing? The less enlightened, less complicated a woman is, the more primitive, and therefore happier, she is. Without question or scruple she ful-fills the natural law that decrees she must be clay for Man, the sculptor. . ."
> With different words, the mature doctor Carlés expressed the same idea as Gracia Dorado, the 'star' of 'Astoria'!

"Yes, Aunt," I agreed. "Whether or not we rebel, we are just the way men want us.") (48)

Eva's positive apprenticeship entails the supplanting of the given interpreta-tion—one that betrays the coercive and hierarchical nature of the prevailing gender ideology—by the normative formulation that imbues female subordi-nation with a positive meaning. In other words, Eva must go from resisting to desiring the confinement implicit in the embodiment of assigned gender roles and reinforce the endorsed view of "feminine surrender" as voluntary rather than compulsory.

The anticipated transformation comes, once again, as a consequence of love, the supreme disciplinarian. However, I would like to contend that in obeying this gender and genre imperative, the novel remains open to interpre-tation. The fact that at the end Eva reformulates tía Evangelina and Gracia Dorado's assertions (instead of simply restating them as has been the case up to this point in the narrative) speaks more of the need to reconcile the dissent-ing views that motivate the character than of the refutation of the original thesis. Thus when Federico Villena makes the claim, "—Creo en ti. . . . Y en que, aun a pesar tuyo, serás como yo quiero que seas. . ." ("'I believe in you. . . . And I believe that, even in spite of yourself, you will be as I want you to be. . .'") (155), Eva (quite in keeping with her role of "censor" (11)), uses the opportunity to make amends for the view that permeates the rest of the narrative: " —¿Cómo. . .?—susurré con un recuerdo a tía Evangelina, a Gracia Dorado, a tantas y tantas mujeres que, menos afortunadas que yo, no alcanzaron el goce de amoldarse, no a la voluntad del varón, sino a la del hombre amado y digno" ("'How?' I whispered, remembering Aunt Evangelina, and Gracia Dorado, and so, so many women who, less fortunate than I, had not had the pleasure of molding themselves, not to the will of the male, but to that of the beloved and worthy man") (155). Perhaps the most readily available reading of this statement is "capitulation" (Labanyi, "Romancing" 4), but "capitulation" understood less as a "defeat" than a man-ifestation of a number of operating constraints that curtail narrative possibili-ties. Eva's pronouncement may also be read as an attempt to mollify feminine surrender by insisting that it be to a worthy man; or as a denunciation meant to underscore that "tantas y tantas mujeres" ("so, so many women") are vic-tims of existing models of female socialization; and finally as a sign of tex-tual indeterminacy or of a reluctance on the part of the narrator-protagonist to divest her story of complexity in favor of any one interpretation. Thus, Federico's assertion which Eva interrupts and which I have likewise delayed, reads as: " —Creo en ti. . . . Y en que, aun a pesar tuyo, serás como yo quiero que seas. . . [Eva's response]—feliz" ("'I believe in you. . . . And I believe that, even in spite of yourself, you will be as I want you to be. . .' [. . .]—'happy'") (155). The effect of this hiatus, introduced by Eva, is twofold: it places emphasis on the part of Federico's claim that is consonant with Gracia Dorado and tía Evangelina's allegation—that women are as men want them to be; and it portends Eva's resolution to assimilate the prescribed ideal. In addition, the deferred reference to "happiness" renders it secondary in a way that can be read as either irrelevant or given. The latter interpretation would be in keeping with the genre, where legitimate love invariably leads to happiness, but if this is so, happiness is not something to which Eva yields unreluctantly:

> Me detuve a corta distancia del ventanal de la biblioteca. Sonaba la masculina voz de Federico, definitivo factor originario de mi dicha o de mi espiritual hundimiento. Y sentí miedo . . ., un miedo en cierto modo dulce, grato, pues que nacía de la seguridad de mi amor, que transformaba en dios a un hombre, como yo juguete de lo que en el libro de nuestras vidas estuviera escrito.

> (I stopped a short distance away from the window of the library. I could hear Federico's masculine voice, the determining factor in my happiness or spiritual demise. I was afraid . . . in a way that was sweet, and pleasant, as it was born from the security of my love, which transformed a man into a god and me into a plaything of whatever might be written in the book of our lives.) (170)

The representation of male heroes in so-called women's literature warrants a separate study. Here I would only like to remark that both Federico and Miguel (*Un marido a precio fijo*) resemble enlightened despots, men who impose their will without violence (at least, overt violence), infusing their authority instead with the didactic intent and impartiality of someone who knows what is best and is determined to act in the name of higher values, as opposed to self-interest. Both embody all that is "good," which ensures that their own goals and ambitions are attended to by "fortune" or "destiny." Both are willing to make concessions (provided that the desired outcome is secured). Having married Estrella after inheriting her entire fortune, Miguel nobly waits until she is ready to assume her conjugal duties without availing himself of any of her former possessions. Federico, likewise, gives Eva the benefit of the doubt in a number of compromising situations, and when she shows determination to leave the "Astoria," he hints at the possibility of lucrative employment elsewhere: "Quizá logre otra cosa, un empleo brillante bien remunerado y hasta divertido. . . . Si no ofreciera peligros, la recomendaría a Federico Villena, el jefe de la Casa 'Vibra'" ("Perhaps you will find something else, a great job, well paid and even fun. . . . If it weren't dangerous, I would recommend you to Federico Villena, the boss of the Casa 'Vibra'") (36). As Eva later discovers, Inocencio Galván (the man to whom these words are attributed and whose acquaintance Eva makes at doña Carmen's boarding house) and Federico Villena (one of the ten participants in "el juego de silencio" ("the game of silence") in Estoril) are one and the same person. The dangers alluded to by Ino, a.k.a. Federico, are professional—Federico collaborates with the police in the fight against the black market using three different names for cover: "Inocencio, Juan, Ramón, . . . son tres en una persona" ("Inocencio, Juan and Ramón, are three persons in one") (152), he tells Eva in anticipation of his transformation into her idol /"dios" ("god") (170). However, from what we are given to understand, la Casa Vibra is an antique store that Federico has inherited from his father, where Eva may indeed find gainful employment (or will she?): "Abandonaremos el oficio [de detective] para dedicarnos a la abogacía y a cuidar floreros isabelinos y otros objetos de arte, como, por ejemplo . . . niños de carne y hueso" ("We will give up the job [of being detectives] to dedicate ourselves to practicing law and caring for Isabeline vases and other art objects, like, for example . . . children of flesh and blood") (171). Or else, she may form part of his unique collection: "Como mi padre coleccionó objetos artísticos que le sorbieron los sesos y el capital, yo colecciono individuos al margen de la ley. . ." ("As my father collected artistic objects that drained his brain and capital, I collect individuals on the edge of the law. . .") (152). Not exactly on the margin of the law, she is very much on the social fringes, and without his intervention, she is in danger of being introduced into a criminal world, thanks to her remarkable, and not unproblematic, gift for acting.

It may seem counterintuitive in the context of post-war romance fiction to think of "femininity" in terms of practice, and of prescribed models of womanhood in terms of "performance"; however, such readings are quite in keeping with the rhetoric of the time, which encouraged women toward "el disimulo" or "dissembling." To quote Martín Gaite:

> En nuestro paso por las dependencias de Servicios Sociales nos instaba, efectivamente a disfrazarnos de Dulcineas, sin dejar de ser Aldonza Lorenzo. Y durante aquellos ensayos, demasiado largos para lo mal que luego salía la función, ambos disfraces nos pesaban por postizos e irreconciliables. Nos enseñaba, en resumidas cuentas, a representar. No a ser. (64)

> (In our passage through the departments of Social Services, they urged us to disguise ourselves as Dulcinea, but still be Aldonza Lorenzo. And during those rehearsals (far too long for the deplorable quality of the subsequent performance), both disguises weighed down on us because they were false and incompatible. In short, they taught us to play-act. Not to be.)[3]

---

[3] See Margaret Jones' translation of *Usos amorosos* (Lewisburg, PA: Bucknell UP, 2004) 61.

Thus the fact that Ignacio Escobar praises Eva's "arte de representar" ("art of acting") (143), that as a protagonist she graduates from on- to off-stage performance, and that as a narrator she reproduces the view that womanhood entails the embodiment of prescribed ideals (Gracia Dorado enacts the condition of a "vedette" in the same way that others enact the role of a wife or a madwoman—"[t]anto presumir de personalidad y somos sencillamente, hija mía, como los hombres nos quieren") ("[w]e think we have so much personality, my child, but we are just the way men want us"), all seem to suggest that in marrying, Eva assumes a role that haunts her narrative like the shadow or "la Sombra" of Inocencio Galván, a.k.a. Federico Villena (25, 172).

"No puede una mujer sentirse placenteramente feliz" ("A woman cannot feel joyfully happy") reads a women's advice column, "si no es bajo el cobijo de una sombra más fuerte. Más fuerte en todo: en lo sentido y en lo imaginado. Precisa nuestra feminidad sentirse frágil y protegida" ("if she is not under the protection of a stronger presence [literally, "a shadow"]. Stronger in every sense: in what is felt and what is imagined. Our femininity exacts that we feel fragile and protected").[4] In keeping with this cultural narrative, Federico Villena possesses all the qualities necessary to make Eva's surrender desirable and expedient. However, in a move that departs from the institutionalized view, Eva's narrative construes protection as vigilance: "por lo visto nada ignoraba de mí" ("evidently there was nothing he didn't know about me") (30); "lograba ya desasosegarme con su disimulada, pero continua vigilancia" ("he was making me uneasy with his disguised, but continuous vigilance") (92); "¿Por qué hasta cuando no me miraba sentía girar en torno a mi persona el interés del joven?" ("Why even when he was not watching me did I feel the young man's interest revolving around me?") (98). Thus Federico's role of guardian presupposes a degree of surveillance and intervention that are not always welcome: "Pero usted no tiene derecho. . . . Yo se lo prohíbo. . . . ¡Ya es demasiada intromisión la suya!" ("But you don't have the right. . . . I forbid you. . . . Your meddling has gone far enough!") (37). Christened as "la Sombra" ("the Shadow") by Eva and her companions from the Astoria, his shadow looms over the text as a diffuse presence that both monitors and legitimates its function. While on the level of the story, Federico, the police aide and soon-to-be lawyer, ensures that good triumphs over evil; on the level of discourse he prefigures the reader, understood as an implied censor or "the representative of the dominant order, the arbiter of the ideology of gender and its stories of selfhood" (Smith 49). In this respect, "La Sombra" ("the Shadow") refers to the presence that haunts Eva from the fringes to the heart of the narrative, where the game of silence unfolds.

---

[4] See *Medina*'s column "Consúltame" ("Consult me") June 13, 1943 (qtd in *Usos amorosos* 50).

Despite the fact that "mass cultural texts" were under closer scrutiny than the perceived "high art forms," and despite the "hyper-politicization of culture with censors, artists, and public keen to read the political into everything" (Graham and Labanyi 214), to my knowledge, no political[5] readings have been applied to the novels classified as "rosa" save for those that trace correspondence between such texts and hegemonic value systems. One obvious explanation is the convention of the genre, the ready-made interpretations of which have all too often come to replace close readings of the actual texts. Hence, I would like to conclude the present analysis by suggesting that *Como los hombres nos quieren* may be read as an allegory of the political circumstances of its production, characterized and defined by surveillance, censorship, and the manufacture of consent through silencing.

Two-thirds of the novel takes place in Estoril where Eva, trying to pass for her aunt, participates in the game of silence. Organized under the auspices of the so-called "Club de los Silenciosos" ("Club of the Silent Ones"), its participants are all distinguished members of society, a cosmopolitan minority, presided over by the Brazilian Hilario Pimenteira and his right-hand man, Ignacio Escobar. Upon her arrival in Estoril, Eva learns that the organization is dedicated to cultivating "reservas espirituales" ("spiritual reserves")[6] and to raising its members' moral resistance and ability to confront adversities by abstaining from speaking. Gradually, however, as the narrative unfolds and protection manifests itself as vigilance, the purported moral resistance becomes resistance to morality.

The game restricts its members to seven days of imposed silence during which it is their duty to monitor each other, to induce others to speak, and to denounce the infractors. The club's threshold posts the sign: "Prohibido el uso de la palabra" ("Use of words prohibited"). Inside the "palacete" ("country house"), the walls are adorned by further reminders of the prescribed guidelines: "Las paredes oyen. . . . Si habláis a solas para desahogaros, pagaréis *prenda*" ("The walls have ears. . . . If you talk in private to let off steam, you will suffer the consequences") (80).[7] In the library, Eva encounters more

---

[5] I am using the term in its strict sense, defined as "of or pertaining to the state or its government." *The Random House College Dictionary* 1027.

[6] The term "la reserva espiritual de occidente" ("the spiritual reserve of the west") formed part of national-Catholic rhetoric to designate Spain and its unique spiritual mission.

[7] "Las Prendas," also known as "Antón Pirulero," was the name of a popular game that functions as an intertext to Eva's narrative (and for the games in which her narrative engages). Following the rules of the game, its members select a profession or "oficio" and mimic/interpret it while a person chosen as its "orchestrator" or "conductor" sings "Antón, Antón, Antón pirulero/ cada cual, cada cual, atienda a su juego" ("Antón, Antón, Antón Pirulero / everybody, everybody, attend to your game"). Those who fail to act out their part are made to pay "la prenda" ("guaranty or security, but in this case, a punishment"): "y el que no atienda,/pagará una prenda" ("and he who doesn't attend/ will pay the guaranty [suffer the punishment]"). A player

caveats: "varios avisos nos informaban de la prohibición de leer, de escribir y de salir del Club sin ir acompañados de dos o más personas" ("several notices informed us of the prohibition against reading, writing, and leaving the Club without being accompanied by two or more people") (84). Thus, among the effects of "el juego del silencio" ("the game of silence") and the vigilance that it induces in its members is a heightened sense of self-awareness, a fomenting of alternative means of communication, and a continuous need to interpret others' silence(s).

In spite of her disapproval of the game and its strategies, Eva continues to take part in it out of a perceived sense of duty to her aunt and her determination to win 500,000 escudos, a considerable sum, with which she hopes to open a boutique, "Eva. Vestidos. Abrigos. Modas" ("Eva. Dresses. Coats. Fashions") (90):

> Pero ¿podía yo, el más insignificante de sus miembros, protestar, rebe-larme? Debí suponer que una cantidad de dinero como la que exponíamos no caería en nuestras manos como el chorrillo de agua de una fuente. . . . Desazonada y temblorosa, me repetí la necesidad de ganar, de defender los cincuenta mil escudos de tía Lina, de mantenerme vigilante para no incurrir en falta. . . . ¿Qué sería de mí si fracasaba?

> (But could I, the most insignificant of its members, protest, rebel? I had to suppose that the quantity of money at stake would not just fall into our hands like water from a fountain. . . . Uneasy and trembling, I kept remind-ing myself of the need to win, to protect Aunt Lina's fifty thousand escudos, to remain vigilant so as not to incur punishment. . . . What would become of me if I failed?) (101)

Despite the prohibition, Eva resolves to write to her aunt. She does so in the middle of the night, behind closed doors, wary of her light drawing others' attention, and willing to take the risk that she will be able to post the letter undetected:

> . . . y aunque sé que así falto contra el Reglamento del Club, me encierro para escribirte antes de acostarme y, también a escondidas, trataré mañana de echar la carta. ¿Que no tengo derecho a engañar a unos señores que exponen un capital en el juego? Desde luego, tía. . . . Pero se comportan ellos de un modo tan raro, tan fuera de lo corriente y de lo recto, que los adivino capaces de cualquier cosa peor para apoderarse del dinero.

---

is disqualified if he or she fails more than three times. At the end, those who lose are assigned their "prenda" or punishment. Interestingly, the protagonist's first words are directed to the person in charge of announcing the start of the show behind the scenes, the program seller and informant, Antón, whom Eva christens as "Pirulero":—"¡No . . ., no abras, 'Pirulero'!" ("No . . . don't open, 'Pirulero'!") 5.

(. . . and although I know that in doing so I am breaking the Rules of the Club, I am shutting myself in so that I may write to you before I go to bed, and tomorrow I will try to send the letter secretly. Don't I have the right to trick a few gentlemen who wager so much capital in the game? Of course not, Aunt. . . . But they act so strangely, so far from what is ordinary and upright, that I suspect them capable of doing much worse just to get their hands on the money.) (105)

Again, it is on the superior grounds of morality that an infraction is justified and a transgression is recast as an obligation. But the license that Eva grants herself entails limits, as inscribed in her letter are the constraints under which she produces it: "Sin tranquilidad ni tiempo para contarte todo lo que quisi-era—temo que si no apago la luz sospechen y me vigilen—, me limitaré a . . ." ("Without peace or time to tell you everything that I would like—I fear that if I don't turn off the light they will suspect and watch me—, I will limit myself to . . .") (105).

As the story progresses, Eva finds herself in a greater predicament than merely playing a game, the rules of which she disapproves. Believing herself a witness to a crime, she is torn between denouncing it (and thereby disquali-fying herself from the game) and keeping quiet (so as not to compromise her chances of winning). But even as the burden of the choice is conveniently lifted from her (by no other than Federico Villena), it remains plain that the narrative construes silence as a form of complicity, while at the same time exposing the risks involved in breaking it. Thus, it is in curious contrast to all of her roles as "muda confidente" ("mute confidante") (25), the silent per-former (chorus girl), and the silent representative of her aunt, that Eva's is the sole voice heard, the one that mitigates and interprets others', always self-reflexive and ever so cautious.

9

Carmen de Icaza's *Soñar la vida* or the Imperative to Dream

The title of Carmen de Icaza's 1941 novel, *Soñar la vida*, evokes one of the persistent charges leveled at *novelas rosa*: that of escapism. According to Icaza's contemporary, writer and critic Eugenia Serrano, the authors of *novelas rosa* were ersatz apothecaries dealing in bogus dreams to lighten the yoke of quotidian grievances. That is, the reading of *novelas rosa*, as Serrano's disingenuous "Elogio a la novela rosa" ("Praise of the *novela rosa*") suggests,[1] had the insalubrious effect, not unlike sedatives, of drawing young women, especially the women of the lower middle classes, into a counterfeit world of happy endings, far from their crude reality. What follows is an excerpt from the aforementioned article which helps to elucidate the nature of the controversy over the social value and impact that *novelas rosa* purportedly bore on their female audiences:

> Un tranvía de los que hacen el trayecto Progreso–Cuatro Caminos. En un rincón, acurrucada, una mujercita. Tal vez, en su juventud más temprana, haya sido hermosa; tal vez aun sea joven. Pero cuando la vida es dura, la comida poca y las preocupaciones muchas, no hay juventud posible, ni cutis terso, ni cuerpo esponjado, ni ojos y cabello brillantes. . . . Pero suben los últimos viajeros de este principio o final de trayecto, el conductor arranca, y la mujercita saca de su derrengado bolsillo negro un libro encuadernado en rústica. Comienza a leer ávidamente, con un apetito casi físico. A los tres minutos de la lectura es otra . . .
>
> En el hogar estrecho, mal ventilado, insuficiente a la familia numerosa, todos se quejarán del calor; la mujercita no lo sentirá. Ella está en Saint-Moritz . . ., esquiando sobre la nieve eternamente pura. La comida resultó escasa y desabrida para todos; ella no lo sabe. Está bebiendo champán y picoteando vacilante entre una cena fría y un té completo, deliciosos, con pastelería digna de las hadas, servido en uno de esos saloncitos lujosos y confidenciales que ella conoce muy bien . . . por las novelas. . . . Maravilloso mundo sin miseria, sin malos olores, sin facturas por pagar, sin más enfer-

---

[1] The article is dedicated to Carmen de Icaza, the Linares sisters, Julia Maura, and Rafael Pérez y Perez. See *La estafeta literaria* 36 (Nov. 15, 1945).

medades que el leve accidente de automóvil. Bienaventurado mundo, donde los ricos son generosos y los pobres resignados.

Tierras de tarjeta postal, pobladas por galanes caballerosos, madrinas millonarias y jóvenes puras. Tierras, en las que la mujercita vive más que en la realidad, y cuyo ensueño le da fuerzas para soportar su oscura vida de chica sin bienestar y sin amor. Cuando se piensa en sir Rodolf, o el conde Andrescu, o Oscar, el dorado campeón de tenis, ¡qué importan los groseros galanes de la vida real! Las novelas rosa la preparan bien para una altanera soltería, mientras no venga el príncipe soñado; ese ser correcto, al que nunca se verá en mangas de camiseta, tomando el fresco, como en este momento hace el gordo vecino de enfrente.

(A tram on the Progreso–Cuatro Caminos route. In a corner, hunched over, a little woman. Perhaps, in the earliest flower of youth, she was pretty; perhaps she is still young. But when life is hard, food scarce and worries plentiful, there is no youth, nor smooth skin, nor tender body, nor shining eyes and hair. . . . But the last passengers board at this beginning or end of the route, the driver puts the tram in motion, and the little woman takes a paperback out of her threadbare black purse. She begins to read avidly, with an almost physical appetite. After three minutes' reading she is transformed . . .

In her cramped, poorly ventilated home, too small for the large family, everyone will complain about the heat, [but] the little woman won't feel it. She is in Saint-Moritz . . ., skiing on the eternally pure snow. At home, the meal is insipid and scant, [but] she has no idea. She is drinking champagne and idly nibbling on a delicious cold dinner and tea with pastries worthy of fairies, served in one of those luxurious, private little salons that she knows so well . . . from novels. . . . Marvelous world without poverty, without bad smells, without bills, without sicknesses or injury other than an occasional automobile accident. Blessed world, where the rich are generous and the poor resigned.

Postcard lands, populated with courteous gentlemen, millionaire godmothers and pure youths. Lands in which the little woman lives more than she does in reality, whose enchantment gives her strength to endure the lackluster life of a girl without means and without love. When she thinks of Sir Rodolf, or Count Andrescu, or Oscar, the bronzed tennis champion, the vulgar beaus of real life cease to matter. The *novelas rosa* prepare her well for a dignified spinsterhood while she waits for Prince Charming to come, that flawless being who would never be seen in his undershirt, catching the breeze, as the portly neighbor across the street is doing at this moment.) (Serrano 5)

In keeping with this argument, the escapism fomented by popular romance novels had the effect of at once perpetuating the status quo (a criticism masquerading as the rhetoric of social injustice) and distracting young women from fulfilling their transcendental mission (as future wives and mothers). Their ultimate perfidy was supplanting the incentive for action with an irresponsible complacency.

In light of this debate over the functions and uses of *novela rosa*, I propose to read Carmen de Icaza's novel as an instance of position-taking, a stand homologous to Icaza's concurrently dominated and dominant position within the literary field as a bestselling author of popular romance fictions, and as a political activist, an elite member of *Sección Femenina*.[2] As such, *Soñar la vida* appropriates the criticism leveled at *novela rosa* only to give it a positive spin, that is, that dreams are the foundation of change. Drawing on the official view of literature as a vehicle of indoctrination, Icaza imbues the practice of romance writing with political and social commitment, rewriting reality as the materialization of a dream, and the dream itself as an injunction to action.

The novel's protagonist is 30-year-old Teresa Sandoval, whose multiple roles are marked by different appellations. As Teresa, she is a "mujer sensata" ("sensible woman"), "práctica" ("practical"), "realizadora" ("productive"), "seria y de valer" ("serious and of worth") (23). Being the daughter of the president of "la Real Academia de la Historia" (who, as she puts it, "emancipated" her through a sterling education (33)), she is also a *bas bleu* (32, 42) or a *chica rara* ("[c]allada, tristona, insignificante") ("[q]uiet, sad, insignificant") (31). Her view of the world is mediated by glasses—an expedient sign of distinction pointing at once toward the book knowledge and idealism that inform her conduct (33). It is Teresa, and not her brothers, who, when left in abeyance by the death of their parents, intrepidly fends for them all. Last but not least, she is co-founder and director of the women's magazine *Feminidades ("Femininities")*, as well as a trained nurse, who is wounded saving the life of a nationalist soldier in the Civil War. Under the pen name of Juan Iraeta, Teresa is the writer of bestselling *novelas blancas* ("white novels")[3] translated and adapted to film around the world. And as "Resa" she is "merely" a woman—someone who longs to love and be loved—like the protagonists of her own novels.[4]

The feminine ideal embodied by the protagonist of *Soñar la vida* comes closest to the model of womanhood espoused by the leaders of *Sección Femenina*, who saw themselves as architects and agents of change. In light of the heroine's unambiguous subscription to the Falangist ethos, the resonance between her name, Teresa, and that of the patron saint of *Sección Femenina*—Teresa of Avila—would not have been lost on Icaza's readers. A 1938 pronouncement made by Pilar Primo de Rivera explained the affinity between St Teresa and *Sección Femenina* in the following terms:

---

[2] Icaza was among the *Sección Femenina*'s founding members, and her prestige was secured by her privileged background and social provenance.

[3] On the relationship between "novela rosa" and "novela blanca," see pages 87–89 above.

[4] Suggestively, the title of one of Iraeta's novels is "Er, sie und ich" ("He, She and I") (53), bearing a resemblance to the protagonist's tripartite vision of herself as Juan, Teresa, and Resa.

La escogimos para protectora nuestra por su santidad, y porque ella, con su sabiduría, es una de las mujeres que más gloria han dado a España. Y la escogimos también porque vosotras, camaradas de las Secciones Femeninas, tenéis, como ella, misión de fundadoras. Tenéis que enseñar por todas las tierras de España el ansia de Nuestra Revolución. Tenéis que andar[5] por todos los caminos y llevar a todos los espíritus este modo de ser que nos enseñó José Antonio. Pero de una manera callada, sin exhibiciones y sin discursos, porque estas cosas no son propias de mujeres, sino, sencilla-mente, como lo hizo Teresa. Con espíritu misionero y nacionalsindicalista, iréis[6] llevando por todas las tierras que conquistan los soldados de Franco el calor y la hermandad de nuestra doctrina.

(We chose her as our protector because of her sanctity, and because she, with her wisdom, is one of the women who has given most glory to Spain. And we chose her also because you, comrades of the Women's Section, have, like her, the mission of founders. You must teach the urgency of Our Revolution through all the lands of Spain. You have to walk all of the paths and carry to every soul this way of being that José Antonio taught us. Only quietly, without spectacle or speeches, because these things are not proper for women, but simply, like Teresa. Filled with a missionary and national-syndicalist spirit, you will go, carrying the warmth and brotherhood of our doctrine through all the lands that are being conquered by the soldiers of Franco.) (Primo de Rivera, *Escritos* 106)

As this exhortation makes clear, the sixteenth-century nun was chosen not merely for her canonical stature but for her historically unconventional role as a reformer and founder of a Discalced Carmelite order. The connection estab-lished between the saint's unorthodox trajectory and that of the organization's leading members merits further elaboration. Binding them across centuries is the rhetoric of self-abasement wherein the only acceptable means of voicing one's ambitions, merits, and/or accomplishments (when the voice alone may be construed as a breach of authority) is by stressing one's unworthiness (Weber 46–50). Its operative words, so faithful to and yet so revealing of the hierarchy implicit in the reactionary gender ideology, are "quietly," "simply," and "without spectacle," to which we might add "meekly," "humbly," "self-effacingly." Thus the parallel drawn between St Teresa and the leaders of the organization extends from "content" (what: to found, preach, and convert, which while unacknowledged, are demonstrations of exceptional conduct) to "form" (how: silently, unselfishly, without display). In this necessarily para-doxical insistence on greatness and humility, the former is always an attribute

---

[5] Incidentally, Teresa's last name is made up of the verb "andar"—"to walk" (S-*ando*-val→S-*I walk*-val) and if one were to pursue such correspondence even further, her pen name "Iraeta" includes the verb "to go" – "ir."

[6] See note above.

of the other—the ideal (God, fatherland, man)—to which the speaker (a nun, a falangist, a woman), identified by the latter quality, must submit herself. As we shall see, a similar logic is operative in the novel, whose heroine's prerogative to act is indivisible from her unconditional surrender to the good of Spain and her loved ones.

Following the by now familiar argument, *Sección Femenina*'s proselytizing zeal may be regarded as a lay form of apostleship. If St Teresa founded and reformed a women's religious order, the members of *Sección Femenina* were called to found and reform women's political and social roles. An analogous task is carried out by Teresa, the protagonist of *Soñar la vida*, whose serial publications and bestselling novels allow her to shape and edify the hearts and minds of her vast audiences. However, our discussion of the relationship between Icaza's heroine and the patron saint of *Sección Femenina* would be incomplete without a reference to St Teresa's own relationship to the sixteenth-century equivalent of the bestseller. In her *Libro de la vida,* Teresa confesses her fondness for the then popular *libros de caballería* ("novels of chivalry"), a pastime she picked up from and shared with her mother, and one that is presented sympathetically in the surprisingly familiar light of escapism or coping mechanism. "Teresa's mother apparently read the novels of chivalry in the same way that many women now read sentimental romances, such as those in the Harlequin series," remarks Carole A. Slade. "By giving them hope, even if unrealistic, for improvement, the fantasy world of the novels encouraged these readers to remain in their real-life situations" (304). Such was Teresa's own attachment to this pastime that she felt deprived without it—"Era tan en extremo lo que en esto me embebía que, si no tenía un libro nuevo, no me parece tenía contento" ("I was so completely taken up with this reading that I didn't think I could be happy if I didn't have a new book")[7]—and by a few accounts she is said to have written one herself, *El caballero de Avila* (*Knight of Avila*).[8] Not surprisingly, the appeal, danger, and not the least of all, the utility of such readings lie in their blurring of distinction between life and fiction, between self and text. Therefore their value is contingent upon the cultural valorization of their alleged effects. Since for a future saint, these effects included increased interest in external appearances and matters of love, reading similar books could hardly have been considered edifying.

Finally, we must comment on the ambivalence of these, by traditional standards, unconventional models of womanhood as culturally accepted signs. More in keeping with her namesake than the traditional feminine ideal, the

---

[7] See *Santa Teresa. Obras completas* (Burgos: Monte Carmelo, 1994) 13. For the English version, I am using Kieran Kavanaugh and Otilio Rodríguez's translation, *The Autobiography of St. Teresa of Avila* (New York: Institute of Carmelite Studies, 1987) 57.

[8] See Dámaso Chicharro's edition of St Teresa's *Libro de la vida* (Madrid: Cátedra, 1997) 123.

actions of the heroine of *Soñar la vida*—from fending for her brothers to proposing to an impotent man—presuppose full-fledged agency. Reading the
novel, one would be hard pressed to infer that passivity and meekness are
women's best companions. Finally, in a telling twist on the role of "good" and
"bad" readings, which here is tantamount to "good" and "bad" role models, St
Teresa's own writings presented a problem for posterity for fear that other
nuns or easily excitable female lay readers would want to imitate her. While
her visions and ecstasies were authenticated, how could anyone be sure that
such a strong and publicly recognized figure would not encourage a following
in her unconventional and hence generally undesirable practice?[9] And if all
women became St Teresas or all women assumed initiative, what indeed
would become of "all that is good in the world?"[10]

While the use of literary texts (and especially of popular fictions) in the
dissemination of normative models of conduct has been amply demonstrated,
what sets Icaza's text apart from the previously examined novels is that *Soñar
la vida* makes the edifying function of literature its thesis, thereby inscribing
novela rosa into the canon of formative literature and as such legitimating the
very acts of reading and writing *novela rosa*. Teresa is portrayed as "una niña
que todo lo había aprendido en los libros" ("a girl who had learned everything
from books") (34), and her role models are the characters that populate her
own novels and those of the novelists she admires. Finally, her narrative sets
out to meet the Falangist objective of "elevar el nivel de cultura" ("raising the
level of culture")[11] through the many historical and literary references that
populate the text.

The novel is composed of two symmetrical parts, each of which is introduced by a third-person omniscient narrator and followed by what Lanser
calls the first-person "private voice" (15). Each narrator reinforces the other's
judgments as opinions are duplicated, producing a single authoritative voice.
The first part tells the story of Teresa's success as Juan Iraeta. Most of the
action takes place in Romania, at the home of Nadine Ilescu, whose famous
green envelope bestowing on Juan Iraeta the privilege of attending her exclu-

---

[9] In her seminal study of St Teresa's "rhetoric of feminine subordination," Weber points out
that "the same theologian who defended Teresa's works as theologically sound expressed his
reservations about their dissemination: 'But one could reasonably doubt whether it is wise for
this book, which tells of visions, revelations, raptures and other very spiritual and delicate
things, to circulate in the vernacular among the learned and the unlearned, religious and secular,
men and women. For it may offer the occasion, especially for women, to be deceived, if they
wanted to imitate the things that are written in it, or to feign them in order to deceive others.'"
See *Teresa of Avila and the Rhetoric of Femininity* (Princeton: Princeton UP, 1990) 162.

[10] See p. 109 in this study.

[11] See Anronia Luengo Sojo. "El arquetipo de mujer de la *Sección Femenina*: contribución
de la actividad musical a la consecución de un modelo" in *Pautas históricas de sociabilidad
femenina rituales y modelos de representación* (Cádiz (Sp.): Universidad de Cádiz, 1999) 166.

sive literary gathering is accepted by Teresa.[12] It is there that Teresa, passing herself off as Iraeta's niece, meets the rest of the characters—all constituents of the international literary elite (save the famous Alí Tábara of Istanbul, the son of a Spanish diplomat and the Anatolian princess Sahnaz (125), who is destined to fulfill Teresa's purely "feminine" yearnings).[13] Among the guests are: Virginia Landa (a self-made novelist and daughter of a bohemian Spanish painter), Claude Halliérs (a renowned French poet), Denis Graham (an English laureate of "Premio Normand"—an exclusive literary prize reserved for a select readership), Robert Stanley (an American writer distinguished for his humorous prose and the only other author of "popular" texts besides Juan/ Teresa), and Teresa's compatriot Jaime Vivanco (a diplomat brother of Alí Tábara and an accomplished but under-appreciated author, in the judgment of the protagonist). This literary setting serves as a podium for the protagonist and the third-person narrator to elaborate their views about the merits of literature, suggesting that if popular romance novels do not qualify as "high culture" it is not because of their authors' lack of refinement or erudition, but because of their conviction that literary works should be written for, rather than to the exclusion of, wide audiences.

As the narrator-protagonist's diary further illustrates, Teresa's own literary output presupposes the view of the novel as a vehicle for communication, persuasion, and edification. Interestingly, this position is adopted by the American populist Stanley—the only member of the group who merits her approval besides the brothers Vivanco. In her diary Teresa records Stanley's opinions on the differences between restricted and large-scale literary production, which in turn serve to substantiate her own beliefs and practice:

> Literatura para afortunados que pueden permitirse el lujo de hacer tiempo a que les llegue el sueño—me dice Stanley . . .—, pero que no puede degustar la gran masa moderna que tiene que vivir de prisa, que comer de prisa y que dormir de prisa. A esa hay que ofrecerle un *quick-lunch*: extracto, jugo, savia. Hay que hacerla sentir con una sola frase. Reír con dos sílabas. El 'cine' nos ha enseñado a escribir a nosotros, los del momento. Somos homeópatas de la literatura. Mire usted, yo creo que el secreto de mi

[12] Nadine Ilescu's character seems to be fashioned after Countess Anna de Noailles, née Princess Brancovan—a renowned figure in the elite, fashionable, avant-garde literary circles of the time. There is also a mention of Princess Marthe Bibesco, also a writer, whose encounter with Icaza is depicted in the novel. See the author's footnote (116). In light of these and other parallels that can be drawn between Icaza and Teresa's characters, the novel lends itself to autobiographical reading. Furthermore, the entire text is populated with literary and historical figures, which cause one to question the novel's preliminary note stating that the events depicted in it are purely imaginary.

[13] The persistence with which "international elite" makes its way into popular fiction can be accounted for in a number of ways. Here it almost invariably acts as a trampoline for Spanish protagonists who prove it shallow and morally inferior by comparison.

éxito, hablando claro, consiste en que sé concretar. ¡Y que dejo que divague el lector con la cabeza en la almohada! Porque lo que realmente le divierte es la sugerencia, que le incita a ser novelista a su vez. El libro, como el arado, vale por el surco que abre. En nuestros días escasea la pasta de papel, y el hombre Standard lee en el 'Metro'. El defecto de los superintelectuales consiste en despreciar al hombre Standard y al Metropolitano. ¡Y después hablan de elevar la cultura de las masas! Yo, a quien tanto denigran, soy un purificador de mentalidades. Algo así como un laxante disfrazado. Entre el caramelo de lo ameno disimulo el ricino de unos principios fundamentales.

(Literature for the fortunate ones who can afford the luxury of time before dropping off to sleep—Stanley tells me . . .—, but not for the great modern masses who must live hurriedly, eat hurriedly and sleep hurriedly. These must be offered a *quick-lunch*: pith, juice, sap. They must be moved with a single phrase. Laugh with two syllables. Those of us in tune with the times have learned how to write from the movies. We are the homeopaths of literature. Look, I believe that the secret of my success, to put it plainly, consists in knowing how to present things with clarity and precision. Then let the reader drift away once her head hits the pillow! Because what she really enjoys is the suggestion that in turn incites her to be a novelist. Books, like plows, are worthwhile for the furrow that they open. In our days wood pulp is scarce, and the Standard man reads in the 'Metro.' The defect of the super intellectuals lies in looking down on the Standard man and the Metropolitan. And then they talk of elevating the culture of the masses! I, whom they denigrate so much, am a purifier of minds. Something like a disguised laxative. Within the sweetness of honeyed words, I hide the castor oil of some fundamental principles.) (132)

The novel's second part takes place in Turkey, as Resa—this time the invitation is made out expressly in Teresa's name, rather than her pen name—is invited to the house of Alí Tábara, Nadine's former suitor. Both Alí and Jaime Vivanco are portrayed as men of action, whose allegiance to the Nationalist cause is in no way undermined by their residence abroad; both are engaged in partisan activity and edifying work, but unlike the jovial and easygoing Jaime, Alí belongs to the category of men "con complejos" ("with issues") (*Usos amorosos* 39). His apparent severity, dignified bearing, and brittle temper betray ten years of convalescence and the desertion of a would-be wife, Nadine. Injured in the battlefield at the brink of their engagement, Alí spends five years paralyzed from the waist down and another five emerging from his torments with a heightened sensibility and gift of discernment. By the time Nadine and her guests arrive in Istanbul, Alí is able to walk with the help of crutches and his full recovery seems attainable, albeit uncertain.

Slightly longer than the first, the second part of the novel tells the story of Teresa's success as a "woman," that is, the story of how Resa falls in love with and claims her place at Tábara's side—a position all the more meritorious given his complex and demanding character. As we shall see, it is not until Teresa's femininity has been proven independently from her professional success that the two gendered selves (Resa and Juan) are reconciled as one. The novel ends with the narrator-protagonist's final and triumphant revelation that brings together the text's public and private voices: "Juan Iraeta soy yo" ("I am Juan Iraeta") (319).

Each of the novel's two parts begins by introducing three successful female authors in a consecutive and suggestive order. In the first part, this order reflects the hierarchy operative within the literary field to which they all belong. Accordingly, the omniscient narrator first presents Nadine (poetry), then Virginia (experimental novel), and last of all, Teresa (popular romance fiction). In the second part, this sequence is modified to reflect (and reinforce) the narrator's own judgment of the characters, with Teresa appearing first, followed by Nadine and then Virginia. This latter sequence serves to supplant the initial hierarchy with a principle of valorization that is ultimately edifying and utilitarian, and in keeping with the Falangist project of acculturation.

The differences between the three women, like "the cluster of apprenticeships" examined in *Como los hombres nos quieren*, serve, predictably enough, to underscore Teresa's superiority. Thus, while the self-centered Nadine is shut off in her "torre de marfil" ("ivory tower") (10) and Virginia is busy making a name for herself through uninspired prose, Teresa's literary activities are made out to combine the vocation of writing with a life of service. Furthermore, the "disinterest," which within the field of literary production is taken for a mark of distinction, is denounced as a pose—an "interés desinteresado" ("disinterested interest") (16)—its end ultimately self-serving, while Teresa's commercial success is rendered as the fruit of honest labor—its ultimate beneficiaries being the readers.

It is neither Nadine's exquisite verses, nor Victoria's belabored prose, but the protagonists of Juan Iraeta's romance fictions that succeed in forging an ideal woman—Teresa Sandoval—thereby hailing the agents of large-scale cultural production as partners in nation-building, and their fictions as catalysts for change. Thus Virginia's assertion that "la celebridad fácil es una deshonra para los espíritus sutiles" ("easy fame is a dishonor for subtle spirits") (206) is contested by Tábara who, being a "diletante en almas" ("dilettante of souls") (252), esteems Teresa over the other two women for possessing "un espíritu que, bajo su timidez, oculta una cierta delicadeza" ("a spirit that, beneath its timidity, hides a certain delicacy") (252). In this respect, the narrative follows the model of confrontation outlined by Suleiman (102), wherein the literary and political are conflated in the diverging feminine representations:

> Si se hicieran estadísticas para saber qué personas llevan una vida provechosa y útil, es casi seguro, y desde luego lamentable, que los cálculos

serían muy bajos, porque la inmensa mayoría de las gentes vive egoísta-
mente, sin más mira que su convivencia personal, ni más ideal que la satis-
facción de sus propias necesidades. Esta clase de personas no son útiles a
la sociedad ni a la familia, porque encerrados en el círculo estrecho de su
'yo' prescinden de los demás a quien únicamente acuden para pedir ayuda,
pero sin reportar jamás un servicio desinteresado.

(If statistics were compiled in order to know which persons lead a fruitful
and useful life, it is almost certain, and of course lamentable, that the num-
bers would be very low, because the immense majority of people live self-
ishly, caring only about their private affairs, striving only for the satisfaction
of their own needs. Such people are of no use to society or family, because
shut in their narrow circle of self-interest, they ignore everyone else and
approach others only if they need help, never to render a disinterested service.) (*Formación familiar y social* 235)

It is this notion of "disinterest," understood as service, that lies at the base of
both ideal womanhood and ideal fictions. This is where Teresa surpasses
Nadine and Virginia, whose lives are presented as useless or self-serving; and
this is how the charge of "escapism" leveled at popular fictions is reversed
(and the autonomy of art for art's sake denounced as unpatriotic).

Although Virginia (through her father's legacy) and Teresa share the same
nationality, the former is denied her "Spanishness" on the grounds that "[s]er
español no es únicamente haber nacido en tierras españolas, sino saber sentir a
España para poder servirla. Ser español es lo que muchos desgraciadamente
no saben porque el egoísmo no les deja ver más allá de su propio provecho"
("[b]eing Spanish is not only having been born in Spanish territory, but knowing how to feel Spain in order to serve her. Many people unfortunately don't
know how to be Spanish, because selfishness does not allow them to see
beyond their own self-interest") (*Formación* 123). Hence when Tábara
announces that his Spanish friends residing in Turkey, los Gonzáles de Toledo,
wish to meet their compatriot, he is addressing Teresa as "la única española"
("the only Spanish woman") there present (259). Virginia's protest that she too
is a Spaniard is refuted not on the basis of her residence abroad and cosmopolitan milieu (which she has in common with the Vivancos), but for her failure to "ser útil" ("be useful") in a time of need (*Formación* 239), for neglecting
her obligation to subordinate individual interests to the collective cause:

—No—dice, cortante —; no confundamos. Nosotros no somos internacio-
nales en el sentido de falta de arraigue. Nosotros tenemos una Patria, con
la que estamos fuertemente vinculados, y a la que servimos entusiastas a
través del Mundo . . .
  En las manos morenas resaltan los nudillos. Y yo hubiese querido poder
cogerlas entre las mías. ¡Alfonso Tábara se había ganado el derecho a
hablar de España!

> Que Virginia Landa, en cambio, que había seguido nuestra guerra 'con palpitante interés desde París', pretendiese ahora. . .! ¡No! Hoy el galardón de llamarse español ya no es asunto de pasaporte!

> ("No," he says, sharply, "let us not confuse matters. We are not international in the sense of being rootless. We have a Fatherland, with which we are strongly linked, and which we serve enthusiastically throughout the World."
> His knuckles stood out on his dark hands. I would have liked to be able to take them in mine. Alfonso Tábara had won the right to speak of Spain!
> That Virginia Landa, on the other hand, who had followed our war 'with heart-pounding interest from Paris,' should pretend now . . .! No! Today the prize of calling oneself Spanish is not a question of passports!) (260)

These and similar juxtapositions among the three female characters serve to further tighten the relationship between gender, nationality, and literary vocation endorsed by the text.

Unlike Teresa, who trains as a nurse during the Civil War and puts her life in jeopardy to save an unknown soldier, Nadine deserts her own betrothed at the time of need: "Nuestra musa no tiene temperamento de enfermera" ("Our muse does not have the temperament of a nurse") (132). Significantly, her abandonment of Tábara, a response that is deemed inadequate at the very least, is judged against her flawless verses in a manner that suggests that her failings as a woman far outweigh the perfection of her poetry.

> Una ególatra—es la rápida respuesta [de Stanley]—. Una fría enamorada de sí misma. Un indiscutible talento que empobrece una ausencia de generosidad. Siente artificialmente, como si dijéramos, y escribe a impulsos de su inspiración como en un trance. Domina la técnica, posee el soplo divino, pero le falta lo más importante: los acentos humanos—Stanley parece reflexionar—. Yo dudo que haya amado jamás.

> ("An egomaniac," is [Stanley's] immediate response. "A cold woman enamored of herself. An indisputable talent impoverished by the lack of generosity. She feels artificially, so to speak, and writes on impulses of inspiration as if in a trance. She has command of technique, she possesses the divine touch, but she lacks what is most important: the human quality." Stanley seems to reflect. "I doubt she has ever loved.") (136–7)

Thus the imperfections of Nadine's compositions mirror her imperfections as a woman. In other words, her limitations as a writer are interpreted in the light of her unfulfilled gender expectations (her aborted romance keeps her writing from reaching full fruition). In contrast, Teresa's "spontaneous" response upon seeing Tábara on crutches is to prostrate herself at his feet, an edifying reaction meant to underscore the shallowness of Nadine's behavior:

Resa procura imaginarse lo que ella habría resentido en el lugar de Nadine. Y se encoge de hombros. La *grande amoureuse* había fallado lamentablemente a la hora de la lealtad y del sacrificio. . . .

Y Resa se dice que habría sido maravillosamente hermoso haber podido postrarse junto a aquel herido. Haber podido coger aquella cabeza dolorida e inquieta entre unas manos comprensivas. Y haber podido suavizar rebeldías y desesperanzas.

¡Cielos! ¡Poder dar! ¡Poder dar cuando se quiere y lo que se da es recibido con fervor y ternura! ¡Dar, no ya a cuentagotas, en un esfuerzo pobre y gris que nadie reconoce, sino a chorro limpio! ¡Arruinándose en un loco impulso de generosidad, sin tacañerías, egoísmos ni regateos que envilecen al que aporta y al que recibe! . . .

(Resa tries to imagine what she would have felt in Nadine's place. And she shrugs her shoulders. The *grande amoureuse* had failed miserably at the moment for loyalty and sacrifice. . . .

And Resa tells herself that it would have been marvelously beautiful to have been able to prostrate herself next to that wounded man. To have been able to take his aching and troubled head into her understanding hands. And to have been able to ease his restlessness and despair.

Heavens! To be able to give! To be able to give when one wants and to see what is given received with fervor and tenderness! To give, no longer in little drops, in a poor, colorless effort that nobody notices, but in a clean flood! Ruining oneself in a crazy impulse of generosity, without stinginess, selfishness or haggling that debase the one who gives and the one who receives.) (161–2)

When it comes to Teresa's ideological loyalties there is no lack of classifiers, from "Madrid recién liberado" ("newly liberated Madrid"), to the Bucharest of 1939, to which she flies by way of Rome, Munich, and Berlin while being repeatedly referred to as "la mujer del asiento número cuatro, *a la derecha*" ("the woman in seat number four, *on the right*") (26).[14] Teresa's allegedly quixotic disposition, her impulses defined as "locos" ("crazy"), "generosos" ("generous") and "caballerescos" ("chivalrous"), her "afán de independencia" ("zeal for independence") and "de actuación" ("zeal for action") have altogether more in common with the unconventional "virile" woman than with the stereotypically forlorn protagonists of romance fictions. It is therefore all the more significant that the man to whom Teresa commits herself suffers from an emasculating condition, a fact that justifies Teresa's initiative, for it is she who volunteers to be his companion, and displays her Falangist spirit of "servicio y sacrificio" ("service and sacrifice"). Curiously, the service and sacrifice that Teresa so unconditionally offers to her country and her beloved by proposing to marry him, makes impossible the fulfillment

---

[14] My emphasis.

of the kind of service and sacrifice that women were expected to render, and one that made marriage their ultimate goal: childbearing. However, there is no indication that the possibility of remaining childless daunts Teresa in any way. Her disinterested offering therefore reads as yet another element of inconsistency that riddles the discourse on the Falange's new woman (*nueva mujer*). The result is an inversion of the conventional model of male–female dynamics, as it is Alí who must rely on Teresa's valor and fortitude.[15]

As Tábara's interest in Teresa grows, he demands to know more about her life back in Spain. But even when questioned, Teresa remains reticent about her vocation, fearful lest her success (under the guise of Juan Iraeta) become an obstacle to their relationship: "¿Por qué no le hablo de Juan Iraeta? ¿No es éste el momento? ¡No! Me gusta seguir siendo junto a él apagada e insignificante. Temo perder al cruzarme al bando de Nadine y de Virginia" ("Why do I not speak to him about Juan Iraeta? Is this not the right time? No! I want to go on being subdued and insignificant next to him. I'm afraid of spoiling everything if I cross over into Nadine and Virginia's camp") (273). It is when Tábara's condition worsens, and his operation and subsequent confinement to bed become inevitable (and his full recovery remains uncertain) that Teresa, who until then has kept her initiative under check, makes the unconventional first move in committing herself to him:

> —Te ofrezco mi vida al por mayor. No al detalle.
> —No me tientes.
> Los dos, callados, miramos las aguas azules, estriadas de gris.
> —¿En calidad de qué vendrías conmigo?
> —¡De lo que tú dispongas!—quisiera decir, valiente. Pero de nuevo mi timidez:
> —Soy enfermera diplomada, y una buena enfermera, te lo aseguro.

> ("I offer my life to you completely. Not piecemeal."
> "Don't tempt me."
> Silent, the two of us watch the blue water, streaked with gray.
> "In what capacity would you come with me?"
> "In any that you wish!" I want to say, feeling brave. But my timidity resurfaces:
> "I am a trained nurse, and a good one, I assure you.") (303)

---

[15] In a late post-war novel, *La Plaza del Diamante* (1962), by the canonical Catalan author Mercè Rodoreda, the protagonist's second husband is likewise a man rendered impotent by war. The two novels offer interesting takes on the war's emancipating possibilities for women. While in Icaza's novel, the male protagonist's disabling condition serves to authenticate Teresa's initiative cast always in terms of her patriotic zeal for service, in Rodoreda's novel, the subversive potential of the husband's impotence lies in the heroine's fantasy for a world without male hegemony. See Neus Carbonell, "In the Name of the Mother and the Daughter: The Discourse of Love and Sorrow in Mercè Rodoreda's *La Plaça del Diamant*" in *Garden Across the Border: Mercè Rodoreda's Fiction* (Selinsgrove, PA: Susquehanna UP) 18.

Lest Tábara refuse her offer, she asks their mutual friend, Julia Benavides, to intercede on her behalf. But instead of the anticipated support, she finds in Julia veiled misgivings: "Yo te conozco y sé que obras a impulso de una infinita generosidad. Pero date cuenta de que eres tú la que, aprovechando momentos de terrible desconcierto en su ánimo, quieres ocupar junto a él un sitio que no está claramente definido" ("I know you and I know that you are acting on an impulse of great generosity. But understand that you are the one who, in taking advantage of these moments of terrible confusion in his soul, wants to occupy a place by his side that is not clearly defined") (306). But Teresa is not easily swayed. To her tenacity Julia responds with another argument, this time more blatant in its pressure to conform to normative expectations: "el mundo como siempre, habrá dado desde un principio la peor interpretación a tu actitud. . . . Y pudiese ser que un día hasta el mismo Alfonso llegase a dudar de tu desinterés. . . . ¡Déjale correr su suerte! ¡Deja que, si mejora y si está realmente interesado, sea él quien vaya por ti!" ("the world, as always, will have cast your behavior in the worst light from the very start. . . . And it could be that one day even Alfonso will come to doubt your disinterestedness. . . . Let him be! If he recovers and is interested, let him be the one who goes after you!") (307).

Still Teresa doesn't budge. Her resolution to defy conventions is sustained by the superior logic of her impulse, the kind of "irrationality" that is at once censored and revered as "heroic" as well as "quixotic" (306), subordinating gender conventions to national imperatives (and thereby legitimizing otherwise transgressive urges): "Y que pase otra vez solo por esta prueba terrible . . .!—me rebelo—. No Julia; aunque destroce lo que tú llamas mi porvenir, aunque el mismo Alfonso dude del gesto loco que, por lo visto, no puede permitirse una pobre e insignificante señorita Sandoval, yo he de empeñarme en ello" ("And to let him once again go through this terrible trial alone . . .!" I rebel. "No, Julia; even if it ruins what you call my prospects, even if Alfonso himself doubts the motivation behind this crazy gesture that, apparently, poor, insignificant Miss Sandoval cannot afford to make, I must insist on it") (308). But conveniently, Teresa is not "una pobre e insignificante señorita" ("a poor and insignificant young lady"), but the successful, internationally acclaimed, and financially secure Juan Iraeta. And in an ingenious spin, Teresa's public accomplishments go from being seen as an impediment to being recast as a prerogative. Ultimately, what vindicates and links the feminine condition with the writing of *novela rosa* is their common espousal of the nationalist cause, and their shared responsibility to act as instruments of social change and transformation. If then Teresa succeeds in reconciling the two seemingly irreconcilable pursuits—writing and romance—it is because she subscribes to the Falangist conception of life as "lucha entre comodidad y el sacrificio, entre la materia y el espíritu, entre el bien y el mal" ("struggle between comfort and sacrifice, between the material and the spiritual, between good and evil")

(*Formación* 239). This conception informs both her public and private choices, conjoining them in a single legitimating purpose behind every act: service.

As a partisan of the new Spain and a representative of Falange's "minoría selecta" ("select minority"), Teresa exhibits unique persuasive and oratorical skills. Even as the narrator of her own diary, she seldom misses an opportunity to be instructive. Most of her observations about Romania and Turkey could be read as attempts to popularize the Falangist ethos with its particular blend of tradition and modernity:

> He ido por la mañana a Bucarest, a recorrer unas cuantas viejas iglesias. Después hemos asistido todos a la inauguración de la Exposición Internacional 'Munca si Voe Buna', magno muestrario de cómo conciben la alegría y la belleza en el trabajo la mayoría de los pueblos de Europa. Los pabellones modernistas, sonoros de música populares, son un exponente de tradiciones folklóricas. Como un enorme rigodón campesino en que se cogiese de mano lo más genuino de cada nación. Y son todos los goces que elevan y sanean puestos al alcance del trabajador y reflejados en el pabellón del 'Kraft durch Freude' alemán, del 'Doppolavoro' italiano, del 'Honor en el trabajo' húngaro, del 'Alegría no Trabalho' portugués. . . . Y todo un panel cubierto por estampas del esfuerzo de España, a pesar de la guerra reciente. Alegres hogares del Auxilio Social. Campamentos de O. J. [Organización Juvenil de Falange]. Bailes regionales de la Sección Femenina. . . .
>
> Y yo, al atardecer, he ido sola a conocer desde fuera esa Casa Verde, clausurada y desierta, que era la sede de la Guardia de Hierro. Y he depositado un ramo de campestres 'no me olvides' en las tumbas de los camaradas rumanos caídos voluntarios en lucha por un ideal allá, en rudas y heroicas tierras de España.

> (In the morning I went to Bucharest, to see some old churches. Afterwards all of us went to the opening of the International Exposition 'Munca si Voe Buna,' a magnificent example of how the majority of the peoples of Europe conceive of happiness and beauty in labor. The modernist pavilions, echoing with popular music, are full of displays of folkloric traditions. As if all that is most authentic about each nation had been joined in an enormous peasant rigadoon. All of these are pleasures that edify and purify, placed within reach of the worker and reflected in the pavilion, in the German 'Kraft durch Freude,' the Italian 'Dopolavoro,' the Hungarian 'Honor in work' [sic], the Portuguese 'Alegría no Trabalho'. . . . And a whole wall covered with illustrations of work in Spain, in spite of the recent war. Happy homes of Social Aid. Camps of the Falangist Youth Organization, Regional Dances of the Women's Section [of the Falange]. . . .
>
> And at nightfall, I went alone to see that Green House, [now] closed and deserted, that used to be the seat of the Iron Guard. I left a bouquet of wild 'forget me nots' on the tombs of the Romanian volunteer comrades fallen in the struggle for an ideal, there, in the rough and heroic lands of Spain.)
> (141)

Unlike Nadine, who neglects the welfare of her subordinates, Teresa, during her short stay at Nadine's private residence, cultivates a relationship of trust and tutelage with her Romanian housemaid, Anicuza. As a result, Anicuza confides in Teresa (telling her about the detention of her boyfriend), and Teresa, ever solicitous, seizes this as an opportunity to preach the gospel of the Falange:

> Y yo he puesto mi mano en el hombro de la muchacha.
> —Siempre llega un día, Anicuza—le digo muy seria. Y todo aquello que no interesa a mis ilustres compañeros, ocupados siempre de hablar de ellos mismos, lo voy relatando ante la mirada ingenua y admirativa de la novia del legionario de Gopdreano. Y le hablo de nuestros tiempos heroicos, contra todo y contra todos. De José Antonio. Y de los nuevos tiempos heroicos de nuestra guerra, brecha gloriosa por la que avanza la Falange.
> —¡Siempre llega un día, Anicuza! La revolución auténtica es como la lava de un volcán. Nada ni nadie puede cortar su irrupción.
> Anicuza, en un gesto brusco, me ha besado la mano. Y entre mis dedos, como el brillante más bello que pudiera lucir Nadine, tiembla una lágrima.

> (And I put my hand on the girl's shoulder.
> "A day always comes, Anicuza," I tell her gravely. All the things that do not interest my illustrious companions, continuously occupied in talking about themselves, I begin to relate to the innocent and admiring gaze of the Gopdreano legionnaire's girlfriend. I tell her of our heroic times, against everything and everyone. Of José Antonio. And of the new heroic times of our war, the glorious breach through which the Falange is advancing.
> "A day always comes, Anicuza! The true revolution is like a volcano's lava. No one and nothing can stop its eruption."
> Abruptly, Anicuza kissed my hand. And between my fingers, like the most beautiful jewel that Nadine could ever wear, trembles a tear.) (122)

Of the four novels here studied, the protagonist of *Soñar la vida* is the only one who successfully combines a public persona with a private, purely "feminine" vocation. Even so, the treatment of Teresa's success merits closer examination. She is the first to criticize, and in doing so preempt the criticism of her employment: "Soy imbécil—se dice—. ¿Por qué trabajo tanto? ¡Si ya no necesito matarme! Si ya he hecho bastante!" ("I am an imbecile," she tells herself. "Why do I work so much? I don't need to kill myself any more! I've already done enough!") (20) and almost immediately afterwards, reinforcing this very view, the narrator adds, "[l]a verdad es que es absurdo, completamente absurdo, lo que está haciendo. ¿Por qué? ¿Para quién? ¡Si todos lo tienen ya todo resuelto! Y ella misma es de tan pocas ambiciones y de tan escasas necesidades!" ("[t]he truth is that what she is doing is absurd, completely absurd. Why? For whom? Now that everyone's problems have been solved! And she herself has so few ambitions and so few needs!'") (21). It is noteworthy that in both instances the accusation of working too much is accompanied by a vindication for having worked, underscoring the fact that Teresa's "unfeminine" routine has been very much in keeping with her "feminine" vocation as "la mujer abnegada" ("the self-sacrificing woman"). Furthermore, in a manner that is never articulated as contradictory but is not devoid of contradiction (it is Teresa who volunteers to work when other solutions are available, and doesn't cease working once the necessity passes), she longs to "¡Dejar de ser Teresa Sandoval! Ese ser absurdo 'a quien divierte trabajar'" ("Stop being Teresa Sandoval! That absurd being 'who enjoys working'") to become "una de esas mujeres . . . a las que algún hombre ha dicho alguna vez 'te quiero'" ("one of those women . . . to whom, at some point, some man has said 'I love you'") (24). By virtue of opposition, this sequence reiterates the view posited in *Como los hombres nos quieren*, that being loved and being dedicated to one's work for a woman are incompatible pursuits. Tellingly, Teresa's success as director of *Feminidades*, like Aunt Lina's as a director of a health spa, is presented as a byproduct of "el egoísmo de los demás y la inconsciencia familiar" ("the selfishness of others and the irresponsibility of the family") (24) and therefore as an act of sacrifice rather than as a means to personal gain or individual fulfillment:

> En sus memorias, la emperatriz Elizabeth, esa 'Zizí' que Barrés llama 'la emperatriz de la Soledad', dice. . . . 'Yo podría simbolizar mi vida en la de una aldeana de Taelz que vi una vez distribuir la comida a los mozos. Como tenía que llenar constantemente los platos de los demás, el suyo se quedó vacío. . .' Esto me ha pasado a mí hasta ahora.

> (In her memoirs, the Empress Elizabeth, that 'Zizi' whom Barré calls 'the empress of Solitude', says . . . 'My life resembles that of a village woman from Taelz whom I saw once distributing food to the youths. As she constantly had to fill the plates of the others, hers remained empty. . .' That has happened to me up until now.) (300)

And yet the day she buys herself a typewriter she is overcome by "la sensación de que acababa de colocar una primera piedra" ("the sensation of having placed the first stone") (46) toward realizing her childhood dream: "¡Escribir! Desde que tenía uso de razón había escrito. De niña, a escondidas, cuentos raros, fantásticos, tristes en su mayoría. Y que casi siempre acababan mal" ("To write! Ever since she'd been old enough, she had written. As a child she would secretly write strange, fantastic stories, most of them sad. And they almost always ended badly") (42).[16] Despite her father's otherwise

---

[16] It is hard not to take this as a reference to the happy endings of *novelas rosa* and as a way of suggesting that writing popular fictions is a choice informed and conditioned by a range of

indulgent approach to her education, Teresa's first attempt to make public her vocation as a writer meets with his disapproval:

> A los diecisiete años había escrito una novela: 'El patito feo'. Un cuento sentimental y suave que no logró leer a nadie. Un día intentó 'colocárselo' a su padre, pero el presidente de la Real academia, de costumbre tan bondadoso, se revolvió airado:
> —Hay en la familia un Sandoval, el Bueno—dijo con voz tonante—. Y no quiero que haya un Sandoval, el Malo. ¡Tú, a divertirte y a gozar de la vida! Tienen razón tus tías: me vas a resultar un *bas bleu*.
> Y Sandoval, el Malo, volvió a retraerse en su habitual timidez. Guardó el 'Patito feo' en el fondo de un baúl, y sus aficiones de escribir, en ese desván recóndito que una a una vamos amontonando nuestras ilusiones frustradas.

> (By age 17 she had written a novel: 'The Ugly Duckling.' A sentimental and tender story that she couldn't get anyone to read. One day she tried to 'pass it off' to her father, but the president of the Royal Academy, usually so kind, became irate:
> "There is already one Sandoval in the family, the Good one," he said in a thunderous tone. "I don't want there to be another Sandoval, the Bad one. Off you go—have fun and enjoy life! Your aunts are right: you are going to turn out to be a *bas bleu*."
> And Sandoval the Bad retreated into her habitual shyness. She put the 'Ugly Duckling' in the bottom of a trunk, and her love of writing in that remote attic where one by one our frustrated dreams pile up.) (42)

Upon her father's death, with a "tenacidad silenciosa" ("silent tenacity") (41), Teresa commits herself to finding a job and eventually is hired as a translator of commercial letters for the newly launched magazine *Feminidades*. As a precaution, she decides to hold two jobs (in the other, she works as a door-to-door salesperson) until she is certain that the magazine is going to stay afloat; it does, entirely owing to her efforts. From a translator with "pocas pretensiones" ("few aspirations") (specified as such in the advertisement for the job [41]), she becomes the journal's principal motor, transforming its modest beginnings into a prosperous venture. The magazine's success is reflected in its rapidly expanding coverage, from "crónica de modas" ("style column") and "casa grata" ("good housekeeping"), to "cuidemos a nuestros hijos" ("childcare") and "buen yantar" ("eating well") (43). On Teresa's initiative, *Feminidades* launches a "consultorio sentimental" ("romantic advice column" akin to "Dear Abby") featuring Teresa as the *Princesa azul*[17]—a woman with

---

factors, from gender constraints and the demands of the market to one's social and political responsibilities.

[17] The term "la Princesa azul" (literally, "the Blue Princess") is the feminine form of "el

the solutions for any problem, from disguising a pimple to dealing with delicate matters of the heart:

> La 'Princesa azul' era una verdadera enciclopedia. Lo mismo recomendaba una mezcla de vaselina borricada con óxido de cinc para quitar un inoportuno grano en la nariz, como guarnecía de *renards argentés* un abrigo de tarde o aconsejaba métodos para hacerse amar locamente. . . . 'Yo, en el caso de usted, le devolvería sus cartas con unos renglones breves y dignos, no exentos de afecto, pero desde luego terminantes. Si en realidad la ha querido tanto, ¡quién sabe si reaccionará . . .!

> (The 'Blue Princess' was a real encyclopedia. She was just as likely to recommend a mixture of Vaseline fortified with zinc oxide to get rid of an inopportune pimple on the nose, as to adorn an afternoon coat with *renards argentés*, or give advice on how to be loved madly. . . . 'In your place, I would return his letters with a few short, dignified lines, not entirely devoid of affection, but certainly conclusive. If his love for you is so great, who knows, maybe he will respond. . .!) (44)

In effect, Teresa's relationship with Tábara may be read as a blueprint for a male–female dynamic—the "tira y afloja" ("advance and retreat") approach (Martín Gaite, *Usos* 68)—promoted by the "consultorios sentimentales" of women's magazines like *Y* and *Medina*, published under the auspices of *Sección Femenina*.

However, the necessary impetus for Teresa's literary success comes from don Rogelio, an otherwise insignificant employer, who entrusts her with starting a serial novel in *Feminidades*, "uno de esos libros que causan furor, y en los que la señorita pobre se casa al final con un joven apuesto y millonario" ("one of those books that cause a sensation, in which the impoverished young lady marries the young handsome millionaire in the end") (47). Instead, Teresa presents him with her first novel, "El patito feo," a story of "la muchacha fea en quien nadie se fija y que de pronto inspira un maravilloso amor" ("the ugly girl whom everyone ignores and who all of a sudden inspires a marvellous love") (47). The novel meets with don Rogelio's approval and under the spell of his words, "[e]sta novela es de público" ("[t]his novel is made to be read [literally, "belongs to the public"]"), the novel finally comes to light: "Y así fue como 'El Patito'", que tanto había tardado en lograr salir del cascarón de su baúl-mundo, se lanzó intrépida a la vida pública" ("And that is how 'The Ugly Duckling', that had taken so long to emerge from the shell of its trunk-world, was intrepidly launched into public life") (51). The story of "el patito" ("the duckling") functions as a *mise-en-àbime* of Teresa's "public" and "private" success. It may further be read as a simile of *novela rosa* which, with

Príncipe azul," which means "Prince Charming."

the evocative backdrop of Countess Nadine Ilescu's lake, starts off inferior to other genres, only to be proven their equal, if not their superior.

Teresa's anxiety with regard to her authorship parallels the cultural anxiety about female involvement in the public sphere. In a balancing act reminiscent of *Sección Femenina*'s rhetoric, wherein advancement presupposes retreat, Teresa—in order for her story to gain public recognition—defers her claim to fame to Juan Iraeta. As she travels through Italy, Germany and Romania, it is the name of Juan Iraeta that is welcomed. It is he who is sought out in airports, solicited by journalists and fans, and featured on all the billboards, while she passes for an unassuming traveler, basking in the shadow of his glory. "Teresa Sandoval recuesta la cabeza y cierra los ojos. De nuevo esa sensación sentida plenamente en Roma. Cuando la pequeña sombra de mujer, entre los perfumados claroscuros del Pincio, miraba la Ciudad Eterna extendida a sus pies" ("Teresa Sandoval rests her head and closes her eyes. Again she has that sensation felt deeply in Rome, when the small shadow of a woman, among the perfumed *chiaroscuros* of the Pincio, observed the Eternal City spread out at her feet") (54).

The splintering of Teresa's identity becomes both a stipulation and a means for success. Unwilling to give up her vocation and wary of taking credit for it (she fears that don Rogelio's estimation of the novel will change once he learns that she wrote it), Teresa invents Juan Iraeta, settling for anonymity for herself in lieu of his rampant popularity. This move betrays the inconsistencies latent in the Falangist discourse as alluded to earlier, evidenced by the members of *Sección Femenina* who, in spite of their leadership roles, stressed the importance of keeping a low profile, and extolled domesticity while displaying initiative from their pulpits. One way of glossing over these contradictions was by envisioning a woman's life as consisting of two phases: active and passive. The former was considered transitory and the latter, relative to the woman's ultimate purpose in life, permanent:

[l]a Sección Femenina tiene, como si dijéramos, dos partes: una de servicio activo e intensivo, pero que en general es transitorio, y otra de servicio pasivo, pero permanente. Están en servicio activo todas las camaradas que desde sus puestos de Jefes Locales, Jefes de Escuelas de Formación, Divulgadoras Rurales, Delegadas Provinciales, Instructoras de Especialidades y otros, llevan el total de la organización de la Sección Femenina y consiguen con su trabajo y buen espíritu el que sean realidad perfecta todos los servicios a nosotros encomendados. Pero sucede que el 90 por 100 de estas camaradas se casan. Afortunadamente para ellas y para nosotras. Y entonces entran en una nueva fase de servicio a la Falange menos activo, pero más permanente; pero, al fin y al cabo, servicio a la Falange que, como cualquier otro, no puede eludirse.

([t]he *Sección Femenina* has, so to speak, two parts: one of active and intensive service, that as a rule is transitory, and another of passive, but permanent, service. Active service is performed by all the comrades who, from their positions as Local Leaders, Heads of Schools of Formation, Rural Propagandists, Provincial Delegates, Specialty Instructors and others, carry the bulk of the entire organization of the *Sección Femenina* and through their work and good spirit make a perfect reality of all those duties with which we are entrusted. But it so happens that 90 to 100 percent of these comrades marry. Fortunately for them and for us. And then they enter into a new, less active and more permanent phase of service to the Falange; but, when all is said and done, it is a service to the Falange that, like any other, cannot be evaded.) (*Pilar* 42)

Teresa's division into Juan and Resa may thus be viewed as a way of reconciling her active/public and passive/private vocations. By virtue of the estrangement that she experiences, or that she trains herself to experience—"A fuerza de voluntad había logrado su desdoblamiento. Y el hábito había ido dando vida propia a ese su otro 'yo', que cada vez afianzaba con mayores bríos y brillantes trazos su propia personalidad" ("By force of will she had managed to split herself in two. And the habit had given its own life to her other 'I,' which increasingly strengthened its own personality with greater spirits and brilliant strokes") (54)—Teresa is able to maintain the low profile demanded by the stipulated gender hierarchy:

¿Qué tenía de común con la señorita de Sandoval, tan apagada, discreta y comedida, aquel divagante sutil, escéptico o fantásticamente tierno? Juan Iraeta, tras el cual seguía escondiéndose, herméticamente 'un alto prestigio de la literatura española', ése era el triunfador. Resa no le envidiaba [a Juan]. Ni siquiera sentía la tentación, en esta su primera y anhelante partida a la aventura, de posesionarse de golpe de lo que era suyo. De revestir su modestia de esas galas deslumbrantes; que cambiarían de golpe a la cenicienta en la protagonista de reportajes y gacetillas.

(What did he, that subtle, skeptical, fantastically tender wanderer, have in common with the ever subdued, discreet, self-restrained Miss Sandoval? Juan Iraeta, behind whom remained hermetically hidden 'a high prestige for Spanish literature,' he was the triumphant one. Resa did not envy [Juan]. She did not even feel the temptation, in this her first, long-desired sally into adventure, to suddenly take possession of what was hers—to cloak her modesty with those dazzling fineries which would change Cinderella, at a stroke, into the protagonist of articles and gossip columns.) (54–5)

Thanks to Juan's mediation, Teresa remains unspoiled (absolved of such charges as conceit, egotism, arrogance, independence—in short, of all the perceived pitfalls of women whose success rivaled that of their male counterparts): "Por eso, ella seguiría siendo Teresa Sandoval, una mujer cualquiera, que entre los cipreses, los mármoles y las Fuentes del Pinicio, añoraba dolorosamente algo que no era la fama, estampada con letras de fuego en la noche clara de Roma" ("Therefore, she would continue being Teresa Sandoval, a woman like any other, who, amid the cypresses, the marble, and the Fountains of the Pinicio, achingly longed for something that was not fame, stamped with letters of fire on the clear Roman night") (55). In keeping with the rhetoric of the time, Juan's success leaves Teresa feeling unfulfilled, and this sentiment, the yearning attributed to Resa, is the ultimate proof of her femininity. Thus, unlike Virginia and Nadine, who are defined by their literary accomplishments, Teresa is driven by "el eterno afán de Eva: ¡ser amada!" ("the eternal desire of Eve: to be loved!") (113), that stirs the protagonists of her novels. In contrast to Virginia and Nadine, whose public activities get in the way of their femininity, Teresa's achievements, in the end, seal her success as a woman. And it is the fulfillment of this dream that ultimately legitimates her consecration, enabling the final reconciliation of Juan and Resa into a new woman of the Falange—Teresa Sandoval—a dream come true and an example to be followed.

10

Taking Matters into Your Own Hands in María Mercedes Ortoll's *En pos de la ilusión*

En pos de la ilusión (1940), a first-person narrative by another prolific and popular author of *novelas rosa*, María Mercedes Ortoll, is addressed to "muchachas"—female readers of marriageable age (generously extended to early forties) who, according to the Dominican García Figar, dreamed of nothing but "estrenar un vestido" ("wearing a new dress"), "*cazar*[1] un novio" ("finding [but literally, "hunting"] someone to marry"), and "criar un hijo" ("raising a child") (69). Viewed in this light, *En pos* constitutes a guide in its own right on how to obtain a husband. Circulated at a time when the ranks of single women anxious to avoid the ignominy of spinsterhood had significantly surpassed the number of available male candidates, the novel treats marriage less as a sacrament than as a shared concern, the successful resolution of which requires women to use methods that are at odds with the institutionalized, bride-in-waiting image endorsed by the official arbiters of feminine mores.

The conduct manuals and prescriptive texts considered thus far had addressed questions of female socialization from the moral high ground assumed by the clergy and leading members of the women's political organization. However, along with such attempts at national and pastoral care as Emilio Enciso Viana's *La muchacha en el noviazgo* (*The Young Woman in Courtship*) (1947), Francisco Esteve Blanes' *Hacia tu ideal* (*Toward Your Ideal*) (1939), the Jesuit Angel Ayala's *Consejos a las jóvenes* (*Advice To Young Women*) (1947) or the aforementioned Dominican García Figar's *¿Por qué te casas? ¿Para qué te casas? ¿Con quién te casas?* (*Why Do You Marry? To What End Do You Marry? Whom Do You Marry?*) (1944), to mention but a few, there thrived another current of feminine literature of pronouncedly didactic, albeit less edifying content.[2] Its unorthodox appeal consisted in extending the directives for the practice of quintessential feminine virtues to ostensibly practical advice for achieving that single most sought-after condi-

---

[1] The emphasis is mine.

[2] I am using the term "feminine literature" throughout the text to designate works intended almost exclusively for female readership.

tion without which no woman could rightfully consider herself happy: marriage. Hence, along with recommendations on how to be an ideal companion, these works contained tips on how to procure and retain a husband, inciting in their readers the desire to be loved and admired like the heroines of romance fiction. Such a shift in emphasis may have undermined the works' social and edifying value, but it also guaranteed them a loyal following.

Books like Esperanza de Briones' *La belleza: Los problemas que crea y los que resuelve* (*Beauty: The Problems it Causes and Those it Resolves*) (1945) or Cecilia Mantua's *El libro de la mujer* (*The Woman's Book*) (1946), as well as the highly successful and popular translation of Anita Colby's *Tu belleza* (*Your Beauty*) (1952), encouraged and taught women to look after their appearance. Always scrupulously class-conscious (good taste entailed knowing one's place in society), they nurtured a sense of self-worth, autonomy, and individualism in lieu of meekness, subordination, and conformity. By stressing the importance of physical appeal, they fostered the illusion of control over one's destiny founded on the belief that changing one's appearance could change one's life possibilities while challenging, in the process, the accepted correspondence between beauty and goodness. Hence, on their pages—liberating to some, yet decadent to others—beauty and virtue cease being synonymous. While generosity of spirit is seen as a sign of refinement, it is neither a substitute nor fair compensation for the absence of physical charm. "Buena si quieres, sabia si puedes, ¡bella has de ser!" ("Good if you want to be, wise if you can be, but beautiful you must be!") is a maxim that introduces a chapter in Briones' text with this intriguing title: "La resignación es una virtud negativa.—Influencia que ejercen las emociones estéticas.—Cuándo la fealdad constituye una ventaja" ("Resignation is a negative virtue.—The influence of aesthetic emotions.—When ugliness is an advantage"). Briones' views clearly contrast with those held by the clergy and other custodians of feminine virtue[3]—the views adopted, not without ambivalence, by the heroines of popular romance novels:

---

[3] For an institutionalized view, see *Hacia tu ideal* in which Francisco Esteve Blanes offers his female addressees the following words of comfort and caveat: "No eres muñeca, Dios puso en tu cuerpo la suficiente belleza. El, con mucho más arte que tú, acierta a disimular y suavizar los defectos. . . . Pueril, es por lo tanto, tu pretensión de corregir el arte divino que resplandece en tu semblante, añadiendo pinturas y modificando cejas, párpados y cabellos, según el patrón de una moda caprichosa que con frecuencia desfigura, cuando no daña . . . . Eres superior a toda moda y a todo artificio mundano. . . . Tu verdadera elegancia está en la verdadera distinción, y ésta viene del interior" (You are not a doll. God infused your body with sufficient beauty. He, with much greater skill than you, is able to conceal and soften your flaws. . . . Childish, therefore, is your attempt to alter the divine art that shines in your face, adding makeup and altering brows, eyelashes and hair according to the dictates of capricious fashion that frequently disfigures, if not damages. . . . You are above all fashions and all worldly artifices. . . . Your true elegance lies in true distinction, and this comes from within) (12, 21).

Cuando nos encuentran faltas de atractivos naturales, nos aconsejan la resignación. Ahora resulta que la resignación siempre se ha considerado una
suprema virtud . . . para uso de los demás. Es como la modestia, la humildad
y otras buenas cualidades espirituales, que tanto nos agradan cuando no nos
son impuestas a nosotras mismas. Para la mayoría de las mujeres resulta
difícil mostrarse conformes con la Naturaleza cuando ésta se les ha reve-
lado, poco o mucho, como madrastra y no les ha proporcionado las buenas
facciones o la hermosura de la piel a las que creen tener derecho. Nadie
siente gratitud por algo que no ha recibido, y la resignación es una forma—
—pasiva si ustedes quieren—de agradecimiento.

(When they find us lacking in natural charm, they advise us to be resigned
to our lot. Now, resignation always has been considered a supreme virtue
. . . for others to practice. It is like modesty, humility and other positive
spiritual qualities that we admire so much when they are not imposed on
us. For most women, it is difficult to be content with Nature when she has
treated them more or less like a stepmother, and has denied them good looks
or a beautiful complexion, to which they feel entitled. No one is grateful for
something he or she has not received, and resignation is a form—a passive
one, if you will—of gratitude.) (Briones 45)

The heresy of this position resides not in the recasting and reappraisal of
beauty as a physical category—after all, while aspiring to good looks as an
end in itself was considered vain, doing so to please the opposite sex, the proverbial "el deseo de agradar" ("desire to please") was tolerated and even
encouraged—but in its rebuff of resignation as a woman's only acceptable
response to her natural (and sometimes not so natural) circumstances, in its
unapologetic championing of initiative over complacence (even if the reason
for taking the initiative has a legitimate and authorized end, to marry).
Adopting this attitude as a sign of modernity, while drawing heavily on the
familiar repository of traditional feminine virtues, Mercedes Ortoll's novel,
En pos de la ilusión, affords an interesting meditation on the ambiguous and
contradictory role of women in post-war Spain, where docility epitomized the
norm and initiative its necessary infraction.

Before turning to the analysis proper, we must first consider another significant discrepancy between works that, like Briones' *La belleza*, lacked
institutional footing, and texts that, like Blanes' *Hacia tu ideal*, were backed
by religious, political and/or scientific[4] authority—a discrepancy manifest in
the kind of relationship that these two narrative types sought to establish with
their readers. The latter, drawing on their respective forms of capital, espe-

---

[4] Doctors also wrote manuals. See, for example, Dr A. Clavero Núñez's *Antes que te cases*
(Valencia: Tipografía moderna, 1946), which flaunts the following dedication: "A la mujer,
tesoro de encantos y de . . . ignorancia" (To Woman, treasure chest of charms and . . .
ignorance").

cially when these were buttressed by the right gender (male), depicted their addressees (women) as scarcely old enough to read, let alone to think. Luckily, reading the right books (which were of course the ones in question) released women from having to think, by providing the convenience of set guidelines that the readers merely had to observe. Needless to say, these guidelines carried the weight of injunctions. In contrast, beauty guides and other works of auxiliary thrust, primarily written by women and stemming from a culturally liminal, albeit progressively accepted position, constructed their authority on the basis of personal success and experience, or, alternatively, on the anonymous grounds of primordial wisdom (in case the first two were deemed compromising). Accordingly, their pages addressed inexperienced or unsuccessful women, whom the self-appointed female voice of the narrative, offered to guide as equals, not by fate—which was always class-specific—nor by expertise, merit or other qualities deemed necessary for success—but by a common plight.[5]

Diana, the narrator-protagonist of *En pos de la ilusión*, by virtue of being a "perfect maiden" (a category reassembled and extolled by the narrative), beguiles and marries the man she loves. From her success story, readers are to draw a sense of fulfillment and anticipation of their own happy ending, with Diana as their role model. But when it comes to securing the love of the man she fancies, in itself a daring proposition, Diana's conduct strays from orthodoxy in the vein of Briones' model reader, the one who disdains the path of least resistance and welcomes initiative: "dejemos que se conformen resignadamente las personas acostumbradas a solucionar su vida por la línea de menor Resistencia y hablemos para las demás" ("Let those accustomed to leading their lives by following the path of least resistance conform resignedly, while we speak for the rest") (Briones 45).[6]

Named after the pagan goddess of the hunt, Diana is unwilling to leave her chance of happiness—*ilusión*[7]—to destiny's uncertain hands or, for that matter, to the wavering feelings of her target, so much so that the title, *En pos de la ilusión* (or, *In Pursuit of the Dream*) develops quasi-polemical (or ludic, depending on the interpretation) undertones. An unmistakable allusion to the

---

[5] On a purely conjectural level, one could argue that behind the auxiliary impetus of these women-authored texts lies an understanding of what it meant to be a female in post-war Spain, an understanding that imbues their narrative voice with a sense of complicity that, while not equally appealing to all, could be gratifying and even empowering to some.

[6] Curiously, such a contentious proposition finds validation in the Falangist rhetoric that bade women never to give up in the face of adversity. Accordingly, Briones' text invites one to read "ugliness" as a vicissitude that must be overcome, denouncing resignation as a lack of combative spirit.

[7] The word "ilusión" in the post-war years had many different meanings, from dreams, to illusions, to hopes, fulfillment, and happiness. See "Nubes de color de rosa" in *Usos amorosos* (139–60). Its translation here will vary based on the context and my own interpretative choices.

love–marriage dyad, the title-phrase "en pos de la ilusión" designates that innocuous, culturally accepted, and strictly feminine mind-set that young women were likely to adopt, if not by dint of nature, then through persuasion, example, and convention. However, when viewed in light of post-war courtship practices—practices that for women entailed most notably the politics of concealment—this perfectly admissible disposition, consisting of young women's dreams of marriage, opens the possibility of rather more brazen conduct, a figurative quest turned literal, a pursuit not of a dream, but of its embodiment—a man, or to be more precise, a future husband. Thus seen, *En pos* plays out two contradictory and competing versions of the courtship protocol for women: a conventional one, which instructed them to desist from any artifice or initiative, and a controversial one, which bade them to take matters into their own hands, be it through cunning or cosmetics. The unfeasibility of reconciling these two blueprints in a single character (Diana) leads to a subplot, where the more polemical of the two views is allowed to persist, without any obvious threat to the accepted and ultimately celebrated attitude.

The story takes place in a secluded coastal village, "el último confín del mundo, con el campo a un lado y al otro el mar" ("in the middle of nowhere, with fields on one side and the sea on the other") (6) where, to her remorse, Diana is confined to a perfectly decorous and peaceful existence with her younger sister, Irene, her spinster aunt, Nati (short for Natividad), and the matriarch of the family, grandmother Dora (Dorotea). The housemaid Otilia, gardener Máximo, and a cat, Pitusa, complete this idyllic picture of which Diana, despite her protestations, is rather fond. The two sources of disquiet, clouding her otherwise carefree existence, relate to the tyrannical presence of tía Nati and the conspicuous absence of a fitting suitor. It is the news of Mr Berkeley's arrival, met with Diana's wistful "si fuera él" ("what if he's the one?") (33), that simultaneously initiates the narrative and interrupts the implicit monotony of former days.

For her readers, conceived of as novices and well-wishers, Diana embodies the "perfecta soltera"—a model maiden—of the times; a model concocted with the painstaking fastidiousness befitting a mentor. Most of the expected and controversial topics of the traditional conduct literature—including domestic activities (needlework, cleaning, and playing an instrument), disputed pastimes (reading, sports, fashion, dancing), friendships, love and dealings with the opposite sex—receive their due treatment. The necessary conclusions are drawn (Diana herself needs only to draw one—that she is fine as is), and a welcomed new beginning heralded.

A model modern maiden is someone whose appearance and conduct are in tune with the times, yet whose guiding principles are timeless. "Créame, amiga mía" ("Believe me, my friend [f.]"), writes a columnist of the contemporaneous publication *El español*, "aprovéchese de todos los adelantos de la civilización en cuanto a lo físico: el teléfono, la radio, el automóvil, pero en cuanto al espíritu, déjele con miriñaque y polisón, cuídele como a un niño, trátele como a un novio" ("make the most of civilization's advances in terms of material goods: the telephone, the radio, the automobile, but with regard to the spirit, keep it under crinoline and bustle, protect it like a child, treat it like a beloved") (qtd in Martín Gaite 150). As the overview of the feminine type advocated by the leaders of the *Sección Femenina* has shown, achieving this apparently simple synthesis of form and content was no mean feat. In fact, some of the novel's peculiarities (the extent to which the text "acts as a guide to and constraint on the activity of reading"[8] and its deployment of five female characters as the springboard for one) can be explained as functional choices for its realization.

Not surprisingly, all exemplary heroines are strategists, and Diana— together with her unruly, but unspoiled, sibling Irene—excels in the art, partly because the latter's shortcomings are construed as the other's strengths, and partly because the differences between them are conciliatory. Irene, despite being only two years younger than her 18-year-old sister, is systematically dismissed as a wild child—"una chiquilla" and "loquilla"—epithets that serve to pass off cunning and manipulation as mere impishness. From this position of a girl-child, someone who does not yet have stakes in the highly regulated realm of male–female relations, Irene is licensed to voice opinions that could be construed as inappropriate were they to stem from the narrator-protagonist. In this respect, Irene's age is neither trivial nor fortuitous, for she must be young enough to be able to make certain statements at no cost to her own reputation, yet old enough to engage in a kind of ventriloquism (as Diana's other).

Among the mandatory stratagems of female role models, and here we must include Diana, are poise, caution, mistrust, discretion, restraint, and congeniality. By extension, the single most auspicious trait is dissimulation, the ability to affect innocence, ignorance, and affection.[9] While all three categories constituted requisite attributes of every bride-to-be, their practice was inconvenient at best. Thus when Diana's future husband contends that it is far more estimable for a woman to remain oblivious to her charms than to use them to ensnare men, Diana retorts: "Puede ser también que el mérito esté en saberlas [estas cosas] sin dejarlo sospechar" ("It also may be that the merit is in knowing [how to do] these things without anyone suspecting it") (159). Although in this case the remark is intended to betray innocence by affecting experience, the underlying premise, reaffirmed by Diana's aunt, remains the same: "La mujer que deja traslucir sus pensamientos está perdida" ("The woman who allows her thoughts to show through is lost") (162).

---

[8] See Prince, "Notes on the Text as Reader" 226.

[9] See Martín Gaite, *Usos amorosos* 168. Those interested in the topic will find Chapter 8 full of insightful and amusing observations.

Next to the three generations of women, the two male figures whose right-ful presence is denied in this matriarchal household are the grandfather, Dorotea's husband, whose "genio avinagrado" ("sour disposition") (11) is attributed to tía Nati, and the father, whose weak constitution is inherited by Irene to her apparent disadvantage. With the exception of the gardener, all the other male characters act as potential suitors, even though only one is seen through rose-tinted spectacles. Another missing character is Diana and Irene's mother. While the premature deaths of the would-be heads of the family allow for the concentration of power in the hands of two women—grandmother and tía Nati—the lamented absence of this female character gives rise to nostalgic recollections about the virtues of an ideal mother whose prototype could scarcely improve on the reminiscence:

> A mi padre apenas lo recordamos, pero a mamá. . . . ¡Oh! ¡Qué mamá más ideal! Una de esas madres que todos quisieran tener. Afectuosa, compren-siva, llena de bondad y paciencia. Para nosotras, a pesar de nuestra juven-tud, fué una hermana mayor, una amiga discreta e inteligente. Fué nuestra maestra y consejera; no se enfadaba nunca, no nos reñía; nos hacía ver nuestras pequeñas faltas con suavidad, sin palabras violentas ni tonos brus-cos.

> (We scarcely remember my father, but mother. . . . Oh! What an ideal mother! One of those mothers that everyone would like to have. Affectionate, understanding, full of goodness and patience. To us, despite our youth, she was like an elder sister, a wise and intelligent friend. She was our teacher and counselor; she never got angry with us or scolded us; she made us see our faults gently, without jarring words or a sharp tone of voice.) (11)

In the absence of both parents, the responsibility for Diana and Irene's education falls upon the grandmother and the aunt. The role that the two women assume in the girls' upbringing, and the measure of authority they display in the process, are intriguing when viewed against the backdrop of the post-war political climate. If the grandmother is considered a weak but benign force, with a seldom yet judiciously exercised power, tía Nati is lik-ened to a usurper whose uncompromising attitude and staunch ways incite tension, injustice, and defiance. Unaccustomed to such austerity, the siblings manage to resist their aunt's formidable supervision for six years, the time they arrange to spend away at a boarding school.[10] Still, upon their return, Diana and Irene find it necessary to adapt to tía Nati's sense of propriety

---

[10] If one were to take 1940, the year of the novel's publication, as concurrent with the narrated present so as to estimate the date of other narrated events, then the six years that the girls spent "free from their aunt's tyranny" ("libres de la tiranía de tía Nati" (12)) suggestively point to the period between 1930 and 1936.

sustained at the cost of "censurar" (censoring), "reglamentar" ("regimenting"), "limitar" ("limiting"), "criticar" ("criticizing"), "desconfiar" ("distrusting"), "decidir (régimen de vida moral y material)" (determining (the rules of moral and physical conduct)), "someter" ("subjugating"), and "imponer" ("imposing") (11, 12).

Despite her overbearing presence, the narrative portrays tía Nati as a woman of small consequence. Her compulsion to rule is at once explained and undermined by her spinsterhood, a condition deemed dangerous on many accounts, not the least for being contagious. The prospect of becoming like tía Nati, assailed by "manías" ("peculiarities"), of which presumably no respectable single woman is spared beyond a certain age—"¿Qué más da esta manía si, a su edad, por fuerza ha de tener alguna. . .?" ("What's one more quirk, if at her age she is bound to have some?") reasons Nati's mother when confronted with her daughter's routine cleaning spree (32)—is so alarming to her niece that Diana makes a concentrated effort to prevent it from ever happening: "Aunque yo no llegue a casarme—en realidad, es mi mayor aspiración—, nunca seré una solterona como ella ni llevaré una vida tan inútil" ("Even if I never marry—actually, it's my greatest ambition—I will never be a spinster like her, nor will I lead such a useless life") (14). A living reminder of what, despite her best intentions, may be Diana's future if she does not marry, tía Nati unwittingly bolsters her niece's initiative, thereby underscoring Diana's modernity, understood as a novel attitude governing male–female relations and a category in need of the other against which to define itself. In this case, the boundaries of Diana's modernity are marked by tía Nati, who represents the pole of antiquity, and by Eva, Diana's urbane cousin, who, as we shall see, embodies the opposite pole. These boundaries curb and prefigure the reader's understanding of the acceptable, ensuring that the protagonist's dispositions appear moderate, even at times when these stray from the norm. Furthermore, the diminutives applied to Natividad (Nati) and Evangelina (Eva) reinforce the reader's need to rely on the protagonist's judgment and interpretation of the narrated events. When these appellations are used, it is to supplant the otherwise latent connotations of their full names (both ultra-Catholic and old-fashioned) with the corollary meaning stemming from their relationship to Diana. The modern-sounding "Nati" (so unlike "Natividad") echoes the heroine's repeated attempts at softening and modernizing her aunt; as for Eva, she is no "good news" as her full name would suggest, but a temptress of whom both women and men must be wary.

Thus, on the surface, what tía Nati both lacks and rejects are tokens of modernity as presented in and defined by women's contemporaneous magazines – fashion, make-up, sports, and a positive attitude. The main point of contention, however, is tía Nati's belief (apparently rooted in her lack of appeal) that a woman must never take the first step, a belief further challenged by the narrator:

Tía Nati no fué bonita. . . . Pienso alguna vez que . . . debe haber sufrido
mucho por esta causa y eso contribuyó a amargar su carácter. Ignoro si en
otros tiempos pensó casarse. Supongo que sí. Una a una fué deshojando sus
ilusiones. Pasaron los años y tía Nati se ha convertido en una desagradable
solterona; no obstante, si no se peinara con los cabellos tan tirantes, si no
llevara esos vestidos tan largos y anticuados, si se arreglara un poco el
rostro y fuese más amable, tengo la convicción de que mejoraría mucho su
aspecto, pero tía Nati no quiere saber nada de estas innovaciones modernas,
porque alega que ya no son propias de su edad . . . ¡Ah, si tía Nati quisi-
era!

(Aunt Nati was never pretty. . . . Occasionally, I think . . . she must have
suffered a lot because of this, and that contributed to embittering her character. I don't know if there ever was a time when she intended to marry. I
suppose so. One by one she discarded her dreams. Years went by and Aunt
Nati turned into a disagreeable spinster; nonetheless, if she didn't keep her
hair so tightly pulled back; if she didn't wear such long, outmoded dresses;
if she put some make-up on and were a little nicer, I believe she would look
much better, but Aunt Nati doesn't want to have anything to do with these
modern innovations, because she claims they are inappropriate for a woman
of her age. . . . Ah, if only Aunt Nati wanted to!) (14)

The physical transformation effected in tía Nati—thanks to her nieces' unre-
mitting efforts to initiate their aunt into the *savoir faire* of every modern
woman, irrespective of her age—parallels the transformations in her attitude.
Under attack are tía Nati's provincial mentality manifest in her proclivity for
gossip and criticism, her inclination to think the worst of others in stark contrast to the high opinion she holds of herself, and the habit of seeing her own
insufficiencies as virtues to the detriment of those who, for the lack of these
limitations, are judged less virtuous: "¡Líbrese el que pueda de tía Nati . . .! Al
que su vista alcance, está perdido. Tía Nati, no lo dudéis, lo criticará; aunque
sea un respetable padre de familia, aunque sea el hombre o la mujer más
insignificante del universo, estad seguros: tía Nati lo criticará" ("Let all who
can, flee from Aunt Nati! Anyone caught within her range of sight is lost.
Without a doubt, Aunt Nati will criticize them; whether it is a respectable
head of household or the most insignificant man or woman on the face of the
earth, you may be certain: Aunt Nati will criticize them") (15). Tía Nati's
attitude of perpetual disapproval foregrounds the proverbial "el qué dirán"
("what will people say") and its power to regulate the conduct of individuals
through their subjection to conventional, ready-made systems of interpretation. An awareness of these preexisting interpretations does not necessarily
change their instrumentality as a mechanism of containment; it is, however, a
necessary precondition for any resistance from the receiving end. For the narrator, the knowledge of how tía Nati is likely to interpret a given act, which
incidentally coincides with how it ought to be interpreted by reigning conven-

tions, entails mistrust and circumspection: "De mutuo acuerdo Irene y yo nos negamos siempre a escucharla y jamás hacemos en su presencia el menor comentario" ("By mutual agreement, Irene and I always refuse to listen to her and we never express the slightest opinion in her presence") (15).

The narrator-protagonist's anxiety over how she is perceived lays bare the degree to which the act of telling a story is inextricably linked with the process of self-representation. The manifest need to reconcile a given object of representation, in this case both the narrating and narrated 'I's, with the authorized patterns of representation, conditions the meaning and importance conferred on individual acts as these necessarily reflect upon the character. Therefore, when reading these novels, it is expedient to differentiate between the desires inscribed in the marriage plot (e.g., the desire to fall in love and marry) that endow the narrator-protagonist's voice with legitimacy and those competing or illicit desires (e.g., physical desire or the desire to be self-sufficient) that have the opposite effect of compromising her narrative authority. Thus, when Irene arranges for her sister to be alone with Humberto Berkeley, Diana, who observes this, claims not to comprehend Irene's motives: "Irene retrocedió, no sé aún por qué motivo" ("Irene went back, I still don't know why") (85). For the narrator-protagonist to acknowledge the intentions behind Irene's conduct would be equal to admitting complicity; however, such complicity, given the proscribed nature of the circumstances—destined to grow from questionable (being alone with a man) to racy (being alone with him in a bathing suit on a distant crag in the middle of the sea on a tempestuous afternoon)—is likely to reflect negatively on her character. Similarly, the pleasure of physical contact experienced by Diana while sitting side by side with the man she fancies, previously always in the conciliatory presence of her grandmother, now (in view of missing witnesses and clothes) can only be expressed through disavowal. On both occasions Diana loses consciousness just as she is about to be retrieved from the water by Humberto. The first time, the sudden cramps in her foot prevent her from reaching the shore. Her last thoughts prior to fainting are for God and not Humberto, even though it is the latter's help she seeks, desires, and anticipates. By the time she regains consciousness, Diana has been successfully rehabilitated:

> Mi último pensamiento fué para Dios. No sé lo que sucedió después. Cuando volví a la realidad—no recuerdo en qué regiones ignotas estuve— me encontré sobre el peñón, muy cansada, y Humberto me frotaba las sienes para que reaccionara. Me explicó que había tenido que someterme a la respiración artificial y que me había puesto con la cabeza más baja que los pies para que devolviera el agua que había tragado.

> (My last thought was for God. I don't know what happened after that. When I regained consciousness—I don't remember in what mysterious regions I

had been—I found myself on the crag, feeling very tired, with Humberto rubbing my temples to bring me round. He explained how he had given me mouth to mouth resuscitation and he'd placed me with my head lower than my feet so that I could cough up all the water I had swallowed.) (85)

The titillating pleasures of this prolonged encounter—after all, the story is addressed to girls who, like Diana, dream of just such misfortunes—is enhanced by the understanding that the protagonist has no choice in the matter and, having thus been rendered helpless by circumstances, she must satisfy their curiosity and succumb to her own fantasy. (This is where the traditional conduct manuals saw the danger of unchaperoned outings and why they advised against the reading of *novelas rosa*): "Humberto empezó a darme masaje, pero yo le detuve.—No, no; si alguien supiera . . ." ("Humberto began to massage my limbs, but I stopped him. 'No, no; what if someone were to find out . . .'") (85). It is left up to Humberto to defy the conventions, at once accentuating Diana's sense of propriety and absolving her of the need to comply: "Niñita—me dijo con severidad—, en momentos decisivos no sea usted víctima del eterno 'qué dirán'. Aquí no hay más testigo que el mar, y yo seré discreto" ("'Little girl,' he said to me sternly, 'in decisive moments do not fall prey to the perpetual 'what will people say.' There is no other witness here but the sea, and I shall be discreet") (86). Nature herself seems to corroborate his judgment, as the violence of the approaching storm frees Diana of the necessity to feel further scruples. The subsequent pages reproduce Diana's moral conflict—"¡Dios mío!—gemí, como hubiera hecho cualquier muchacha—, ¡qué imprudencia!" ("'My God!' I moaned, just as any girl in my place would have done, 'how imprudent!'") (86)—in the corresponding terms of struggle against nature:

> Negras nubes corrían vertiginosamente arrastrando la tempestad, empujadas por el viento. . . . Brilló, zigzagueante, un relámpago y estalló un formidable trueno que repercutió en todo el espacio.—¡Humberto. . .—exclamé, amedrentada—, Humberto!— . . . Empezó a llover violentamente, furiosamente. Aquello era el diluvio. Los relámpagos y los truenos se repetían incesantes.
>
> (Pushed by the wind, black clouds raced, bringing on the storm with dizzying speed. . . . Zigzagging lightning flashed and a tremendous thunderclap cracked, resounding throughout the whole area. "Humberto. . ." I called out, petrified, "Humberto!" . . . It started to rain violently, furiously—it was the deluge. The thunder and lightning continued unabated.)[11] (86, 87, 88)

---

[11] The entire account is laden with anxiety. Its cause, interestingly enough, is not the flood itself, but what the flood here prefigures: misconduct. Whereas the Biblical Flood is sent as a divine retribution, here the order is inverted and the flood sets the stage for the breach of conduct. Nonetheless, Diana's depiction of her surroundings, with its apocalyptic overtones, is telling of

This meteorological extravaganza is homologous to the moral intemperance of which Diana may expect to be accused and of which accusation this very linguistic exuberance must exonerate her. Furthermore, the recurring infractions of the inviolable laws of convention are punctuated by equally regular invocations of God: "¿Sabe usted rezar, Diana?—Sí.—pues encomiéndenos a Dios. Se nos prepara un mal rato; ahora, que no pierda usted el valor y tenga confianza" ("'Do you know how to pray, Diana?' 'Yes.' 'Then commend us to God. There's trouble ahead; be brave and have faith") (88). And through a few narrative tweaks, censurable conduct is converted into a trial and display of personal valor: "Henos por fin allí arriba, mojados, extenuados y dispuestos, sin embargo, a proseguir la lucha" ("Finally, there we were at the top, wet, exhausted, yet willing, all the same, to continue the struggle") (89). One cannot overestimate the positive connotations of the word "lucha" ("struggle" or "fight"), understood as a resistance to obstacles, in post-war Spain. Life itself, as we have seen in previous chapters, was conceived in terms of a battle between good and evil, and those who prevailed (the victors) were good. An action couched in these terms—putting up a good fight, not giving in, facing up to what may come—was commendable, and therefore likely to deflect criticism if not elicit sympathy and respect. By this point, Humberto's arm is tightly wrapped around Diana's shoulders as the two lie prostrate on the uppermost tip of the crag, drenched by the waves and rain.

The second time Diana loses consciousness is after the storm has passed. The rescue party arrives in the form of the lighthouse keeper, his son, and Humberto's servant Jacobo, and the sodden, skimpily dressed heroine must face the world (in addition to three men) outside her romantic misadventure. When Diana comes to her senses, she is already in the comfort of her own home; the clock from her bedroom has been mysteriously removed and the feeling of enchantment thus prolonged. By the time Diana confronts the designated voice of "el qué dirán" in the person of tía Nati, the latter's judgment has been so thoroughly discredited that it can hardly jeopardize Diana's claims to felicity.

Diana's less than irreproachable conduct is further ameliorated by the timely appearance of her cousin, Eva. Eva's representation, subservient to that of the narrator-protagonist's, is exaggerated, verging on burlesque. She is the "pescadora con anzuelo" ("fisherwoman with a hook") (1092), the "veraneante fresca" ("brazen vacationer") (1091), the "superficial sin sustancia" ("trifling one without substance") (1097) of the Jesuit Angel Ayala's zealous imaginings. Evangelina's lapdog, Fifí, is enough to throw tía Nati into an apoplectic fit, and understandably so, as the author of the following diatribe is keen to certify:

how these circumstances ought to be perceived by the protagonist who, being aware of the censurability of her own actions, anticipates signs of reprisal.

Fuera gatos. Y, sobre todo, fuera chuchitos y falderillos, en quienes se pone
el corazón de tal manera, que no pueden sus dueñitas salir a tomar el aire
sin que las acompañe el inevitable y horroroso gozque. . . . Remedando un
dicho vulgar, puede decirse que a quien Dios no le da hijos, el Diablo le da
un perrito. Es una especie de apéndice de solteronas y de matronas que, no
teniendo a quién querer, se enamoran de un falderillo. ¡Adulteración de cosa
tan alta como el amor!

(Out with cats. And above all, out with mongrels and lapdogs that are doted
on so much that their little mistresses cannot even take a breath of fresh air
without the company of these inescapable, frightful yappers. . . . To mimic
a popular saying, to whom God grants no children, the Devil gives a min-
iature dog. It is a kind of appendage of spinsters and matrons who, having
no one to love, become besotted with a lapdog. Adulteration of something
as elevated as love!) (Ayala 1054–5)

Doubts about Evangelina's character are introduced as soon as her intentions of vacationing in the countryside become known to the grandmother.
Thus, even before her arrival, readers, and with them Diana (even though she
chooses to ignore the caveat), are alerted to Eva's questionable company.
Those who until now may have judged Diana and Irene's habits and dispositions to be bold and irreverent need only meet Evangelina to gain the "right"
perspective:

Una, dos, tres maletas, una sombrerera de piel azul, una caja de bombones,
un libro, varios periódicos y revistas, un perrito pequinés y, detrás de aquel
bagaje, Evangelina. Os imaginaréis en seguida a Evangelina si os digo dos
palabras acerca de ella. Llevaba un trajecito sastre azul marino, un sombre-
rito verde, una blusa blanca y transparente. . . . Esbelta, pintada, con el
cabello rubio platino, los ojos negros, la boca muy grande y la dentadura
magnífica, la vi descender del tren alegremente, con su agilidad de muchacha deportista.

(One, two, three suitcases, a blue leather hat-box, a box of chocolates, a
book, several newspapers and magazines, a small Pekinese, and behind that
baggage, Evangelina. You will be able to picture Evangelina at once if I tell
you just a few words about her. She was wearing a cute little navy-blue suit,
a cute little green hat, a transparent white blouse. . . . Slender, made-up, with
platinum blond hair, black eyes, an enormous mouth and magnificent teeth,
I watched her descend cheerfully from the train, with the agility of a girl
athlete.) (114)

Unlike tía Nati, who considers Eva "demasiado extravagante" ("too flamboy-
ant") (44), which is to say intolerable, Diana finds her cousin "muy elegante,
muy culta y muy moderna" ("very elegant, very sophisticated and very modern") (113). Despite their apparent difference of opinion, both find it impos-

sible to describe Eva in moderate terms. As a result, the repeated qualifier "*muy*" ("very"), together with the diminutives employed in conveying the narrator's impressions of Eva, produce the effect of undermining what they seem to laud.

A textbook example of reprehensible modern ways, not to be confused with the purportedly modern views espoused by Diana, Eva carries around a photo of her date, Sergio. In Spanish he is referred to as a "flirt," which as the name suggests, was someone unlike a "novio" or a "boyfriend" in that the latter category denoted a formal relationship between a man and a woman, whereas a "flirt" referred to a fling. What keeps Sergio from achieving the status of a "boyfriend," according to Eva, is her reluctance to commit, for fear (or hope) of finding someone even more attractive: "Me gusta mucho, mucho, pero no estoy decidida, porque no sé si puedo encontrar otro que me guste más" ("I like him very, very much, but I can't make up my mind, since I don't know if I might meet someone I like more") (118). For Diana's taste, which the reader is expected to share, Sergio's undeniably good looks are spoiled by an attitude "un poco . . . peliculero" ("a little . . . showy [literally, "movie-like]") (118), an attitude that suggests a rehearsed look that in men was considered at best vain, and at worst effeminate. Another term that Eva's character helps to clarify is "el coqueteo," or flirting, of which tía Nati accuses her niece, Diana. Insulted by what she deems unfair judgment of herself, the narrator is keen to draw a line between legitimate flirting and censurable flirting, with the result that "coquetear" with a boyfriend or a potential suitor receives a positive sanction, whereas its practice with strangers or mere acquaintances is admonished as a sign of frivolity. Finally, if Diana is brazen enough to pursue a man she loves (or is willing to love), an attitude that the novel at once adopts and repudiates as modern, Eva is a tease; if Diana's initiative is endowed with a legitimate purpose, marriage, Eva's is presented as an end in itself—she is an idle pursuer driven neither by noble sentiment nor the worthy goal of her cousin.

Although Diana and Eva coincide in their view of tía Nati—both find her frightfully old-fashioned—in Eva's estimation, Diana too is guilty of falling behind times: "¿Sabes lo qué te digo? Pues que tienes que saber arreglarte, cambiar el peinado, pintarte más, quitarte ese sabor antiguo que tienes de otro modo no triunfarás entre los hombres y créeme, a ellos les gusta la mujer de hoy" ("You know what I'm saying? You have to learn how to fix yourself up, change your hair style, put on more make-up, get rid of that old-fashioned look or else you're not going to be successful with men, and believe me, they like modern women") (119). What we may infer from this judgment in particular and from the narrative at large is that there are two types of modern women, one a perversion of the other. The differences between them owe less to Diana and Eva's views, than to the motives that drive them, or to be more precise, the social value ascribed to their respective choices. One seeks a diversion, the other love, and of the two, only the latter is a conduit to marriage. Hence, the same action will elicit the label of frivolous in Eva and of steadfast in Diana. "Los hombres—me confió mi prima con aire doctoral— son dóciles animalitos que la mujer maneja como quiere, sin dejarles comprender que son dueñas de su voluntad" ("'Men,' my cousin confided to me with a knowledgeable air, 'are docile little creatures that a woman controls as she wishes, without letting them know that she is in charge'") (122). In fact, it is not Eva but her cousins, Diana and Irene, who come close to substantiating this statement. Meanwhile, in the presence of Evangelina, the narrator-protagonist chooses to adopt a demure attitude toward the object of her desire: "Prefiero que el destino siga su curso, sin poner ningún esfuerzo de mi parte" ("I prefer that destiny take its course, without any work on my part") (123). Her words, which reproduce the institutionalized attitude regarding courtship, are contradicted by her opinions and subsequent actions:

> Desde entonces, no hago más que pensar en sus palabras y he ensayado ya ante el espejo cinco peinados diferentes, a cual más atrevido, pero quiero que mi transformación sea más completa. Y por lo tanto, heme aquí leyendo concienzudamente mi gran libro con sus ochenta y tres recetas de belleza.

> (Since then, all I've done is think about her words. Already I've tried out five different hairdos in front of the mirror, each more daring than the last, but I want my transformation to be more complete. And so, here I am diligently reading my fine book with its eighty-three beauty formulas.) (119)

The striking self-referentiality of *En pos* stems partly from its narrator-protagonist's proclivity for reading.[12] As if to disclose this questionable habit, the news of Mr Berkeley's arrival has the predictable effect of activating Diana's imagination, revealing her to be a consumer of popular romance fictions. "Tengo impaciencia por conocer al señor Berkeley y no sé todavía su nombre. He escogido al azar una de mis novelas favoritas y he buscado el nombre del protagonista: se llama Heriberto. ¿Se llamará también así el señor Berkeley? No suena mal . . . Heriberto Berkeley" ("I can't wait to meet Mr Berkeley and I still don't know his first name. I picked out one of my favorite novels at random and looked for the name of the protagonist: It's Heriberto. Could that also be Mr Berkeley's name? It doesn't sound bad . . . Heriberto Berkeley") (15). As we come to find out, Mr Berkeley's first name is Humberto— not precisely a stretch from Diana's imaginings, but a detail laden with the implication that Humberto Berkeley's exotic name owes less to ethnic origins than to genre conventions.

---

[12] On the fascinating topic of "reading heroines" in Spanish literature, see Stephanie Sieburth's *Inventing High and Low*.

Similarly, we are given to understand that the aforementioned readings infuse Diana's character with hopes and expectations proper to the protagonists of romance novels, just as they provide her narrating 'I' with a way to interpret and structure her narrative. When, gazing lethargically at an empty road, Diana catches herself thinking, "esta vida no es la que yo he soñado" ("this life is not the one I dreamed of") (18)—a thought she does not share with her grandmother (who is engrossed in reading St Teresa)—what she seems to lament and allude to at the same time is the discrepancy between her own existence (prior to the arrival of Mr Berkeley) and that of her heroines'. Immediately after disclosing the link between her readings, life, and narrative, Diana nonetheless is keen to indicate that she is not the credulous reader that one might suppose her to be on account of this very revelation. Owning up to the suggestive power of literature (the mutually constitutive relationship between her fiction and persona) does not make her susceptible to everything she reads, or detract from her ability to discern between life and fiction. Because her narrative is mediated by other texts, Diana must ensure that her narratees (and readers) come to trust her interpretative ability and rely on her reading competence. Accordingly, the books Diana mentions in her narrative are subjected to a test of experience, and when they fail to withstand it, they bring disillusionment. Curiously, the example chosen to prove that one cannot believe everything one reads comes from the work of a French author:

> En un libro de una autora francesa leí que si durante ocho días se dicen unas palabras determinadas habiendo creciente y a la octava noche se duerme con un espejo debajo de la almohada, se sueña con el hombre que ha de ser nuestro marido. Irene y yo lo ensayamos, pero la verdad es que no obtuvimos el resultado que esperábamos. Yo no soñé siquiera; Irene soñó que un ratón enorme le había estropeado uno de sus mejores dibujos. Quedamos algo desilusionadas . . .

> (I read in a book by a female French author that if for eight days when the moon is waxing you say the designated words and on the eighth night sleep with a mirror under your pillow, you will dream about your future husband. Irene and I tried it, but the truth is, we didn't get the results we'd hoped for. I didn't dream at all; Irene dreamed that a gigantic mouse had destroyed one of her best drawings. We were somewhat disillusioned . . .) (16)

Another work waiting to be put to the test at this point in the narrative is the controversial *Aparecer bonita sin serlo*, containing eighty-some beauty formulas, twenty-five aerobic exercises, three preparations for a *toilette*, numerous hair-do and make-up tips, and miscellaneous advice for women of all ages, organized in accordance with the time of day, place and occasion.

> Lo tengo guardado en el fondo de un cajón, donde nadie pueda encontrarlo, debajo de unas cuartillas llenas de apuntaciones de álgebra, y pienso leerlo

concienzudamente y llevar a la práctica lo que me convenga. Desde luego, no le he dicho nada a Irene de esta adquisición, pues me avergonzaría un poquitín que pudiera adivinar mis propósitos de conquista. Porque se trata de esto: he resuelto conquistar al señor Berkeley. Y como yo, en realidad, no me considero ser una mujer tan atractiva como las que él habrá conocido, ni tengo arte suficiente para despertar su interés, he comprado un libro con magnífica encuadernación y letras doradas, que se titula *Aparecer bonita sin serlo*, la obra—dice en una de sus primeras páginas—que debe figurar en la biblioteca de todas las mujeres, la ciencia que ninguna mujer debe ignorar.

(I have it hidden in the bottom of a drawer where no one can find it, under some papers covered with algebra notes, and I plan to read it carefully and put into practice whatever suits me. Of course, I haven't said anything about this acquisition to Irene, because it would be a little embarrassing if she guessed at my strategy for conquest. Because that's what it is: I have resolved to conquer Mr Berkeley. And since I don't think I am as attractive as other women he has met, nor do I have sufficient charm to awaken his interest, I have purchased a book with a magnificent cover and golden lettering called *How to Look Pretty Even If You Aren't*, the work—as it says on one of the first pages—that ought to be in every woman's library, the knowledge that no woman should be without.) (76)

What remains of the novel can effectively be read as an argument for and against the application of *Aparecer bonita sin serlo*, a test of its true worth, only this time, the consequences are less conclusive, and together constitute a cultural bone of contention to which Ortoll's work lends its own voice. The two complementary views questioned, affirmed, and faulted in tandem may be summed up in the following assertions imputed to the designated voice of convention, tía Nati: "hijas mías, las mujeres no nos casamos cuando queremos, sino cuando quieren ellos" ("My darlings, we women do not marry when we want, but when they (men) want") and "receta de belleza solo hay una: la naturalidad" ("there is only one formula for beauty: being natural") (127, 168). In the converse argument, upheld by a host of other characters, among them Eva, Irene, and Diana (in the order of least to most authoritative), beauty is understood more broadly as a set of implements available to women for making themselves alluring and, as such, a strategy deployed in the pursuit of men. This premise implicit in Diana's reading and her ensuing narrative destabilizes the approved norms of socialization both on the diegetic and extradiegetic levels (where it enjoyed only marginal popularity alongside the aforementioned, more traditional, and widely endorsed view, which equated beauty to nature, nature to passivity, and passivity to virtue). These divergent attitudes are played out in two independent applications of Diana's furtive findings: ". . . Lo he hojeado con mucha rapidez para tener idea de lo que decía, pero esta noche me encerraré en el estudio y lo leeré despacio. Al mismo tiempo, no dejaré de tomar nota por si hay algo que pueda interesar a tía Natividad. Irene y yo hemos pensado casarla" (". . . I have skimmed it hastily to get the gist of its contents, but tonight I will lock myself in the study and read it slowly. At the same time, I will be sure to note anything that might interest Aunt Nati. Irene and I have decided to marry her off") (76). As was stated earlier, such a split allows *En pos* to introduce alongside the obvious and expected resolution (epitomized in the case of Diana), an alternative (in the example of tía Nati). The irony is that the "solutions" are mismatched, and inconsistent with the preferences manifested by the characters, seeing as it is tía Nati and not Diana who ultimately benefits from the book and what the book represents.

Diana and Irene's decision to marry off tía Nati is inspired by the arrival of Humberto Berkeley's tutor, and tía Nati's former acquaintance, don Ramón. The successful execution of this plan is the most obvious refutation of the beliefs upheld by their aunt in favor of the view, articulated by Humberto and Diana respectively, that "lo que una mujer se propone, lo consigue" ("whatever a woman sets her mind to, she achieves") (78) and that "ellos quieren [casarse] cuando nosotras nos lo proponemos" ("they [men] want to marry us when we set our mind to it") (127). The plan, sustained by Irene's generous and Diana's conservative interventions, consists of inducing don Ramón to take notice of tía Nati, and of compelling tía Nati to look after her own appearance. This latter task includes confronting tía Nati's staunch beliefs about acceptable feminine conduct, beliefs rendered outmoded time and time again:

> —En mi tiempo, la muchacha que se arreglaba para gustar a un hombre era una descocada.
> —Tal vez. Hoy, la que no lo hace es una descuidada, una abandonada. Además—esto lo decía yo—tú no te arreglas para gustarle, puesto que le gustas de todas maneras, sino por estar bien.
>
> ("In my day, the girl who fixed herself up in order to please a man was a brazen hussy."
> "That may be. Nowadays, the girl who doesn't keep up her appearance is considered careless and slovenly. Plus," it was I who spoke, "you are not making yourself attractive in order to please him, since he likes you anyway, but to feel good.") (127)

The truth known to Diana, however, is that don Ramón is not interested in tía Nati in the slightest. In order to remedy this situation, which is to say, in order to alter his perception, Irene invents a love story of melodramatic proportions resorting to the hackneyed categories and stock phrases that prevailed in the aftermath of the war, and that stood for the acceptable attitudes between men and women. Her choice is revealing of what she considers to be the most convincing arguments for her audience:

Le dije . . . 'Aquí tiene usted a tía Natividad, fiel a su recuerdo, siempre enamorada de la misma imagen. . .' . . . Le hice ver lo triste que era estar encadenada a una pasión en silencio. . . . Le convenceré de que, por su culpa, ella ha sido siempre muy desgraciada. Y creo que se compadecerá.

(I told him . . . 'Here you have Aunt Nativity, faithful to your memory, always in love with the same image. . .' . . . I made him see how sad it was to be chained to a single passion in silence. . . . I shall convince him that it is his fault that she has always been very unhappy. And I think he will be sympathetic.) (80)

In her rendition of the story, tía Nati is a willing martyr to true love conceived and borne silently for years. "Ese cariño constante, silencioso, sumiso y desinteresado . . . ella supo disimularlo muy bien, y la admiro; cualquiera de nosotras," she adds appreciatively, "habría sido más impulsiva" ("Such constant, silent, meek, unselfish love . . . she learned to conceal very well, and I admire her; any of us girls would have been more impulsive") (113). The object of her alleged affection, harbored with patience, discretion, fidelity and only a modest hope of ever reaching fruition is, of course, don Ramón. In reproducing this all too familiar line of thought in the context of a hoax, Irene lays bare the ubiquity and bathos of such discourse, denouncing the purportedly high-minded notions as hollow rhetoric. Following this logic, don Ramón, now privy to tía Nati's most intimate and guarded sentiments, must himself rise to the occasion. His reluctance to do so seems to undermine the sacrosanct grounds sustaining such categories. Furthermore, it shows don Ramón, a man about to marry while still unencumbered by love or chivalry, through something less than rose-tinted spectacles. Whether or not one can suppose such a portrayal to be more candid than that of the traditional heroes of *novelas rosa* modeled after the fairy-tale *príncipe azul* ("Prince Charming"), the fact remains that don Ramón does not fit the archetype, and that apart from serving as the butt of the joke, he and tía Nati together come to fulfill the pretensions of realism on the part of the narrator, who is conscious of such conventions:

En las blancas novelas de mi biblioteca, había visto siempre que eran, los protagonistas del amor, ella, bonita, joven, dulce, con ojos donde vibraba la ilusión; él, fuerte, arrogante, decidido y enérgico. En la vida también me figuré que una novia tenía que ser necesariamente linda y moza, para llevar los blancos velos de desposada, y él, muy varonil y guapo, para tener el privilegio de llevarla al altar. Hoy, mirando a tía Nati y a don Ramón, empiezo a pensar que la vida no se sabe nunca cuándo está en su plenitud y cuándo declina. . . . Si vierais a tía Nati pensaríais todos lo mismo. ¿Cómo es posible que vaya a casarse? Flaca, nerviosa, sin atractivo físico alguno, sin feminidad, sin dulzura de carácter, sin ser ni interesante ni afectuosa. Pero ¿le conocéis a él? Abotagado, cegato, grueso, con su tos sospechosamente asmática, sus manías y su imbecilidad.

(I had always read in the white [romance] novels on my shelves that the heroines of love stories are pretty, young, sweet, their eyes vibrant with hope; while the heroes are strong, proud, resolute and energetic. So I imagined that in real life too a bride would have to be lovely and young to wear the white veil, and the groom very manly and handsome, to have the honor of leading her to the altar. Today, looking at Aunt Nati and Don Ramon, I am beginning to think that one never knows when life is in its prime or when it is in decline. . . . I am sure if you saw Aunt Nati, you would all think the same. How could she be getting married? Skinny, jumpy, devoid of physical attractiveness, without femininity or sweetness of character, neither interesting nor affectionate. But have you seen him? Bloated, nearsighted, stout, with his suspiciously asthmatic cough, his peculiarities and his imbecility.) (163)

When don Ramón at last resolves to propose to tía Nati, it is for reasons entirely unimaginable to Irene. Rather than a sign of tokenism or narrative susceptibility to the reigning conviction that women deliberate, but men make decisions, the incident lends itself to some interesting observations about acceptable incentives for marriage. If Irene cannot conceive of don Ramón's motives, if the reasons she imputes to him are in stark contrast with the ones he comes to allege, it is because they are operating under separate, gender-differentiated sets of conventions. Hence, when don Ramón concedes to Irene that there are times when he misses female company, he conjures up in her a model of companionate marriage, which, as we have seen, had been appropriated by the *Sección Femenina* as a way of ennobling the implicit and endorsed hierarchy of male–female relations.

> —Yo no soy ya joven, Irene, y he organizado mi vida de una manera muy apacible e invariable, pero a menudo, en las pequeñas cosas de la vida, he echado de menos la compañía de la mujer.
> —Es natural. Cuando ha llegado usted a su casa cansado, con necesidad de expansión espiritual, hubiera usted querido tener a su lado una esposa comprensiva e inteligente. (130)

> ("I'm no longer young, Irene, and I've organized my life to be placid and unchanging, but often, in the small things of life, I have missed female companionship."
> "That's natural. Whenever you've come home tired, seeking a spiritual outlet, you would have wanted an understanding, intelligent wife by your side.") (130)

But being a man, and an older one at that—age denoting perception unmediated by illusions, and hence a glummer but ostensibly more realistic outlook (not surprisingly, this aging man must change his glasses before he can propose to tía Nati (135))—don Ramón is under no compulsion to accept this embellished view of conjugal responsibilities. Instead he unwittingly demystifies the model proposed by Irene for what it is, subservience disguised as partnership:

> —No, no, Irene, las mujeres no pueden ser ni comprensivas ni inteligentes; si me he sentido en este estado de ánimo, he encontrado suficiente compensación en mis libros, en mis estudios, en el silencio de mi casa. Yo he dicho que la echaba de menos en las pequeñas cosas de la vida.
> Irene no sabía a qué pudiera referirse.
> —Una mujer, para los desempeños naturales de su sexo, es insustituíble. A mí me hubiera gustado tener la ropa arreglada, la mesa bien servida, la sala de estudio en orden, la casa administrada a conciencia. No he tenido nada de eso y por esta razón he admitido que el matrimonio es necesario cuando se llega a cierta edad.

> ("No, no, Irene, women aren't capable of being either understanding or intelligent; whenever I've been in that frame of mind, I have found sufficient solace in my books, in my studies, in the tranquility of my house. I said that I missed having a woman in the small things of life."
> Irene could not figure out what he was referring to.
> "A woman is indispensable for fulfilling the duties natural to her sex. I would have liked my clothes to be clean and ironed, the table well served, the study in order, the house looked after with care. I have not had any of this, and for this reason I've accepted that marriage is necessary once you reach a certain age.") (130–1)

Marriage for don Ramón is convenience turned necessity, and accordingly, he synchronizes his wedding plans with the anticipated departure of his maid, Manuela.

As these observations show, don Ramón and tía Nati's relationship constitutes a departure from the "rosa" norm. Its incentive is not love, but a mutual desire to satisfy respective needs. Interestingly, for tía Nati, this need is seen as rooted in conventions, while for don Ramón it is conceived as a matter of personal preference. Their happiness is contingent on the fulfillment of these perceived exigencies, which can only be satisfied in marriage. It is this stipulation, the rendering of marriage as the only viable end for don Ramón and tía Nati, that this model shares with the archetypical couple of *novela rosa.* That marriage invariably leads to happiness and a new beginning in these novels, at once betrays the novels' formulaic nature, and in the case of Ortoll's work, denounces the illusory/fictional status of the narrative: if life indeed begins after marriage,[13] then the narrative in question abides in the margins of the "real," oscillating between daydreams and social imperatives. Consequently,

---

[13] See the criticism leveled at *novela rosa* by Julia Maura in the opening paragraph of "La imperfecta casada."

the readers, just like the narrator-protagonist, will be well served not to believe everything they read, including Diana's own narrative; at least, not without testing it. But, the narrator warns, such a test may fail and lead to disillusionment. To prevent such an outcome, the principal daydream of *En pos de la ilusión* (marriage) is infused with practical tips on procuring a husband. These tips, which can be summed up as calls for initiative, are necessary in order for the narrative to withstand the test of experience.

A force juxtaposed to personal—namely, female—initiative in matters of love and courtship is "fate," often interchangeable with "male." "Deja obrar al destino y no te inquietes. Si el señor Berkeley ha de ser para ti, lo será, a pesar de todas las dificultades" ("Let destiny do its work and don't worry. If Mr Berkeley is meant for you, he will be yours despite all the impediments"), proffers Diana's grandmother (142). "Aquí tienes mi ejemplo. Durante años enteros no he recibido más que miradas de indiferencia, y por fin, la mano del destino ha hecho su obra. Tú debes tener igual confianza" ("Take me, for example. For years I've received nothing but indifferent looks, until finally, destiny's hand has intervened. You should have the same confidence") (142), corroborates tía Nati, oblivious to the fact that in her case, destiny's role has been supplanted by her nieces. "¿Cómo decirle a tía Nati que la única mano que ha intervenido en la realización de sus sueños ha sido la de Irene?" ("How can I tell Aunt Nati that the only hand that intervened to make her dreams come true belongs to Irene?") (142). But while female initiative triumphs quietly, on the fringes of the main storyline, unbeknown even to tía Nati, Diana is bid to proceed as a model heroine, despite the inconsistencies with her conceptions of a modern maiden. Diana's reluctance to assume the expected path, her ensuing rebellion and its predictably botched outcome, reveal the ultimate incompatibility of these two qualifiers, the model and the modern, that the narrative tries desperately to reconcile.

In refusing to accept her grandmother's advice, Diana operates under the conviction, tacitly fortified by the example of tía Nati, that it is artifice, tenacity, and resolve, not patience or resignation, that bear results. She therefore decides to end the ambivalence of her situation by jarring her beloved into action. As her only accomplice in this unorthodox endeavor, Diana enlists her handbook on beauty. With its help she intends to assert her individuality, dazzle everyone present (the occasion being her coming-of-age party), and dispel once and for all any reservations inhibiting Mr Berkeley. The painstaking preparations that follow, the recounting of the instructions and their careful application, merely augment the only outcome they can achieve in view of their deflection from the central precept that "receta de belleza solo hay una: la naturalidad" ("there is only one formula for beauty: being natural") (168). The changes in the book's valorization likewise reflect the primacy of this view. The latter undergoes a transformation from its initial status as a "must have" (76), a "useful" (167), and a "celebrated" find (174) to "deceptive"

(185), "detestable" (190), and "common" (191). Sensitive to the needs and intentions of its users, the book resembles a fairy-tale object endowed with supernatural properties. The same source that helps to embellish tía Nati, in Diana produces garish results; if the former, aided by her nieces' intervention and the tips drawn from the book, succeeds in attracting don Ramón, Diana, following the same instructions on her own initiative, comes close to thwarting her chances for happiness.

"¿Qué pecado es que una muchacha destinada al matrimonio quiera parecer bien y se esmere con el arte de realzar la naturaleza? Ninguno" ("Is it a sin for a bride-to-be to want to look good and to take pains to enhance her natural features? Of course not"), contends the moralist Ángel Ayala, but what happens, he adds, is that "se sobrepasan los límites de un modo absurdo, no solo contra el decoro, sino contra el sentido común: no hay ni moralidad ni arte. ¡Qué pinturas, cielo santo! ¡Qué ojera! ¡Qué cejas! ¡Qué uñas! Parecen caricaturas de ellas mismas. ¡Y tan contentas! ¡Figurándose que están bellas!" ("to an absurd extreme, they exceed the limits not only of decorum, but of common sense: there is neither morality nor art. Heavens, what make-up! What rings under the eyes! What brows! What nails! They look like caricatures of themselves. And how pleased they are! Imagining themselves to look beautiful!") (1024). This in short, is the lesson exemplified by Diana: "La pintura se me había corrido de los labios, el *rimmel* me escocía en los ojos, el cabello estaba aplastado y en desorden y suponía que debía parecer una caricatura grotesca" ("Lipstick had smeared around my lips, mascara was stinging my eyes, my hair was messily plastered to my head, and I figured I must look like a grotesque caricature") (183). Lesson imparted and happy end in sight, Diana confesses to Humberto that she had resorted to all manner of ruses to win his affection. And lest her ridiculed attempt at worldliness, her fatally sophisticated *toilette*, were not eloquent enough signs of proscription, Humberto makes the final correction in reiterating this moral of the story: "El secreto de ser bonita, Diana, está en serlo, no en los consejos de un vulgar libro de bellezas . . . deja que te examine . . ., ¡pero si estás maravillosa, Diana!" ("The key to being pretty, Diana, is in being pretty, not in heeding the advice of some vulgar handbook on beauty. . . . Let me look at you . . . but you look gorgeous, Diana!") (191). But *this* moral is not the only moral. It never is, if for no other reason than the surplus of meaning that is indelible to any literary act, and also for the very specific socio-political context that, acting as a constraining force, marks the production of given works.

When Irene's inquiries regarding the six hours that Diana and Humberto spent alone on the crag receive an exhaustive "Ya lo sabes todo" ("You already know everything") from her sister, Irene feels compelled to clarify: "Desde luego, sí, el relato oficial; pero el otro, el verdadero . . . ¿qué sucedió?" ("I know the official story, of course; but what about the other, the real one . . . what happened?") (98). The distinction between the censored and uncensored versions of the same story is one that holds true for the readers of *En pos* as well. Following the edifying or indoctrinating content of the narrative, works like *Parecer bella sin serlo*, consulted by Diana, are misguided; women must desist from initiative since true beauty is free of artifice and always finds its due reward. The benefit of this lesson being reaffirmed at the end is that it implies a continuity with the rest of the narrative that is not necessarily present. The content that does not figure at the end even as (or rather because) it contradicts it, the so-called reactionary content, is that resignation is passivity and passivity is sterile; however, even in this case, the potentially destabilizing element has a normalizing effect: with a little help from beauty guides and considerable female initiative (questionable means), tía Nati is liberated from the stigma of spinsterhood through marriage (legitimate outcome).[14] But if the application of beauty guides in the novel is necessarily regulated, can the same be true beyond the narrative boundaries?

In the end we may contend that the didactic impulse of *En pos* is different from the edifying function it shares with the other novels. This impulse is founded in its appropriation of (as a way of intertext) and subscription to what we may call women's support or ancillary literature in the vein of Briones' work. Unlike the conduct manuals written by religious, political or moral authorities, these etiquette books and social guides addressed their readers on the equalizing terms of a mutual desire to be beautiful, successful, and loved, desires that were articulated marginally and consumed widely, for their fulfillment presupposed conditions that were best transcended symbolically, on the pages of a book.

---

[14] This distinction draws on Jameson's analysis of the works of mass culture as concomitantly ideological and utopian. According to Jameson, "the works of mass culture cannot be ideological without at one and the same time being implicitly or explicitly Utopian as well: they cannot manipulate unless they offer some genuine shred of content as a fantasy bribe to the public about to be so manipulated" (*Signatures* 39).

CONCLUSION

In writing about women's popular romance novels from the early years of Franco's rule, I have sought to vindicate the reading of works until now disregarded on account of their ideological complicity with the prevailing socio-political order and their alleged narrative transparency. While these assumptions are not all together unfounded, their application as ready-made interpretations has rendered the study of the selected texts futile, or at the very best, redundant. In an effort to debunk this *a priori* judgmentalism, I take the novels' normative function (the endorsement and diffusion of desired feminine models of comportment), and their socio-political conditions of emergence, as my point of departure.

As we have seen, the post-war authors of *novelas rosa* were heavily influenced by the national-Catholic signifying and representational system, especially since it was during this time of political and cultural upheaval, brought about by the Nationalist victory in 1939, that many of the values, conventions, and cultural codes that inform narratives from the early 1940s were instilled as an expedient way of legitimating and consolidating the new order. The comprehensive analysis of Catholic, bourgeois, and Falangist feminine ideals found in the first part of this study establishes the groundwork necessary to understanding the prescribed models of female socialization and the prevailing conventions of representing women in the years immediately following the Spanish Civil War. Susan Suleiman's readings of the ideological novel in terms of positive and negative apprenticeships and Carmen Martín Gaite's writings on the role of post-war romance novels in forging the subjectivity of their contemporary female readers provide tools for examining the relationship between "cultural production and social power" (Sieburth 8)—between selected women-authored texts and the constraints that shape them.

Given the complex matrix of post-war Spain, the national-Catholic agenda, and the ubiquitous gender and genre expectations, an examination of four novels from the early 1940s by bestselling Spanish authors of *novelas rosa*—Luisa-María Linares, Concha Linares-Becerra, Carmen de Icaza, and María Mercedes Ortoll—offers a model for reading post-war female representations in terms of exemplarity. The advantage of this model is that it is in keeping with the black-and-white representational system endorsed by the regime, which saw literary texts as a means of social control and edification—a function further regulated by censorship—without, however, limiting our understanding of these texts to the ways in which they act as instruments of ideological reproduction. "The object of the critic," writes Catherine Belsey,

> is to seek not the unity of the work, but the multiplicity and diversity of its possible meanings, its incompleteness, the omissions which it displays but cannot describe, and above all its contradictions. In its absences, and in the collisions between its divergent meanings, the text implicitly criticizes its own ideology; it contains within itself the critique of its own values, in the sense that it is available for a new process of production of meaning by the reader, and in this process it can provide a knowledge of the limits of ideological representation. (109)

As the present analyses show, what the selected novels have in common is their "conformist–contestatory ambivalence" (Labanyi and Graham 170). While their protagonists offer "positive" or legitimate models of selfhood, upon closer examination the novels' apparent coherence and lack of ambiguity are fraught with contradictions, paradoxes, and inconsistencies. The reinforcement of a given norm often presupposes its prior transgression, with an unclear effect as to whether the departures from the norm are enabling conditions for the reinstatement of the status quo, or whether the normative and normalizing elements in the narrative license the transgression of cultural givens elsewhere in the novel. Likewise, the conventional happy endings of *novelas rosa* function less as dénouements than as a kind of *deus ex machina*, or as prescribed and legitimating ends for the otherwise unconventional storylines. Finally, these readings substantiate the view that any study of constraints is also the study of the limits of selfsame constraints.

It is my hope that the present work opens the field for further, and much warranted, inquiries in the area of women's writing from post-war, Francoist Spain. Constraints of time and scope have only allowed for skimming the surface of a vast corpus that remains unexplored. Limitations notwithstanding, the hermeneutic model presented in this study may be used in interpreting any number of post-war narratives by women and, in so doing, help to address the lack of readership and scholarly attention to Francoist cultural production in general, and to post-war women's narratives in particular.

BIBLIOGRAPHY

Abellán, Manuel L. *Censura y creación literaria en España (1939–1976)*. Barcelona: Península, 1980.

"Agency." *A Dictionary of Sociology*. Eds John Scott and Gordon Marshall. 3rd edn. Oxford: Oxford UP, 2005.

Aldaraca, Bridget. *El Ángel del Hogar: Galdós and the Ideology of Domesticity in Spain*. Chapel Hill: U of North Carolina P, 1991.

——. "*Tormento*: La moral burguesa y la privatización de la virtud." *Textos y sociedad: Problemas de historia literaria*. Eds Bridget Aldaraca, Edward Baker, and John Beverley. Amsterdam: Rodopi, 1990. 215–229.

Alted Vigil, Alicia. "La mujer en las coordenadas educativas del régimen franquista." *Ordenamiento jurídico y realidad social de las mujeres*. Madrid: UNAM, 1986. 425–438.

Althusser, Louis. *Lenin and Philosophy and Other Essays*. 1971; New York: Monthly Review P, 2001

Alvarez, Blanca. "Corín Tellado: mantilla y matrimonio." Martínez de la Hidalga 147–153.

Alvarez Junco, José, and Adrian Shubert, eds. *Spanish History since 1808*. London: Arnold, 2000.

Andreu, Alicia. *Galdós y la literatura popular*. Madrid: Sociedad General Española de Librería, 1982.

——. "La obra de Carmen de Icaza en la difusión de un *nuevo* concepto de nación española." *Revista hispánica moderna* 1 (June 1998): 64–71.

Armstrong, Nancy. *Desire and Domestic Fiction: A Political History of the Novel*. Oxford UP, 1987.

Ayala, Angel. *Consejos a las jóvenes*. Madrid: Studium, 1947.

Balfour, Sebastian. "The *Desarrollo* Years, 1955–1975." Alvarez Junco and Shubert 277–288.

——. *The End of the Spanish Empire 1898–1923*. Oxford: Clarendon P, 1997.

——. "The Loss of Empire, Regenerationism, and the Forging of a Myth of National Identity." Graham and Labanyi 25–31.

Ballarín Domingo, Pilar. *La educación de las mujeres en la España contemporánea (siglos XIX–XX)*. Madrid: Síntesis, 2001.

Barthes, Roland. "Myth Today." *Mythologies*. 1972. New York: Farrar, Straus & Giroux, 1987. 109–158.

Beaujour, Michel. "Exemplary Pornography: Barrès, Loyola, and the Novel." *Reader in the Text*. Ed. Susan Suleiman. Princeton: Princeton UP, 1980. 325–349.

Belsey, Catherine. *Critical Practice*. London: Methuen, 1980.

Bennett, Tony. "Texts in History: The Determinations of Readings and their Texts." *Reception Study: From Literary Theory to Cultural Studies*. James L. Machor and Philip Goldstein, eds. London: Routledge, 2001. 61–74.

Bergmann, Emilie. "Reshaping the Canon: Intertextuality in Spanish Novels of Female Development." *Anales de la literatura española contemporánea* 12.1–2 (1987): 141–156.

Best, Steven and Douglas Kellner. *Postmodern Theory: Critical Interrogations*. New York: Guilford, 1991.

Bieder, Maryellen. "Intertextualizing Genre: Ambiguity as Narrative Strategy in Emilia Pardo Bazán." Brownlow and Kronik 57–75.

Blanco, Alda. "Domesticity, Education and the Woman Writer: Spain 1850–1880." *Cultural and Historical Grounding for Hispanic and Luso-Brazilian Feminist Literary Criticism*. Ed. Hernán Vidal. Minneapolis: Institute for the Study of Ideologies and Literature, 1989. 371–394.

——. "Escritora, feminidad y escritura en la España de medio siglo." *Breve historia feminista de la literatura española (en lengua castellana)*. Coord. Iris M. Zavala. Vol. 5. Barcelona: Anthropos, 1998. 9–38.

——. *Escritoras virtuosas: Narrativas de la domesticidad en la España Isabelina*. Granada: Granada, 2001.

——. "The Moral Imperative for Women Writers." *Indiana Journal of Hispanic Literatures* 2.1 (Fall 1993): 91–110.

Bourdieu, Pierre. *Distinction: A Social Critique of the Judgment of Taste*. Trans. Richard Nice. Cambridge, MA: Harvard UP, 1984.

——. *The Field of Cultural Production*. New York: Columbia UP, 1993.

——, and Jean-Claude Passeron. *Reproduction in Education, Society and Culture*. 1977. London: Sage, 2000.

Boyd, Carolyn P. *Politics, History, and National Identity in Spain, 1875–1975*. Princeton: Princeton UP, 1997.

Briones, Esperanza de. *La belleza: Los problemas que crea y los que resuelve. Conocimiento cultivo y conservación de la estética personal*. Madrid: Afrodisio Aguado, 1945.

Brown, Joan L., and Crista Johnson. "Women Writers in the Hispanic Novel Canon in the United States." *Hers Ancient and Modern: Women's Writing in Spain and Brazil*. Eds Catherine Davies and Jane Whetnall. Manchester: U of Manchester P, 1997. 45–56.

Brownlow, Jeanne P., and John W. Kronik, eds. *Intertextual Pursuits: Literary Mediations in Modern Spanish Narrative*. Lewisburg, PA: Bucknell UP, 1998.

Burdiel, Isabel. "Lo imaginado como material interpretativo para la historia: A propósito del monstruo de *Frankenstein*." *Literatura e historia cultural o Por qué los historiadores deberíamos leer novelas*. Valencia: Episteme, 1996. 1–22.

Butler, Judith. *Gender Trouble: Feminism and the Subversion of Identity*. New York: Routledge, 1999.

Carbonell, Neus. "In the Name of the Mother and the Daughter: The Discourse of Love and Sorrow in Mercè Rodoreda's *La Plaça del Diamant*." *Garden Across the Border: Mercè Rodoreda's Fiction.* Eds Kathleen McNerney and Nancy Vosburg. Selinsgrove, PA: Susquehanna UP, 1994. 17–30.

Carlston, Erin. *Thinking Fascism: Sapphic Modernism and Fascist Modernity.* Stanford, CA: Stanford UP, 1998.

Carr, Raymond, and Juan Pablo Fusi Aizpurua. *Spain: Dictatorship to Democracy.* London: George Allen & Unwin, 1981.

Castillo, Debra. "Mercedes Salisachs, Ideal Womanhood, and the Middlebrow Novel." Brownlow and Kronik 97–125.

Castillo y Cortázar, Blanca. "Antropología bíblica de la feminidad en *La perfecta casada.*" *Fray Luis de León: IV centenario (1591–1991).* Madrid: Ediciones escurialenses, 1992. 193–208.

Catalina del Amo, Severo. *La mujer.* 1858. Buenos Aires: Espasa-Calpe, S.A., 1954.

Charlo, Ramón. "La novela sentimental." *La novela popular en España.* Ed. Fernando Martínez de la Hidalga, et al. Vol. 2. Madrid: Robel, 2000. 177–231.

Charnon-Deutsch, Lou. *Narratives of Desire: Nineteenth-Century Spanish Fiction by Women.* University Park, PA: Pennsylvania State UP, 1994.

Christian-Smith, Linda K. *Becoming a Woman through Romance.* London: Routledge, 1990.

Clavero Nuñez, A. *Antes que te cases. . . Un texto de formación prenupcial con la explicación sencilla y clara de los procesos sexual y generativo humanos.* Valencia: Tipografía moderna, 1946.

Colby, Anita. *Tu belleza.* Trans. María Teresa Luaces de Fontinalla. Barcelona: Daimon, 1954.

Cruz-Cámara, Nuria. "'Chicas raras' en dos novelas de Carmen Martín Gaite y Carmen Laforet." *Hispanofilia* 139 (Sept. 2003): 97–110.

Culler, Jonathan. *Literary Theory: A Very Short Introduction.* Oxford: Oxford UP, 1997.

Davis, Catherine. "Spain under Franco: Women and the Authoritarian State." *Spanish Women's Writing 1849–1996.* Atlantic Highlands, NJ: Athlone, 1998. 173–197.

De Grazia, Victoria. *How Fascism Ruled Women.* Berkeley: U of California P, 1993.

Delegación Nacional de la Sección Femenina de F.E.T. y de las J.O.N.S. *Formación familiar y social.* 2nd edn. Madrid: Magisterio Español, 1945.

Di Febo, Giuliana. "La condición de la mujer y el papel de la iglesia en la Italia fascista y en la España franquista: Ideologías, leyes y asociaciones femeninas." *Ordenamiento jurídico y realidad social de las mujeres.* Madrid: UNAM, 1986. 439–452.

——. *Ritos de Guerra y de Victoria en la España franquista.* Bilbao: Desclée de Brouwer, 2002.

——. *La santa de la raza: Un culto barroco en la España franquista.* Barcelona: Icaria, 1987.

——. "El tiempo de las mujeres durante el franquismo: De los manuales 'de formación' a la narrativa femenina." Congreso internacional: "En el sentido de la vida." Alicante, 1990.

Durán, María Angeles. "Lectura económica de Fray Luis de León." *Nuevas perspectivas sobre la mujer. Actas de las primeras jornadas de investigación interdisciplinaria organizadas por el Seminario de Estudios de la Mujer*. Vol. 2. Madrid: Universidad Autónoma, 1982. 257–273.

Edgar, Andrew, and Peter Sedgwick, eds. *Cultural Theory: The Key Concepts*. London: Routledge, 1999.

Elam, Diane. *Romancing the Postmodern*. London: Routledge, 1992.

Ellwood, Sheelagh M. *Spanish Fascism in the Franco Era: Falange Española de las Jons, 1936–76*. New York: St Martin's P, 1987.

Enciso Viana, Emilio. *La muchacha en el noviazgo*. Madrid: Studium, 1946.

Enders, Victoria L. "Nationalism and Feminism: The Sección Femenina of the Falange." *History of European Ideas* 15: 4–6 (1992): 673–680.

——. "Problematic Portraits: The Ambiguous Historical Role of the *Sección Femenina* of the Falange." Enders and Radcliff 375–397.

—— and Pamela Beth Radcliff, eds. *Constructing Spanish Womanhood*. New York: State U of New York P, 1999.

Esteve Blanes, Francisco. *Hacia tu ideal: Unas palabras a una joven*. Barcelona: Subirana, 1939.

Everding, Robert. G. "Shaw and the Popular Context." *The Cambridge Companion to George Bernard Shaw*. Ed. Christopher Innes. Cambridge: Cambridge UP, 1998. 309–333.

Falange Española de las J.O.N.S. *Doctrina e historia de la revolución nacional española*. Barcelona: Editora Nacional, 1939.

Foucault, Michel. *The Archaeology of Knowledge*. New York: Pantheon Books, 1972.

——. *The Uses of Pleasure: The History of Sexuality*. Vol. 2. New York: Vintage Books, 1990.

Franco, Jean. "Plotting Women: Popular Narratives for Women in the United Status and in Latin America." *Reinventing the Americas: Comparative Studies of Literature of the United States and Spanish America*. Eds Bell Gale Chevigny and Gari Laguardia. London: Cambridge UP, 1986. 249–268.

Galerstein, Carolyn L., ed. *Women Writers of Spain: An Annotated Bio-Bibliographical Guide*. New York: Greenwood Press, 1986.

Gallego Méndez, María Teresa. *Mujer, falange y franquismo*. Madrid: Taurus, 1983.

García Figar, Antonio. *¿Por qué te casas? ¿Para qué te casas? ¿Con quién te casas?* Madrid: Editorial bibliográfica española, 1944.

Genette, Gérard. "Plausibility and Motivation." *The Princess of Clèves: Contemporary Reactions, Criticism*. Trans. John D. Lyons. New York: Norton, 1994. 178–185.

Gentile, Emilio. "La sacralización de la política y el fascismo." *Fascismo y Franquismo cara a cara: Una perspectiva histórica*. Eds Javier Tusell, et al. Madrid: Biblioteca Nueva, 2004. 57–68.

Godsland, Shelley and Nickianne Moody. *Reading the Popular in Contemporary Spanish Texts.* Newark, DE: U of Delaware P, 2004.

Gómez-Ferrer Morant, Guadalupe. *Hombres y mujeres: El difícil camino hacia la igualdad.* Madrid: Complutense, 2002.

Gonzales, María Teresa. *Corín Tellado medio siglo de novela de amor (1946–1996).* Oviedo (Sp.): Pentalfa, 1998.

Graham, Helen. "Gender and the State: Women in the 1940s." Graham and Labanyi 182–194.

——, and Jo Labanyi, eds. *Spanish Cultural Studies: An Introduction.* Oxford: Oxford UP, 1995.

Griffin, Roger. *The Nature of Fascism.* London: Routledge, 1991.

Hall, Stuart. *Representation: Cultural Representations and Signifying Practices.* London: Sage, 2000.

Herzberger, David. *Narrating the Past. Fiction and Historiography in Postwar Spain.* Durham, NC: Duke UP, 1995.

Hobsbawm, Eric. *The Age of Capital: 1848–1875.* New York: Charles Scribner's Sons, 1975.

Icaza, Carmen de. *Soñar la vida.* 2nd edn. 1943. Buenos Aires: Juventud, 1944.

Jagoe, Catherine. *Ambivalent Angels: Gender in the Novels of Galdós.* Berkeley: U of California P, 1994.

——, Alda Blanco, and Cristina Enríquez de Salamanca, eds. *La mujer en los discursos de género: Textos y contextos en el siglo XIX.* Barcelona: Icaria, 1998.

Jameson, Fredric. *The Political Unconscious: Narrative as a Socially Symbolic Act.* Ithaca, NY: Cornell UP, 1981.

——. *Signatures of the Visible.* London: Routledge, 2007.

Johnson, Carroll. "Ideology, Economy and Feminism." *San Juan de la Cruz and Fray Luis de León: A Commemorative International Symposium.* Newark, DE: Juan de la Cuesta, 1996. 129–144.

Jones, John A., and Javier San José Lera, eds. *A Bilingual Edition of Fray Luis de León's La perfecta casada: The Role of Married Women in Sixteenth-Century Spain.* Lewiston, NY: Edwin Mellen, 1999.

Jover, José María, and Guadalupe Gómez-Ferrer. "Sociedad, civilización y cultura." *España: Sociedad, política y civilización (siglos XIX–XX).* Eds José María Jover Zamora, Guadalupe Gómez-Ferrer Morant, and Juan Pablo Fusi Aizpúrua. Madrid: Areté, 2001. 203–258.

Kirkpatrick, Susan. *Las Románticas: Women Writers and Subjectivity in Spain, 1835–1850.* Berkeley, CA: U of California P, 1989.

——. "The Female Tradition in Nineteenth-Century Spanish Literature." *Cultural and Historical Grounding for Hispanic and Luso-Brazilian Feminist Literary Criticism.* Ed. Hernán Vidal. Minneapolis: Institute for the Study of Ideologies and Literature, 1989. 371–394.

Kitts, Sally-Ann. *The Debate on the Nature, Role and Influence of Woman in Eighteenth-Century Spain.* Lewiston, NY: Edwin Mellen, 1995.

Labanyi, Jo. "Censorship or the Fear of Mass Culture." Graham and Labanyi 207–214.

——. "Resemanticizing Feminine Surrender: Cross-Gender Identifications in the Writings of Spanish Female Fascist Activists." *Women's Narrative and Film in Twentieth-Century Spain: A World of Difference(s)*. Eds Ofelia Ferrán and Kathleen M. Glenn. London: Routledge, 2002. 75–92.

——. "Romancing the Early Franco Regime: The *novelas románticas* of Concha Linares Becerra and Luisa-María Linares." Working paper, 5 Mar. 2004. [consulted 30 Oct. 2006] <http://repositories.cdlib.org/cgi/viewcontent.cgi?article=10508&context=ies>.

Lannon, Frances. *Privilege, Persecution, and Prophecy: The Catholic Church in Spain, 1875–1975*. Oxford: Clarendon P, 1984.

Lanser, Susan. *Fictions of Authority: Women Writers and Narrative Voice*. Ithaca, NY: Cornell UP, 1992.

León, Fray Luis de. *La perfecta casada*. 1583. Buenos Aires: Espasa-Calpe, 1940.

——. *Obras completas castellanas de Fray Luis de León*. Ed. P. Félix García. Madrid: B.A.C., 1967.

——. *The Perfect Wife*. Trans. Alice Philena Hubbard. Denton, TX: College P [T.S.C.W. Texas State College for Women], 1943.

Linares, Luisa-María. *Un marido a precio fijo*. 10th edn. 1940. Barcelona: Juventud, 1979.

Linares-Becerra, Concha. *Cómo los hombres nos quieren*. 6th edn. 1944. Madrid: Ediciones C.L.B., 1962.

López, Francisca. *Mito y discurso en la novela femenina de posguerra en España*. Madrid: Pliegos, 1995.

Lorenzo Arribas, Josemi. "Fray Luis de León: un misógino progresista en la 'querella de las mujeres'. Relectura de *La perfecta casada*." *Feminismo y misoginia en la literatura española: Fuentes literarias para la Historia de las Mujeres*. Madrid: Narcea, S.A., 2001. 59–79.

Luengo Sojo, Antonia. "El arquetipo de mujer de la *Sección Femenina*: contribución de la actividad musical a la consecución de un modelo." *Pautas históricas de sociabilidad femenina rituales y modelos de representación*. Eds Mary Nash, María José de la Pascua, and Gloria Espigado. Cádiz (Sp.): Universidad de Cádiz, 1999. 163–173.

Malo Segura, Francisco. *Los derechos de la mujer en la legislación española: Contiene las disposiciones canónicas, civiles, penales y mercantiles relacionadas con los derechos de la mujer, expuestas en forma práctica y de fácil comprensión*. Santander (Sp.): Fasan, 1950.

Mantua, Cecilia. *El libro de la mujer*. Barcelona: Albón, 1946.

Manzano Badía, Benjamín. "Carmen de Icaza, una apología pequeño-burguesa y conservadora de la familia." Villalba Álvarez, 107–121.

Maravall, José Antonio. *Estado moderno y mentalidad social*. Vol. 2. Madrid: Revista de Occidente, 1972.

Martín Gaite, Carmen. *El cuarto de atrás*. 1978; 10th edn. Barcelona: Destinolibro, 1994.

——. *Desde la ventana*. Madrid: Espasa Calpe, 1987.

——. *Usos amorosos de la postguerra española*. 1986; 8th edn. Barcelona: Anagrama, 2001.

——. *Courtship Customs in Postwar Spain*. Trans. Margaret E.W. Jones. Lewisburg, PA: Bucknell UP, 2004.

Martínez de la Hidalga, Fernando, et al. *La novela popular en España*. 2 vols. Madrid: Robel, 2000.

Mayock, Ellen C. *The 'Strange Girl' in Twentieth-Century Spanish Novels Written by Women*. New Orleans: UP of the South, 2004.

Miller, Nancy. *Subject to Change: Reading Feminist Writing*. New York: Columbia UP, 1988.

Modleski, Tania. *Loving with a Vengeance: Mass-Produced Fantasies for Women*. London: Methuen, 1984.

Montejo Gurruchaga, Lucía, and Nieves Baranda Leturio, eds. *Las mujeres escritoras en la historia de la literatura española*. Madrid: UNED (Universidad Nacional de Educación a Distancia), 2002.

Morales, María Pilar. *Mujeres (Orientación femenina)*. 2nd edn. Madrid: Imprenta Sáez, 1954.

Morcillo Gómez, Aurora. "Shaping True Catholic Womanhood: Francoist Educational Discourse on Women." Enders and Radcliff 51–69.

——. *True Catholic Womanhood: Gender Ideology in Franco's Spain*. De Kalb, IL: Northern Illinois UP, 2000.

Mosse, George L. "Fascist Aesthetics and Society: Some Considerations." *Journal of Contemporary History* 31.2 (1996): 245–252.

Nash, Mary. *Mujer, familia y trabajo en España (1875–1936)*. Barcelona: Anthropos, 1983.

——. "Pronatalism and Motherhood in Franco's Spain." *Maternity and Gender Policies: Women and the Rise of the European Welfare States, 1880s–1950s*. Eds Gisela Bock and Pat Thane. London: Routledge, 1991. 160–177.

——. "Towards a New Moral Order: National Catholicism, Culture and Gender." Alvarez Junco and Shubert 289–300.

——. "Un/Contested Identities: Motherhood, Sex Reform and the Modernization of Gender Identity in Early Twentieth-Century Spain." Enders and Radcliff 25–49.

Nielfa Cristóbal, Gloria, ed. *Mujeres y hombres en la España franquista: Sociedad, economía, política, cultura*. Madrid: Complutense, 2003.

O'Byrne, Patricia. "Spanish Women Novelists and the Censor (1945–1965)." *Letras Femeninas* 15.1–2 (1999): 199–212.

Ortoll, María Mercedes. *En pos de la ilusión*. Barcelona: Juventud, 1940.

Palacio Lis, Irene. *Mujeres ignorantes: madres culpables. Adoctrinamiento y divulgación materno-infantil en la primera mitad del siglo XX*. Valencia (Sp.): Martín, 2003.

Pastor i Homs, María Inmaculada. *La educación femenina en la postguerra (1939–45): El caso de Mallorca*. Madrid: Instituto de la Mujer, 1984.

Payne, Stanley. *Fascism in Spain: 1923–1977*. Madison: U of Wisconsin P, 1999.

——. *The Franco Regime: 1936–1975*. Madison: U of Wisconsin P, 1987.

——. *Spanish Catholicism: An Historical Overview*. Madison: U of Wisconsin P, 1987.

Porter Abbott, H. *The Cambridge Introduction to Narrative*. Cambridge: Cambridge UP, 2002.

Primo de Rivera, José Antonio. *Obras completas de José Antonio Primo de Rivera*. Eds Agustín del Río Cisneros and Enrique Conde Gargollo. N.p.: Delegación Nacional de Prensa y Propaganda de Falange Española Tradicionalista y de las J.O.N.S., n.d.

Primo de Rivera, Pilar. *Cuatro discursos de Pilar Primo de Rivera*. N.p.: n.p., 1939.

——. *Discursos, circulares, escritos*. Madrid: Sección Femenina de F.E.T. y de las J.O.N.S. [1944?].

——. *Escritos*. 2nd edn. Madrid: Sección Femenina de F.E.T. y de las J.O.N.S. [1950?].

Prince, Gerald. *Dictionary of Narratology*. Lincoln: U of Nebraska P, 1987.

——. "Notes on the Text as Reader." Suleiman and Crosman 225–240.

Rabinow, Paul, ed. *Foucault Reader*. New York: Pantheon, 1984.

Radway, Janice. *Reading the Romance: Women, Patriarchy, and Popular Literature*. Chapel Hill: U of North Carolina P, 1984.

Richmond, Kathleen. *Women and Spanish Fascism: The Women's Section of the Falange, 1934–1959*. London: Routledge, 2003.

Riddel, María del Carmen. *La escritura femenina en la postguerra española*. New York: Peter Lang, 1995.

Rivera, Olga. *La mujer y el cuerpo femenino en* La perfecta casada *de Fray Luis de León*. Newark, DE: Juan de la Cuesta, 2006.

Roca i Girona, Jordi. "Del clero para el pueblo. La Literatura Edificante de Postguerra: un instrumento de divulgación y socialización religiosa." *Revista de dialectología y tradiciones populares* 48.2 (1993): 5–29.

Rodríguez, María Pilar. *Vidas Im/Propias: Transformaciones del sujeto femenino en la narrativa española contemporánea*. West Lafayette, IN: Purdue UP, 2000.

Rodríguez-Puértolas, Julio. *Literatura Fascista Española*. Vol. 1. Madrid: Akal, 1986.

Rueda, Ana. *Pigmalión y Galatea: Refracciones modernas de un mito*. Madrid: Fundamentos, 1998.

Ruiz Franco, Rosario. "La situación legal: Discriminación y reforma." Nielfa Cristóbal 117–144.

Sánchez López, Rosario. *Mujer española, una sombra de destino en lo universal: Trayectoria histórica de Sección Femenina de Falange (1934–1977)*. Murcia (Sp.): Universidad de Murcia, 1990.

Scanlon, Geraldine M. *La polémica feminista en la España contemporánea, 1868–1974*. Madrid: Akal, 1986.

——. "Revolución burguesa e instrucción femenina." *Nuevas perspectivas sobre la mujer*. Vol. 1. Madrid: Universidad Autónoma, 1982. 163–173.

Scott, Joan W. "Gender: A Useful Category of Historical Analysis." *American Historical Review* 91 (1986): 1053–1075.

Servén Díez, Carmen. "Novela rosa, novela blanca y escritura femenina en los años cuarenta: la evolución de Carmen de Icaza." *Asparkía: Investigación feminista* 7 (1997): 91–102.

Shaw, George Bernard. *Pygmalion*. 1916. New York: Amereon House, 1957.

Sieburth, Stephanie. *Inventing High and Low: Literature, Mass Culture, and Uneven Modernity in Spain*. Durham, NC: Duke UP, 1994.

Sinués de Marco, María del Pilar. *El ángel del hogar.* 2 vols. 8th edn. Madrid: Librería General de Victoriano Suárez, 1904.

Slade, Carole A. "'Este gran Dios de las cavallerías' [This Great God of Chivalric Deeds]: St. Teresa's Performances of the Novels of Chivalry." *The Vernacular Spirit: Essays on Medieval Religious Literature*. Eds Renate Blumenfeld-Kosinski, Duncan Robertson, and Nancy Warren. New York: Palgrave, 2002. 297–316.

Smith, Sidonie. *A Poetics of Women's Autobiography: Marginality and the Fictions of Self-Representation*. Bloomington: Indiana UP, 1987.

Soliño, María Elena. *Women and Children First: Spanish Women Writers and the Fairy Tale Tradition.* Potomac, MD: Scripta Humanística, 2002.

Suárez Fernández, Luis. *Crónica de la Sección Femenina y su tiempo.* Madrid: C.I.R.S.A., 1993.

Suleiman, Susan R. *Authoritarian Fictions: The Ideological Novel as a Literary Genre.* 1983. Princeton: Princeton UP, 1992.

—, and Inge Crosman, eds. *Reader in the Text. Essays on Audience and Interpretation.* Princeton: Princeton UP, 1980.

Sunder Rajan, Rajeswari. *Real and Imagined Women: Gender, Culture and Postcolonialism.* London: Routledge, 1993.

Teresa of Avila. *The Autobiography of St. Teresa of Avila.* Trans. Kieran Kavanaugh and Otilio Rodríguez. New York: Institute of Carmelite Studies, 1987.

—. *Libro de la vida.* Ed. Dámaso Chicharro. 11th edn. Madrid: Cátedra, 1997.

—. *Santa Teresa. Obras completas.* Ed. Tomás Alvarez. 7th edn. Vol. 1. Burgos: Monte Carmelo, 1994.

Tusell, Javier, and Genoveva Queipo de Llano. "The Dictatorship of Primo de Rivera, 1923–1931." Alvarez Junco and Shubert 207–221.

Valls, Fernando. *La enseñanza de la literatura en el franquismo (1936–1951).* Barcelona: Antoni Bosch, 1983.

Vigil, Mariló. *La vida de las mujeres en los siglos XVI y XVII.* Madrid: Siglo XXI, 1986.

Villalba Álvarez, Marina. *Mujeres novelistas en el panorama literario del siglo XX: I Congreso de narrativa española (en lengua castellana).* Cuenca (Sp.): Universidad de Castilla-La Mancha, 2000.

Weber, Alison. *Teresa of Avila and the Rhetoric of Femininity.* Princeton: Princeton UP, 1990.

White, Hayden. "The Value of Narrativity in the Representation of Reality." *On Narrative.* Ed. W.J.T. Mitchell. Chicago: U of Chicago P, 1981. 1–23.

INDEX